Westview Special Studies in International Economics and Business

The Sogo Shosha: *Japan's Multinational Trading Companies*
Alexander K. Young

The *sogo shosha*, Japan's general trading companies, are regarded as a key element in the country's rapid economic growth after World War II and its great success in international trade. In Japanese fiscal year 1975, the ten largest *sogo shosha* had total sales of $155 billion, accounting for 56 percent of Japan's exports and imports, 18 percent of domestic wholesale trade, and 31 percent of GNP. On the international level, the transactions of these companies in the same year were 5 percent of world export trade.

This book—the first comprehensive, English-language work on the *sogo shosha*—systematically describes and analyzes the basic characteristics, business methods, sales and profit trends, strategies, national roles, global reach, strengths and weaknesses, and future prospects of these global trading conglomerates. In examining both the national and the global facets of the *sogo shosha*, the author presents the economic and social origins of the ten largest companies, how they differ from the pre-World War II *zaibatsu*, and how they resemble and differ from Western multinational corporations. A wealth of statistical and tabular material supplements his account of the *sogo shosha* as Japan's chief importers of foodstuffs, raw materials, and equipment; as the advance guard of Japanese exports; as a driving force to rationalize the domestic distribution system; and as investor-organizers of multinational overseas natural resource development programs.

Alexander K. Young is professor of international relations at the College of New Paltz, State University of New York. A graduate of the College of Law of the National Taiwan University, he received a Ph.D. from Columbia University, where he is currently an associate of the University Seminar on Modern Japan.

The *Sogo Shosha*: Japan's Multinational Trading Companies

Alexander K. Young

Westview Press / Boulder, Colorado

This book is published in cooperation with the Japan Society, Inc., New York.

*Westview Special Studies in
International Economics and Business*

All rights reserved. No part of this publication may be reproduced or transmitted in any form or by any means, electronic or mechanical, including photocopy, recording, or any information storage and retrieval system, without permission in writing from the publisher.

Copyright © 1979 by Westview Press, Inc.

Published in 1979 in the United States of America by
  Westview Press, Inc.
  5500 Central Avenue
  Boulder, Colorado 80301
  Frederick A. Praeger, Publisher

Library of Congress Cataloging in Publication Data
Young, Alexander K.
  The sogo shosha.
  (Westview special studies in international economics and business)
  Bibliography: p.
  1. Conglomerate corporations—Japan. 2. Export sales—Japan. I. Title.
HD2756.J3Y68   338.8'8'0952   78-18935
ISBN 0-89158-425-0

Printed and bound in the United States of America

To the memory of my father,
a good and just man

Contents

List of Figures xi
List of Tables xiii
Preface xix

Part 1
What They Are and What They Do

1 The *Sogo Shosha*'s Core Business 3
2 The Ten Largest *Sogo Shosha* 23
3 Services and Resources for Conducting Business 57

Part 2
Evolution and Roles

4 Growth Trends and Business Strategies: 1960-1973 83
5 Roles in the Post-World War II Japanese Economy 119
6 Overseas Natural Resource Development Projects 145

Part 3
Challenges and Prospects

7 Strategic Changes Since 1973: Management Efficiency
   and Global Reach 167
8 The *Sogo Shosha* in World Commerce 195

Selected References 235
Index 239

Figures

1.1 Share of the ten general trading companies' commodities trade in Japan's foreign trade, FY 1975 7

3.1 Organizational structure of Sumitomo Shoji Kaisha, March 1974 76

3.2 Mitsui global communications network (September 1, 1973) 78

5.1 Shift in export/production ratio of major commodities, 1954 and 1955 133

8.1 Third-country trade of the ten general trading companies, FY 1956–FY 1976 198

8.2 Model for international strategic planning and control 225

Tables

1.1 Geographic structure of exports of large trading companies, FY 1973 10
1.2 Exports and imports of Japanese traders, FY 1973 14
1.3 Exports of Japanese trading companies by scale of transactions, FY 1973 15
1.4 Imports of Japanese trading companies by scale of transactions, FY 1973 16
1.5 Large non-Japanese trading companies (wholesale and trade), 1976 18
2.1 Sales of the ten general trading companies, FY 1976 26
2.2 Share of various commodities groups in the ten general trading companies' sales, FY 1976 27
2.3 Sales of the ten general trading companies by types of trade, FY 1976 29
2.4 Profits of the ten general trading companies, FY 1976 30
2.5 Share of six conglomerate groups in the total capital stock and total asset of Japanese enterprises (public utilities excluded), March 31, 1974 38
2.6 Members of the President Clubs of the six conglomerate groups, March 31, 1974 39
2.7 Sources of loans of the ten general trading companies, March 31, 1973 43

xiii

2.8	Share of Sumitomo Shoji Kaisha in total sales of the core Sumitomo group manufacturers, September 1971–March 1974	45
2.9	Subsidiaries (stock ownership exceeding 50 percent) of six general trading companies classified by industries, March 31, 1974	47
2.10	Stocks of three general trading companies analyzed by shareholders, March 31, 1975	52
2.11	Stocks of three general trading companies analyzed by number of shares, March 31, 1975	53
2.12	Major shareholders of six general trading companies and their weight, 1973	54
3.1	Commercial credit created by the ten general trading companies, fiscal six months ended March 31, 1974	59
3.2	Short-term and long-term loans extended by the ten general trading companies, March 31, 1974	60
3.3	Bank loan guarantees made by the ten general trading companies, fiscal six months ended March 31, 1974	61
3.4	Employees of the ten general trading companies, September 1976	69
3.5	Capital structure of the ten general trading companies, March 31, 1974	72
3.6	Top five financial institutions lending to six general trading companies, March 31, 1974	73
4.1	Annual sales of the ten general trading companies, FY 1960–FY 1976	85
4.2	Share of the ten general trading companies in Japan's foreign trade, FY 1963–FY 1976	87
4.3	Share of domestic, foreign, and overseas (third-country) trade in sales of six general trading companies, 1955–1977	88
4.4	Share of various products in sales of six general trading companies, 1955–1977	91

Tables

4.5	Own capital as percentage of total capital employed, six general trading companies, 1939-1974	94
4.6	Net profit rates of six general trading companies, 1966-1974	96
4.7	Shifts in trading companies' and manufacturers' share of Japanese exports and imports, FY 1952-FY 1973	101
4.8	Gross National Product of Japan, 1955-1972	103
4.9	Structure of Japanese household expenditure, 1955-1972	104
5.1	Breakdown of wheat import contracts by fifteen trading companies and by countries of production, FY 1973	121
5.2	Volume of iron ore imported by Japanese general trading companies for Japanese steel makers, FY 1973	122
5.3	Volume of coking coal imports signed by trading companies, 1973	123
5.4	Machinery import of general trading companies and manufacturers and share of Japan's total machinery import, FY 1957-FY 1973	126
5.5	Japanese imports of foreign technology, 1950-1970	127
5.6	Percentage participation of the general trading companies in Japanese import of foreign technology, FY 1971 and FY 1972	128
5.7	Export growth factors of major countries, 1955-1970	134
6.1	Japanese imports of major raw materials, 1960-1968	146
6.2	Import dependence rates for Japan's major natural resources, FY 1960-FY 1972	147
6.3	Direct foreign investments (DFIs) of the ten general trading companies, FY 1972-FY 1975	156
7.1	Domestic stock holdings of the ten general trading companies and holdings exceeding limits proposed	

	by the Japan Fair Trade Commission in 1974	171
7.2	Loans of Japanese banks to the ten general trading companies and amount in excess of the limits imposed by the Ministry of Finance as of March 31, 1974	173
7.3	Trading activities of Japanese firms in the United States, FY 1970 and FY 1973	186
7.4	Trading activities of Japanese firms in Taiwan, FY 1970 and FY 1973	187
7.5	Capital stock of six general trading companies' North American headquarters, March 1971–March 1976	190
8.1	Consumption and import shares of Japan, the United States, and West Germany in the world's major primary products, 1974	196
8.2	Third-country trade of the ten general trading companies, March 1971–March 1977	199
8.3	Overseas trade (third-country and overseas domestic trade) of the ten general trading companies by commodities	200
8.4	Share of the ten general trading companies in Japan's plant exports, 1966-1974	203
8.5	Sales, assets, income, and equity of American affiliates of six general trading companies, 1973-1976	206
8.6	Transactions of C. Itoh & Co. (America) by types of business, 1974-1976	207
8.7	Trade with Japan, C. Itoh & Co. (America) and Mitsui & Co. (U.S.A.), 1975-1976	207
8.8	Export and import transactions of Nissho-Iwai American Corporation and Mitsui & Co. (U.S.A.), 1975-1976	208
8.9	Transactions of C. Itoh & Co. (America) by types of business and commodities, year ended December 31, 1976	208
8.10	Number of employees of U.S. affiliates of the ten	

Tables xvii

      general trading companies, March 31, 1976 210
8.11 Number of offices operated by affiliates of the ten
      general trading companies, March 1976 211
8.12 Wholly-owned affiliates in selected countries of
      three general trading companies 213
8.13 Trends in Japanese industrial production, 1970-
      1985, 1970 price basis.............................216
8.14 Trends in commodities exports of Japan, 1970-
      1985 219
8.15 Trends in commodities imports of Japan, 1970-
      1985 220

Preface

Former U.S. Secretary of Commerce Peter Peterson was correct when he referred to Japan's large general trading companies as "probably the world's most efficient marketing channel." These general trading companies, known as the *sogo shosha*, have played a key role in Japan's extraordinary economic growth since World War II and in its subsequent outstanding success as an international trader.* As an indication of their scope, the ten largest *sogo shosha* had gross sales of $155 billion in the Japanese fiscal year that ended March 1976. This was 31 percent of Japan's gross national product. They handled about 56 percent of Japan's imports and exports and almost 20 percent of the total domestic wholesale trade in Japan. The export and overseas transactions of the *sogo shosha* in the same year amounted to slightly over 5 percent of total world export trade.

Despite their obvious significance in the Japanese economic system and in world commerce, there is no other book-length objective study of the *sogo shosha* in English. The many studies in Japanese of the *sogo shosha* are inaccessible to the English

---

*The ten largest general trading companies, ranked by decreasing size of sales in fiscal 1975, are: the Mitsubishi Corporation, Mitsui & Co., C. Itoh & Co., the Marubeni Corporation, Sumitomo Shoji Kaisha, Nissho-Iwai Co., Toyomenka Kaisha, Kanematsu Gosho, Ltd., Ataka & Co., and Nichimen Company. After this book was typeset, word was received that Sumitomo Shoji Kaisha, Ltd., had changed its official English title to Sumitomo Corporation. It was not possible to make this change in the text, but I hope the reader will bear the new title in mind.

reader. Some also tend to be either ideologically based attacks or uninformative public relations defenses.

Perhaps the sheer size and complexity of the *sogo shosha* has prevented their adequate description and analysis. On the one hand, they are integral parts of Japanese society and culture, with historical roots extending as far back as the early 1870s, when their mission was to assist Japan—recently opened to the Western world—to industrialize and become politically independent. Their roles in the Japanese economy, always central, evolved and expanded during the first half of the twentieth century. During the period of economic recovery following World War II, the *sogo shosha* emerged as Japan's primary importers of food and raw materials, the advance guard of its export drive, modernizers of the incredibly complex Japanese domestic distribution system, and organizers-investors of huge natural resource development projects abroad.

On the other hand, the *sogo shosha* have always been externally oriented—they are, after all, trading companies. They have long had global networks for sales and communication. Responding to the challenges of the 1970s, they have chosen to become international enterprises, globally active in the trading of commodities, capital, technology, managerial skills, and labor. Today, the *sogo shosha* seem to be moving away from being solely an integral part of "Japan, Inc."—that interlocking network of government, manufacturers, finance, and trade—and are becoming part of a more inclusive network of international trade and finance.

Individually and collectively, the *sogo shosha* are complex and evolving parts of one of the world's most productive economic systems. The goal of this book is to present the reader with an accurate description of what the general trading companies are, how they developed, and what the future is likely to hold for them.

The author has no ideological axe to grind for or against the *sogo shosha*. If this book has a thesis, it is simply that the Japanese general trading companies warrant the close attention of businessmen, economists, government officials, and the educated public outside Japan. As the second largest economy in the free world and as a vital and creative democratic society, Japan is

Preface

indisputably one of the most influential participants in the international community of nations. For too long have too many of its primary institutions remained shrouded from international attention. The Japanese *sogo shosha* are among the most significant phenomena of contemporary world commerce. The present volume aspires to describe them accurately and to place them in their appropriate contexts of Japanese society and international business.

The *sogo shosha* are already in many ways global traders and investors. In many other ways, they remain uniquely Japanese. However, as their global orientation develops and extends, it seems likely that they will fully enter into the international economic system. In a day when terms such as "global reach" and "multinational corporation" are widely bandied about, it would seem the better part of wisdom to understand the origins, roles, and prospects of Japan's giant overseas trading companies.

This book has three principal parts. Part 1 examines the *sogo shosha*'s core business (Chapter 1), describes the origins and defining characteristics of the big ten *sogo shosha* (Chapter 2), and explores the extended network of services and resources they provide for conducting business (Chapter 3). Part 2 describes the growth trends and business strategies of the general trading companies from 1960 to 1973 (Chapter 4), elaborates on their roles in the post–World War II Japanese economy (Chapter 5), and looks in detail at their overseas natural resource development projects (Chapter 6). Part 3 examines the strategic changes the *sogo shosha* have made since 1973 with their new emphasis on management efficiency and global reach (Chapter 7) and portrays their present role and likely future place in world commerce (Chapter 8).

The book focuses on the period between the mid-1960s and fall 1977. One of the ten firms, Ataka & Co., merged with another general trading company, C. Itoh & Co., in October 1977. Inasmuch as the manuscript was practically completed in the fall of 1977 and many of the tables were compiled on the ten-firm basis, statistics have not been revised to reflect the new situation. This has not, however, affected the descriptive analysis or views of the book.

The dollar-Yen exchange rates used in this study are as follows: 1:360 prior to December 1971; 1:308 between December 1971 and September 1972; 1:265 between October 1972 and February 1974; and 1:300 between March 1974 and December 1976. Strictly speaking, only the Yen figures form a relatively, though not absolutely, accurate basis for evaluating the transactions, assets, and profits of the general trading companies because of the two Yen revaluations after 1971 and the continuing float of major world currencies since the spring of 1973. For this reason the Yen figures in many tables have not been converted into U.S. dollars.

* * *

I would like to thank the Japan Society, Inc., of New York for sponsoring the publication of this book. In particular, I would like to thank the society's Executive Director David McEachron, Deputy Executive Director Robert Ruenitz, and Education and Communications Director Peter Grilli for their deep interest, encouragement, and support. I would also like to thank Rodney Armstrong, the Japan Society's former executive director, now of Armstrong, Byrd and Associates, for being among the first to believe in the importance of the subject.

The book could not have been written without the keen personal interest and support of Tatsuzo Mizukami (president of the Japan Foreign Trade Council, Inc.), Chujiro Fujino (chairman of the Mitsubishi Corporation), and Hisashi Tsuda (honorary chairman and director of Sumitomo Shoji Kaisha, Ltd.). Naoji Harada, Zenji Kyomoto, and Yoshishige Murakami (respectively senior managing director, managing director, and information director of the Japan Foreign Trade Council, Inc.) were most helpful in arranging interviews and in providing other forms of assistance. Eiichi Hashimoto (chairman of Mitsui & Co., Ltd.), Masaoki Kojima (managing director of the Marubeni Corporation), Gyota Machida (chairman of Kanematsu Gosho, Ltd.), Toshio Takeuchi (president of Toyomenka Kaisha, Ltd.), Seiki Tozaki (president of C. Itoh & Co., Ltd.), Hisao Tsuchihashi (managing director of Nichimen Company, Limited), and Mitsuo Ueda (president of Nissho-Iwai Co., Ltd.), too, extended courtesy and much appreciated cooperation. I hope that they and the numerous other officials of Japanese general trading companies and business organizations who assisted me will find the book sympathetic yet objective in analysis and interpretation.

Daniel Stein and Alfred Marks have provided deeply appreciated editorial assistance. Martin Labbe of the State University of New York at New Paltz, Masao Okamoto (director of Normura Research Institute), Misag Tabibian (partner of Touche Ross & Co.), and William V. Rapp (vice president of Morgan Guaranty Trust Company) read the manuscript and made valuable comments. It goes without saying that I alone bear responsibility for the interpretations and facts contained in this book.

Finally, my profound appreciation goes to my wife and children for their patience, understanding, and cooperation.

—*Alexander K. Young*

The *Sogo Shosha*

Part 1
What They Are and What They Do

1
The *Sogo Shosha*'s Core Business

Traders, Trading Intermediaries, and Developers

Japan's huge general trading companies have been characterized in Japan and abroad by all sorts of appellations, ranging from "Japanese-type conglomerates," "Japan's new *zaibatsus*," "Japanese-type multinationals," "modern monsters with worldwide communications networks rivaling that of the Pentagon," "mammoth traders handling 10,000 commodities from instant noodles to missiles," "speculators in stocks, rice, land, lumber and other necessities," to "action think tanks." These characterizations are only partial and misleading descriptions of the *sogo shosha*'s business, organizational structure, resources, and behavior. Outsiders and even many company insiders see thousands of puzzle pieces, but not the whole picture nor, more important, how the pieces fit together. In reality, the *sogo shosha*'s basic business is amazingly simple. Once one grasps the core business, it becomes easy to understand their complex services, resources, strategies, operations, and organizational structure.

The general trading company's basic business has always been and still is trading. Specifically, this includes independent selling and buying as well as being a trade intermediary between sellers and buyers—in other words, serving as a channel connecting demand and supply. The *sogo shosha* are more than mere traders and trade intermediaries, however. They are also active creators of long-term demand and supply to ensure stability and to generate new business opportunities. They create demand and supply by organizing huge joint ventures, such as overseas development of industrial raw materials (e.g., iron ore, coal, bauxite), with giant producers. These ventures increase producers' demands for transportation, construction, and mining equipment, which the trading companies can then sell as principals or as agents. They also ensure the long-term supply of natural resources to various industries and thus open additional sales opportunities to the *sogo shosha*.

Enormous Power in Japanese and World Trade

Japan's big general trading companies are commercial giants possessing enormous power in Japanese and world trade. During the 1975 Japanese fiscal year (April 1, 1975 to March 31, 1976) the ten largest general trading companies ("the big ten") had gross sales amounting to nearly $155 billion. They handled 56.4 percent of Japan's total exports, 55.6 percent of its import total (exports and import totals are both figured on a customs clearance basis), and approximately 18 percent of the domestic wholesale total. Their export and overseas (i.e., third-country trade) transactions accounted for slightly over 5 percent of world trade (export).[1]

A Highly Diversified Business

The big ten handle an almost infinite number of products. As one of their officials stated jokingly, "We buy and sell everything under the sun except people and coffins." Each trading company handles from 10,000 to 20,000 products. Furthermore, in addition to selling and buying, they engage in numerous other types of business.

Consider, for example, the extensive business ventures of the Mitsubishi Corporation as listed by its semiannual financial report for the fiscal half year ended March 31, 1974:

 1. Purchase, sales, export, and import of the following:
    a. coal, petroleum, gas, other fuels and manufactured products of above;
    b. iron, nonferrous metals, manufactured products of above, ores and minerals;

c. machinery, equipment (including gauge and medical equipment), locomotives, ships, airplanes, and parts of above;
   d. food, liquor and other beverages, fat, resin, tobacco, salt, and other agricultural, marine, forestry, livestock and natural products and finished products of above;
   e. fertilizer, feed, and raw materials of above;
   f. textile products and raw materials;
   g. lumber, wood products, cement, glass and other kiln products;
   h. chemical products, cosmetics and pharmaceuticals (drugs, poison and explosives, etc.); and
   i. rubber, leather, pulp, paper, manufactured products of above, and sundry goods.
2. The development, prospecting, production, manufacturing, processing, growing, and subcontracting of each of the items above.
3. Repair and installation, subcontracting, leasing and management of machinery, equipment, locomotives, ships, airplanes, and parts.
4. Construction business.
5. Purchase, sales, leasing, and management of real estate.
6. Purchase and sales of antiques.
7. Warehousing.
8. Land transportation, maritime transportation, and air transportation.
9. Agency, brokerage, and wholesale of each of the items above.
10. Agency for liability insurance and for automobile insurance based on the automobile liability insurance law.
11. All and every business related to each of the items above.[2]

The financial reports of the other nine general trading companies show that each of them engages in similarly diversified business ventures, except for C. Itoh & Co., Ltd., which omits manufacturing as a line of business. Indeed, additional ventures were listed by other firms: travel agencies by Toyomenka Kaisha, Ltd., and Ataka & Co., Ltd.; analysis and dissemination of information by Kanematsu Gosho Ltd.; purchase and sale of precious metals by Nissho-Iwai Co., Ltd.; and acquisition of securities and extension of credits and funds (i.e., loans) by Nichimen Company, Limited. Actually all the *sogo shosha*, even those not listing them, engage in these additional activities although they may suspend some ventures from time to time.

A systematic examination shows that the big ten have been primarily large-volume, first-stage wholesale traders of industrial raw materials and grains and of such standardized intermediate products as steel, synthetic fiber, and fertilizer. Price, speed of information, and economies of scale are of primary importance in these kinds of sales, which require little engineering service to manufacturers, minimum sales promotion, and minimal repair and other after-service to retail consumers. The big ten are not large traders of machineries or consumer products (e.g., automobiles, electronic equipment, cameras, etc.) characterized by multiplicity of products, product differentiation, sales promotion, and various technical customer services.

During FY 1975 ended March 31, 1976, the ten largest general trading companies had an overwhelming weight (81.8 percent) in Japan's metal exports, more than a majority share in the country's chemicals and textiles export (64.7 percent and 60.8 percent, respectively), but less than a majority share (42.7 percent) of machineries and an insignificant share (35 percent) in the export of all other commodities groups. The import business of the big ten shows a similar pattern. They dominated three groups of Japanese imports: foodstuffs (81.3 percent), chemicals (78.2 percent), and textiles (73.5 percent). They also had a majority share in Japan's import of metal raw materials and fuel. Their weight in machineries and "others" was insignificant. Figure 1.1 provides specific figures.

Global Spread of Business

The *sogo shosha* buy and sell as principals or agents not only at home but all over the world. They trade with all geographic regions: North America; Central and South America; East, Southeast, and Western Asia; Oceania; Near and Middle East; Africa; and Eastern and Western Europe. They have extensive business dealings with both the industrialized democracies and the Communist bloc countries. At any moment, several thousand well-dressed *sogo shosha* men from the Japanese headquarters are

Figure 1.1 Share of the ten general trading companies' commodities trade in Japan's foreign trade, FY 1975

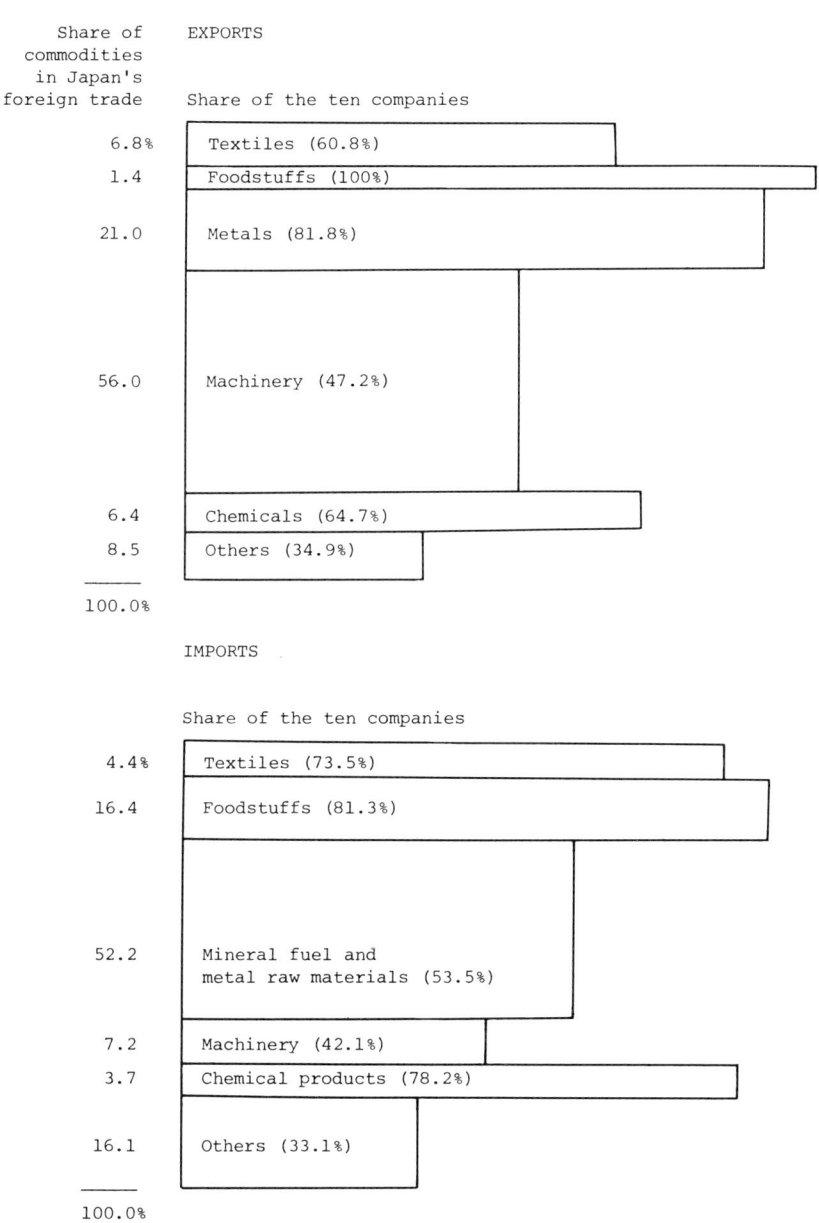

Note: Unit = %.
Source: Information and Research Department, Mitsui & Co., Nihon keizai ni okeru shosha no yakuwari: genjo to tenbo (Tokyo: Mitsui & Co., 1976), p. 7.

abroad working in their Park Avenue offices in New York, flying to Buenos Aires with attaché cases in hand, huddling with customers at Taipei's Grand Hotel, eating at restaurants along Toronto's Yonge Street, or drinking at bars in Mexico City. Drinking, dining, or laughing, they are always ready to make a deal. Each spring and autumn hundreds of them travel to the Canton trade fairs to sell to and to buy from the Chinese. Top officials, such as Honorary Chairman Hisashi Tsuda of Sumitomo Shoji Kaisha, Ltd., and President Seiki Tozaki of C. Itoh & Co., Ltd., spend much of their time traveling to the four corners of the world conferring with government and business officials and attending economic conferences.

Young company officials may show up in Libya to buy oil for export to Japan or in Kenya to negotiate a huge airport construction project. They turn up in South Africa as "honorary whites" to negotiate a deal for export of chrome and diamonds to Japan or other countries. Since the oil crisis they have been flocking to the Middle East's money and action to conclude business ventures ranging from oil imports to joint oil development projects to the construction of huge petrochemical complexes. Whether it be a remote area in Alberta, Canada, Davao in the Philippines, Minas Gerais in Brazil, central Java in Indonesia, or Lake Leroy in Western Australia, trading company officials are there—or will soon arrive—if a business opportunity beckons.

Despite the global spread of the *sogo shosha's* business, the preponderance of their share in Japan's foreign trade has been in trade with the developing countries and the communist bloc nations rather than with the industrialized countries of North America and Western Europe. The two major exceptions are their dominance in the import trade from North America (because of their overwhelming weight in the import of American grains and industrial raw materials), and their insignificant share in oil imports from the Middle East (because of the long predominance of major international oil companies).

According to statistics of the Ministry of International Trade and Industry (MITI), during FY 1973 a dozen or so large trading companies handled 61 percent of Japan's exports to Latin America, 61 percent of exports to Western Asia (India, Pakistan, etc.), 56 percent of exports to the communist bloc, and 53 percent of the nation's exports to Southeast Asia, but only between 40 and 44 percent of Japan's exports to North America, Western Europe, and Oceania. They accounted for 75 percent of Japanese imports from Oceania, 72 percent of imports from Latin America, 71 percent of imports from North America, and 53 percent of imports from both the communist bloc and Southeast Asia, but less than 40 percent of Japan's imports from Western Europe and Western Asia.[3] (See Table 1.1)

Multiple Types of Trade

The *sogo shosha* engage in many types of trade. Single product sales remain basic. However, multiproduct sales to single customers are also numerous. Nissho-Iwai Co., Ltd.'s export to a Mexican electric power company of not only boilers, turbines, and accessories but power transmission equipment, electric wires, and cables is an example of a multiproduct sale. Furthermore, the *sogo shosha* are increasingly involved in more complex transactions such as assembly or package trade. An example was the export of a huge petrochemical plant to the government of Singapore on a turnkey basis. The deal required a package sale of equipment, technology, and consulting services of numerous manufacturers. Similar deals may involve the construction of a plant or the sale of an entire plant.

The trading companies conduct simple one-way trade and two-way seller-buyer transactions. They try as much as possible to develop two-way trade: to buy a huge quantity of iron ore and coal from an Australian mining company and sell it mining and transportation equipment in return; or to import grains from the U.S. and sell fertilizer to U.S. farmers; or to buy molybdenum from AMAX and sell it equipment and money in the form of development loans.

The *sogo shosha* have also been increasingly involved in third-country trade—i.e., trade between two foreign countries handled (negotiation, contract, and financial settlement) by Japanese firms without direct involvement of Japan as a source of supply or market—and trade involving many nations. Selling U.S.-manufactured gas turbines to Indonesia, exporting U.S. scrap iron to the People's Republic of China, importing Rumanian

Table 1.1 Geographic Structure of Exports of Large Trading Companies, FY 1973 (annual exports exceeding 100 billion Yen)

	Southeast Asia	Western Asia	Western Europe	North America	Latin America	Africa	Oceania	Communist bloc
(A) Japan's total import[a]	31,511	7,250	20,344	35,195	10,111	14,280	5,853	8,504
Large trading companies:								
No. of firms	12	12	12	12	11	12	12	12
(B) Export[a]	16,723	4,425	8,396	14,030	6,189	6,444	2,580	4,768
Percent of B in A	53.1	61.0	41.3	39.9	61.2	45.1	44.1	56.1

Source: Tsusho Sargyosho (MITI), 1974 Boeki gyotai tokeihyo (1974 Foreign Trade Statistics by Industries) (Tokyo: Tsusho Sangyo Chosakai, 1975), pp. 148-149.

Note: See footnote 3 on p. 21 on the double accounting system of Japan's foreign trade transactions used in MITI's Boeki gyotai tokeihyo.

[a] In hundred million Yen.

urea into Bangladesh, or exporting Brazilian gasoline to the U.S. are a few examples of third-country trade.

They search all over the world, using their offices in numerous countries, to meet the needs of their customers. For example, upon receiving a request from a Brazilian textile manufacturer for polyester fibers, a large general trading company approached a major American chemical company. The chemical firm was willing to supply the fibers but was short of ethylene glycol, an essential raw material. The general trading company asked a French firm to supply the necessary ethylene glycol, but was informed that they could do so only if the trading firm could provide them with benzene. The general trading company turned to firms in the U.S. and Holland and obtained the benzene for the French manufacturer, who then supplied the trading company with ethylene glycol. Thus, the American chemical concern was finally able to provide the Brazilian textile maker with polyester fibers. The transaction involved four countries and five different trading company offices. It was concluded in one week.

In addition to normal commercial transactions that involve financial settlements between seller and buyer, the giant trading firms also conduct so-called "barter trade" (exchange of goods between two countries without the use of money) and "switch trade" (import of goods from a second country through the use of a third country's currency as a currency of settlement). One firm arranged the export of wheat from a poor agricultural country, intent on industrialization but short of foreign exchange, to Japan in a barter exchange for a small Japanese steel plant. Another helped Rumania acquire a paint manufacturing plant, part of whose cost was defrayed in the form of fine chemicals and machine tools because Rumania preferred payment in goods rather than hard currency. The firm then found buyers for the products elsewhere. Yet another firm arranged the use of Indonesian currency as the currency of settlement for imports of high precision machinery from West Germany to Japan, thus reducing Indonesia's trade deficit vis-à-vis Japan.

Trading Conglomerates Rather Than Manufacturing Conglomerates

The extensive and highly diversified business ventures

portrayed by the ten largest *sogo shosha* in their financial statements are impressive. They paint a picture of themselves not only as agents, commission merchants, brokers, and wholesalers in domestic and foreign trade, but as principals engaged in purchases, sales, export and import of raw materials, foodstuffs, and intermediary and finished manufactures of a broad range of product groups. More important, they claim that they are more than service industries engaged in commerce and in providing financing, information, project organization, transportation and other services. They also claim to be prospectors, developers, manufacturers, and processors of and subcontractors for numerous product groups from textiles to ferrous and nonferrous metals, chemicals, oil and natural gas, machinery, food, and nearly everything else under the sun. The trading companies' claims give the public the impression they are American-style manufacturing conglomerates similar to ITT or Litton Industries. Both their supporters and critics also have sometimes characterized them as manufacturing conglomerates.

This is incorrect. It is the source of much confusion, misunderstanding, and criticism of the *sogo shosha*, including attacks on them in Japan by the Japan Fair Trade Commission, the politicians, the mass media, scholars, and the general public between 1972 and 1975. *The ten sogo shosha have been and remain trading conglomerates, not manufacturing conglomerates.* This is true despite the numerous products they handle, the global spread and multiple types of their business, the broad range of services they provide, and the enormous resources they command.

The *sogo shosha* own hundreds of small subsidiaries and large joint ventures in Japan and all over the noncommunist world that engage in resource prospecting and development, manufacturing and processing, construction, financing and leasing, and subcontracting. But all are owned and run for one primary purpose: to support the core business of selling and buying and to generate new business opportunities—not for development and manufacturing purposes per se. The broad range of services they supply for customers and the immense resources they possess, described below, also have as their purpose to support and expand the core business. For this reason, a majority of subsidiaries controlled by

Japan's ten largest trading companies are in sales, warehousing, transportation, and other service industries. Furthermore, most were acquired by mergers after lengthy consultation among the parties involved (including banks) rather than by outright takeovers, or established as new firms to develop new businesses for what the Japanese call expanded acquisition of "commercial rights" (*shoken*) rather than for manufacturing purposes per se.

By contrast, U.S. and Western European conglomerates are centered around manufacturing industries. Furthermore, their primary objectives generally are improved cash flow and profit maximization from capital gains through outright takeovers or sales of business firms.

If a clear understanding of the *sogo shosha*'s core business is the first imperative, a clear grasp of the firms as trading rather than manufacturing conglomerates is the second imperative.

A Comparison with Other Types of Japanese Trading Companies

The *sogo shosha* are not the only Japanese businesses engaged in export and import, nor are they the only trading companies. According to statistics compiled by MITI, Japan had 9,743 firms (including 270 firms under foreign control) that engaged in foreign trade during Japanese FY 1973. About 70 percent of them (or about 6,800 firms) were wholesalers and retailers; 28 percent (or about 2,700 firms) were manufacturers. These two categories accounted for about 98 percent of the total, while department stores and "others" accounted for only 2 percent.[4]

The *sogo shosha*, which MITI called "large trading companies," differ from wholesalers, retailers, department stores, manufacturers, and others by their overwhelming weight in Japan's foreign trade. The big ten had a startling 53 percent share of Japan's export total on a customs clearance basis and 64 percent of Japan's total imports on a customs clearance basis during FY 1973 (note that the big ten's share during fiscal 1973 was even larger than during fiscal 1975). Their share in Japan's foreign trade was smaller in MITI's categories of industries, but was still a not insignificant 48 percent of the 9,734 firms' export total and 57 percent of these firms' import total, while the manufacturers'

Table 1.2 Exports and Imports of Japanese Traders, FY 1973

	Firms		Exports		Imports	
	Number	Percent	Million Yen	Percent	Million Yen	Percent
Wholesalers and retailers	6,734	69.8	8,919,425	67.1	10,629,450	77.5
Department stores	19	0.2	4,901	—	29,541	0.2
Manufacturers	2,703	27.8	4,285,078	32.2	2,976,037	21.7
Others	215	2.2	95,419	0.7	75,977	0.6
Total	9,734	100.0	13,304,823	100.0	13,711,005	100.0

Source: Tsusho Sangyosho (MITI), *1974 Boeki gyotai tokeihyo* (1974 Foreign Trade Statistics by Industries) (Tokyo: Tsusho Sangyo Chosakai, 1975), pp. 4-5.

Table 1.3 Exports of Japanese Trading Companies by Scale of Transactions, FY 1973

Scale of export transactions[a]	Firms Number	Percent	Share in exports (percent)
Less than 10 million	587	14.6	—
10-50 million	838	20.9	0.3
50-100 million	558	13.9	0.5
100-500 million	1,235	30.7	3.4
500-1,000 million	361	9.0	2.9
1,000-5,000 million	355	8.8	7.8
5-10 billion	35	0.9	2.7
10-50 billion	31	0.8	6.4
50-100 billion	5	0.1	3.5
More than 100 billion	12	0.3	72.5
Total	4,017	100.0	100.0

Source: Tsusho Sangyosho (MITI), *1974 Boeki gyotai tokeihyo* (1974 Foreign Trade Statistics by Industries) (Tokyo: Tsusho Sangyo Chosakai, 1975), p. 14.

[a] In Yen.

weight was much smaller (32.2 percent of the export total and 21.7 percent of the import total).

The difference between the *sogo shosha* and the approximately 6,000 other incorporated Japanese trading companies (wholesalers, retailers, and department stores as defined by MITI) was even more striking. During fiscal 1973, of 4,017 Japanese trading companies that engaged in export (not all the 5,874 incorporated Japanese trading companies were involved in *both* export and import business), the twelve largest firms had a lopsided 72.5 percent share of the export firms' export total. Of 4,099 Japanese trading firms that engaged in import business, eleven had a 74.5 percent share of the import firms' import total.

The *sogo shosha* differ from specialized trading firms because they are highly diversified rather than focusing on product groups or geographic areas. As defined by MITI, specialized product traders are those whose transactions in one product group (food, beverage, and tobacco; textiles; lumber, pulp and paper; coal, crude oil and other fuels; chemicals; ferrous and

Table 1.4   Imports of Japanese Trading Companies by Scale of Transactions, FY 1973

Scale of import transactions[a]	Firms Number	Percent	Share in imports (percent)
Less than 10 million	819	20.0	—
10-50 million	1,054	25.7	0.3
50-100 million	491	12.0	0.3
100-500 million	1,017	24.8	2.3
500-1,000 million	303	7.4	2.0
1,000-5,000 million	317	7.7	6.3
5-10 billion	44	1.1	2.7
10-50 billion	39	0.9	3.9
50-100 billion	4	0.1	2.7
More than 100 billion	11	0.3	74.5
Total	4,099	100.0	100.0

Source: Tsusho Sangyosho (MITI), *1974 Boeki gyotai tokeihyo* (1974 Foreign Trade Statistics by Industries) (Tokyo: Tsusho Sangyo Chosakai, 1975), p. 14.

[a] In Yen.

nonferrous metals; machinery, etc.) exceed 50 percent of their total transactions. Specialized regional traders are those whose transactions in a given geographic area (North America, South America, Southeast Asia, East Asia, Western Europe, Africa, the communist bloc, etc.) exceed 50 percent of total transactions. The *sogo shosha* are highly diversified in product groups, business ventures, and geographic spread. Furthermore, the scale of their transactions, resources, and functions is vastly larger than that of specialized traders.

The general trading companies are also distinct from Japan's traditional domestic wholesalers, the *tonya*. *Tonyas* are primary wholesalers specializing in the collection of a vast variety of finished goods from a large number of small producers for distribution to secondary (regional) and tertiary (local) wholesalers. General trading companies are huge wholesale intermediaries between large manufacturers on the one hand and small producers and the *tonya* wholesalers on the other hand. The *sogo shosha* supply large volume raw materials from overseas and parts and components from small- to medium-sized domestic producers to huge manufacturers. They also distribute intermediate producer goods from large manufacturers to small- to medium-sized producers and finished products to *tonyas* for further distribution to numerous retailers. The scale and diversity of the *sogo shosha*'s business and resources are incomparably larger than those of the traditional domestic wholesalers.

Comparison with U.S. and European Trading Companies

It is well known that the giant American and Western European manufacturing industries (steel, automobile, computers, shipbuilding, rubber, and others), oil industry, and financial institutions prefer assuming their own direct supply and marketing responsibilities when possible rather than using intermediaries. Manufacturers prefer direct purchases of industrial raw materials and direct marketing not only at home but abroad. Thus, for example, International Business Machines (IBM) employs its own completely controlled sales subsidiaries, such as IBM Americas/Far East Corporation, IBM World Trade/Middle East/Africa Corporation and others, for the worldwide marketing of its computers, peripheral gear, and software. Other industrial and financial giants follow a similar pattern.[5]

In contrast, Japan's general trading companies are huge traders and supply and sales intermediaries, not manufacturers or financial institutions per se, although, as discussed later, they are also giant financial intermediaries.

The strong preference by giant U.S. and Western European enterprises for direct supply and marketing activities, however, does not mean a lack of trading intermediaries in the rest of the world or, for that matter, in the United States and Western Europe. Twelve large multiproduct trading companies exist in Sweden, Finland, Canada, Hong Kong, Switzerland, and Singapore. These include such well-known old firms as Jardine Matheson. They are all far smaller than the *sogo shosha* in sales if not in profit margins. Only three had sales exceeding $1,000 million during 1976, whereas each of Japan's big ten had sales between about $5 billion and nearly $33 billion during the fiscal

Table 1.5   Large Non-Japanese Trading Companies
             (Wholesale and Trade), 1976

Company	Country	Sales ($1,000,000)	Earnings per share ($1)
Kesco	Finland	1,718	0.32
Beijerinvest	Sweden	1,555	2.18
KF (Kooperativa Förbundet)	Sweden	2,950	NA
C. F. Bally	Switzerland	287	95.85
Acklands	Canada	270	1.17
Provigo	Canada	502	1.18
H. Russel	Canada	287	0.90
Wajax	Canada	96	2.50
Westburne International	Canada	864	2.27
Jardine, Matheson	Hong Kong	584[a]	0.31
Bousteadco	Singapore	32	0.08
Inchcape	Singapore	250	0.04

Source: *Business Week,* July 25, 1977, pp. 81-98.

[a] 1975 figure.

year ended March 31, 1977. Total annual sales of the largest non-Japanese trading company (Kooperativa Foroundel of Sweden) amounted to $2,950 million, equal to about one-tenth of the Mitsubishi Corporation's and one-half of Nichimen Company, Limited's. Sales of the remaining nine non-Japanese trading companies were far smaller, ranging between $32 million (Bousteaco of Singapore) and $584 million (Jardine Matheson of Hong Kong; 1975 figure).

Large American nonindustrial trading companies are generally specialized commodities traders handling grains, sugar, coffee, and other products. Furthermore, while the sales scale of such well-known grain traders as Continental Grains, Cook Industries, Cargill, and Bunge—to use the grain trade as an example—is of considerable size, they cannot match the *sogo shosha*'s sales aggregate or diversified business.

Other types of trading companies also exist in the United States. A quick perusal of import firms based in New York, the world's commercial center, reveals that most of them are of small or medium size. The 1970 *Directory of New York Importers* listed approximately 2,000 import firms. None seems to be a member of the Board of Directors of the powerful U.S. Foreign Trade Council or is on the *Fortune 500 Non-Industrial Companies* list. Most of them appear to be importers specializing in one commodity group or another, although many individual products are on their import commodity lists. Furthermore, a careful analysis of about 180 firms whose first initial is A (the *Directory* is compiled alphabetically) indicates that all are limited in how they conduct import trade. The sole exception is Ataka America, Inc., the U.S. affiliate of a *sogo shosha* firm. Ataka America, Inc. was the only firm on the A list that imported for its own account, as an agent of foreign suppliers, as an agent of U.S. purchasers, and as a broker. All the others run their import business only in one or two capacities, not in all four capacities.[6]

In sum, Japan's ten largest general trading companies are unique global trading institutions, whether compared with Japanese or non-Japanese trading companies—unique in terms of the scale of transactions, the almost infinite number of products they handle, the global spread of their business, the multiple types of their trade, and, equally important, in terms of the services they provide and the enormous resources they command for conducting and expanding their businesses. The *sogo shosha* are an important economic institution the Japanese have devised and refined to serve their national and corporate needs.

Notes

1. Statistics supplied by the Japan Foreign Trade Council, Inc. Figures for the *sogo shosha* are for the Japanese fiscal year; figures for world export trade are for the calendar year. The abbreviation FY will be used in this book for fiscal year.

2. See the Mitsubishi Corporation's financial report for the fiscal half year ended March 31, 1974, p. 16.

3. The author has encountered formidable research problems in writing this book: limited data, incomplete breakdowns by either

geography or commodity, and lack of uniformity in the commodity classification standards used by the general trading companies.

The series of mergers the *sogo shosha* have gone through since 1952 make it virtually impossible for an outsider to gather a complete set of semiannual financial reports from which data on trade can be collected and analyzed. In addition, the reports that are available provide statistics by different types of trade (i.e., domestic transactions, imports, exports, and overseas transactions) and by commodity groups (metals, chemicals, machinery, etc.). They do not provide individual commodity breakdowns for domestic and foreign trade transactions. Major countries from which commodities are imported and to which goods are exported are named, but no statistical data are given by any trading company except Ataka & Co., Ltd.

The most serious barrier to an exact analysis, however, has been the lack of uniformity in the firms' commodity classification standards. While the Mitsubishi Corporation and Kanematsu Gosho, Ltd., provide the most detailed statistical breakdowns, giving separate entries for fuel, iron and steel, and nonferrous metals, other firms lump iron and steel and nonferrous metals together in financial reports for March 1974. The Marubeni Corporation, C. Itoh & Co., Ltd., and a number of other firms lump fuel and chemicals together. Construction is a separate entry for the Mitsubishi Corporation and for Toyomenka Kaisha, Ltd., but it is grouped together with machinery by the Marubeni Corporation, C. Itoh & Co., Ltd., and the Nichimen Company, Limited. On close inspection, Mitsui & Co., Ltd.'s category for "others" turns out to cover lumber, pulp and paper (listed by most firms as "materials" or *shizai*), as well as crude oil, gasoline, cement, and others.

Fortunately, the annual *Foreign Trade Statistics by Industries (Boeki gyotai tokeihyo)*, published by the Ministry of International Trade and Industry (MITI), despite incompleteness in several areas, provides a limited but workable solution. These annual foreign trade yearbooks for every fiscal year since 1952 do not give breakdowns by individual firms. However, they do provide a detailed statistical analysis by categories of traders (wholesalers, retailers, department stores, manufacturers, and others), by commodity groups, and by geographic origin of imports and direction of exports (although geographic breakdowns were not given before the mid-1960s). The statistical analysis by categories of traders is in turn given more detailed breakdown by rank of capital and by rank of transaction volume, with one separate entry for what MITI officials call "large trading companies." The number of "large trading companies" varies from year to year. However, they can be considered *sogo shosha*

Sogo Shosha's *Core Business* 21

firms and serve as a basis of analysis because they were named as *sogo shosha* by MITI in the 1956 *Tsusho hakusho (1956 International Trade White Paper)*. They have had an overwhelming share of Japan's foreign trade since the early 1950s despite the fact that they constitute no more than 1 percent of all Japanese trading companies. Their number in the *Foreign Trade Statistics by Industries* has been down to ten since fiscal year 1966, the number of the top ten *sogo shosha*.

Unfortunately, there is one problem: the double or even triple accounting system of foreign trade transactions. According to Yoshishige Murakami of the Japan Foreign Trade Council, each domestic concern involved in a given export process, from the manufacturer of a given export item to the trading company that handles it, reports to the MITI the same export shipment in the multistage export process for inclusion in *Foreign Trade Statistics by Industries*. As a result, export figures in *Foreign Trade Statistics by Industries* are larger than export figures on customs clearance basis; and shares of general trading companies in Japanese exports in *Foreign Trade Statistics by Industries* are smaller than those on customs clearance basis. Once the double or triple accounting system and its implications are borne in mind, MITI's annual *Foreign Trade Statistics by Industries* can be used to analyze the *sogo shosha*'s import and export trends over the past twenty years.

4. MITI places the *sogo shosha* under two categories: (1) as wholesalers-retailers under categories of industries; and (2) as trading companies by types of foreign traders (i.e., exporters, importers, and exporters-importers).

5. Most of the giant U.S. firms are members of the powerful U.S. National Foreign Trade Council, Inc. The firms that served on the council's board of directors during 1975 read like a *Who's Who* of American industry. The oil industry was represented by Exxon, Texaco, Gulf, Mobil, Standard Oil of California, and Caltex Petroleum; the steel industry by Bethlehem and Armco; the electric industry by General Electric and Westinghouse; the automobile industry by General Motors and Ford; the computer data processing and communications industries by IBM, NCR, Xerox, and ITT; the chemical industry by du Pont, Union Carbide, and Monsanto; the rubber industry by Firestone, Uniroyal, B.F. Goodrich, and Goodyear; the consumer products industry by Coca Cola, Colgate-Palmolive, Gillette, Proctor & Gamble, and United Brands; and the financial institutions by the Citibank, Chase Manhattan, Chemical Bank, Bank of America, Morgan Guaranty Trust Co. of New York, Manufacturers Hanover, and Continental Illinois National Bank and Trust. Other board members include, among others,

Johnson and Johnson, Del Monte, Otis Elevator, Pan American, United States Lines, Caterpillar Tractor, International Harvester, and Eastman Kodak.

    6. See *Directory of New York Importers,* 1970 (New York: Commerce and Industry Association Institute, Inc.), pp. 1-12.

2
The Ten Largest *Sogo Shosha*

This chapter examines the ten largest general trading companies at close range. We will look into their origins in Japanese history and culture, the individual histories of some of the companies, the complex interlocking worlds of group enterprises and subsidiaries in which they operate, the important question of whether they are monopolies or oligopolies, and their business records during the fiscal year ended March 31, 1977. Such an examination is a necessary prelude to putting the pieces of the *sogo shosha* puzzle together to form a coherent whole. Once we have sketched in the origins of the ten largest companies and the environment in which they operate, we can delve further into the analysis of other significant features they share, features often hidden from the public by the sheer complexity of the firms' operations and by their confusing rhetoric and self-descriptions.

Japan's ten largest general trading companies, ranked by gross sales during fiscal 1976 ended March 31, 1977 (not by total capital employed or earnings), were: Mitsubishi Corporation; Mitsui & Co., Ltd.; Marubeni Corporation; C. Itoh & Co., Ltd.; Sumitomo Shoji Kaisha, Ltd. (now Sumitomo Corporation); Nissho-Iwai Co., Ltd.; Toyomenka Kaisha, Ltd. (or Tomen); Kanematsu Gosho Ltd.; Nichimen Company, Limited; and Ataka & Co., Ltd. In the fall of 1977, C. Itoh & Co., Ltd., absorbed the $2-billion steel and chemical business of Ataka & Co., Ltd., and passed its longtime rival, Marubeni Corporation, to become the third-largest trading company. Major trading companies on the way to becoming *sogo shosha* are the Okura & Co., Ltd.; Chori Co., Ltd.; Toshoku Ltd.; Nozaki & Co., Ltd.; Kinsho Mataichi Corp.; and Itohman & Co., Ltd.

The Origins of the Big Ten

The ten largest general trading companies are all well known today in world trade. Not all of them enjoyed worldwide reputations before World War II. However, Mitsui & Co., Ltd., and the Mitsubishi Trading Company (name changed to Mitsubishi Corporation in 1971), and their trademarks, were well known in international trade by World War I. Mitsui & Co., Ltd., the largest trading company in pre–World War II Japan, initiated its third-country trade in 1908 with a sale of Manchurian soybeans to Western Europe. Between 1937 and 1943 Mitsui & Co., Ltd., had 18.3 percent of Japan's annual foreign trade, while the Mitsubishi Trading Company had a 10.3 percent share.[1]

The origins of the trading companies date back to the early 1870s, when Japan, under the control of the new Meiji government, resumed international trade after two centuries of self-imposed isolation under the Tokugawa shogunate. As international contacts expanded, perceptive government and business leaders were quick to realize that Japan not only lagged considerably behind the West in industrial development but also was in a very weak position in external trade. The young but farsighted government leaders embarked on an industrialization program to build a strong independent nation through the development of foreign trade. The task was not easy. Inexperience and unfamiliarity with foreign trade customs and procedures, insufficient import and export market information, and a lack of foreign language skills seemed almost insuperable obstacles. Moreover, foreign importers and exporters stationed in Nagasaki, Kobe, Yokohama, and other Japanese cities took advantage of the difficulties and succeeded in gaining a near monopoly of Japan's foreign trade (about 96 percent) soon after its resumption in the 1860s.

Not long after the inauguration of the new Meiji government in 1868, government leaders and industrialists began actively to support the establishment of Japanese trading companies. They had three purposes: (1) to reduce the near monopoly of Japan's foreign trade by foreign business; (2) to develop external trade to supply raw materials, industrial equipment, technology, and other goods to Japan's budding industries and to develop overseas outlets for manufactured products; and (3) to build a system of division of labor in which Japanese manufacturers could concentrate on manufacturing and leave supply and marketing functions to the trading companies with their foreign trade specialists.

How Big Are the Big Ten?

Before pursuing the discussion of the historical development of the *sogo shosha* in more detail, it is important to establish both the absolute and relative sizes of the ten largest general trading companies. An analysis of their sales and profits during FY 1976 (ended March 31, 1977) is revealing. Two firms (Mitsubishi Corporation and Mitsui & Co., Ltd.) had annual sales in excess of $30 billion; three firms (Marubeni Corporation, C. Itoh & Co., and Sumimoto Shoji Kaisha, Ltd.) were in the $20- to $22-billion range; and one firm (Nissho-Iwai Co., Ltd.) was in the $15-billion range. Three firms had annual sales below $10 billion but larger than $6 billion. Ataka & Co., Ltd., with sales totaling only $5.1 billion—an unbelievable $1.7-billion drop from fiscal year 1975—was a special situation because of the agonizing reorganization made necessary by the default of the huge financing it provided the bankrupt Newfoundland Refining Co. of Canada.

The ten general trading companies are highly stratified. While sales of Nichimen Company, Limited, were a huge $6.2 billion (twice the size of those of the largest non-Japanese general trading company, Kooperative Foroundel of Sweden), the four smallest trading firms are dwarfs compared with the Mitsubishi Corporation and Mitsui & Co., Ltd., each of whose sales exceeded $30 billion. Each of the two giants had yearly sales exceeding the combined total of Toyomenka Kaisha, Ltd., Kanematsu Gosho, Ltd., Ataka & Co., Ltd., and Nichimen Company, Limited, or about five times the size of Nichimen Company's and twice the sales of Nissho-Iwai Co., Ltd. Together, the big five had about two-thirds the combined sales of the top ten firms. Sales of the Mitsubishi Corporation amounted to 5.7 percent of Japan's gross national product; those of Mitsui & Co., Ltd., to 5.3 percent. In a strict sense, the big ten should not only be distinguished from the nearly 6,000 other small incorporated Japanese trading compa-

Table 2.1   Sales of the Ten General Trading Companies, FY 1976

Company	Million Yen
Mitsubishi Corporation	9,609,009
Mitsui & Co.	9,024,958
Marubeni Corporation	6,438,242
C. Itoh & Co.	6,332,657
Sumitomo Shoji	5,825,444
Nissho-Iwai Co.	4,527,070
Toyomenka	2,521,751
Kanematsu Gosho	2,335,713
Nichimen Company	1,810,546
Ataka & Co.	1,490,174
Total	49,915,564

Source: Financial statements of the firms, March 31, 1977.

nies but also should themselves be divided into four hierarchical groups: first-class, second-class, third-class, and fourth-class *sogo shosha*.

Although the big ten are highly diversified and remarkably well balanced in product, all the firms except C. Itoh & Co., Ltd., Toyomenka Kaisha, Ltd., and Kanematsu Gosho, Ltd. enjoy special strength in two product groups, metals and machinery. These two product groups alone had about 50 percent share in the sales aggregate of each of the seven firms; 60 percent for Nissho-Iwai Co., Ltd., and 57.3 percent for Sumimoto Shoji Kaisha, Ltd. C. Itoh & Co., Ltd.'s forte lies in chemicals, including fuel, and textiles. Textiles had the largest weight in the total sales of Toyomenka Kaisha, Ltd., and Kanematsu Gosho, Ltd. While Sumitomi Shoji Kaisha, Ltd., is a powerful trader in metals, machinery, and chemicals, the weight of foodstuffs and textiles in its total sales is the smallest among the big ten. The weight of fuel rose tremendously after the oil crisis of October 1973 because of the quadrupling of oil prices and the relentless efforts of the trading companies to expand the handling of energy. Fuel has forced a significant change in the companies' commodities structures.

Despite some significant changes in the past few years,

Table 2.2 Share of Various Commodities Groups in the Ten General Trading Companies' Sales, FY 1976 (percent)

	Fuel	Metals	Machinery	Chemicals	Foodstuffs	Textiles	Others	Total
Mitsubishi Corporation	18.5	33.4	15.0	8.4	12.9	5.4	6.4	100.0
Mitsui & Co.	7.3	31.7	18.2	12.0	13.9	6.7	10.2	100.0
Marubeni Corporation	14.4	24.5	24.3	—	14.1	14.2	8.5	100.0
C. Itoh & Co.	—	15.0	18.0	27.6	13.3	19.8	6.3	100.0
Sumitomo Shoji	—	33.9	23.4	20.7	8.7	5.3	8.0	100.0
Nissho-Iwai Co.	—	38.3	21.8	—	11.3	8.0	20.6	100.0
Toyomenka	—	21.7	21.0	11.9	19.0	22.0	4.4	100.0
Kanematsu Gosho	13.0	18.0	13.0	—	17.0	27.0	12.0	100.0
Ataka & Co.	—	36.9	12.8	—	14.6	16.9	18.8	100.0
Nichimen Company	—	28.2	22.0	10.3	13.8	17.5	8.2	100.0
Total	7.3	28.8	19.2	10.7	13.2	11.4	9.4	100.0

Source: Financial statements of the firms, March 31, 1977.

Note: For Mitsubishi, "Metals" includes steel, nonferrous metals, and construction equipment; "Others" includes [construction] materials, insurance agency, etc. For Sumitomo Shoji, "Chemicals" includes chemicals and fuel; "Others" includes construction materials, etc. For Nissho-Iwai, "Others" includes fuel, chemicals, lumber, etc. For Toyomenka, "Others" includes lumber, etc. For Kanematsu Gosho, "Machinery" includes construction machinery; "Others" includes synthetic products, lumber, etc. For Ataka, "Metals" includes fuel; "Machinery" includes construction equipment; "Foodstuffs" includes chemicals, agricultural, and marine products. For Nichimen, "Metals" includes fuel.

domestic trade remains the most important component in the big ten's total transactions. It is far larger than the firms' export, import, and third-country trade. The weight of domestic transactions among the big ten averaged nearly 49 percent during fiscal 1976. In only three firms (Mitsui & Co., Ltd., Sumimoto Shoji Kaisha, Ltd., and Ataka & Co., Ltd.) did domestic trade rise above the 50 percent level. The firm with the highest rate of domestic trade to total transactions was Sumimoto Shoji Kaisha, Ltd. (59 percent); the smallest was Toyomenka Kaisha, Ltd. (about 42 percent).

The average share of both exports and imports in the top ten firms' total sales was 21 percent. The Marubeni Corporation had the largest export share (26 percent), while the Mitsubishi Corporation had the smallest (17.3 percent). Ranking, in terms of the proportion of imports in total transactions, was almost exactly the opposite of exports: the Mitsubishi Corporation was the largest (29 percent), while the Marubeni Corporation was the second smallest (17.3 percent), next to Sumimoto Shoji Kaisha, Ltd. The weight of Toyomenka Kaisha's third-country trade in total transactions was an astonishing 18.4 percent—larger than the share of its import trade and twice the big ten's average. Reflecting the large share of its domestic trade, the weight of both import and third-country trade in Sumimoto Shoji Kaisha's total transactions was far below the big ten's average.

Ranking the big ten by profits shows an interesting variation from ranking by sales. The ranking by operating profits was: Mitsubishi Corporation, Marubeni Corporation, Sumimoto Shoji Kaisha, Ltd., Mitsui & Co., Ltd., C. Itoh & Co., Ltd., Nissho-Iwai Co., Ltd., Toyomenka Kaisha, Ltd., Nichimen Company, Limited, Kanematsu Gosho, Ltd., and Ataka & Co., Ltd. Ranking by the all-important yardstick of profits after taxes was: Mitsubishi Corporation, Mitsui & Co., Ltd., Marubeni Corporation, Sumimoto Shoji Kaisha, Ltd., C. Itoh & Co., Ltd., Toyomenka Kaisha, Ltd., Kanematsu Gosho, Ltd., Nichimen Company, Limited, and Ataka & Co., Ltd. (which suffered a $46-million loss over fiscal 1975). The standout was Sumimoto Shoji Kaisha, Ltd., which ranked higher by profits (both operating profits and earnings after taxes) than by sales. Three trading firms (Sumitomo Shoji Kaisha, Ltd., Mitsubishi Corporation, and

Table 2.3 Sales of the Ten General Trading Companies by Types of Trade, FY 1976 (percent)

	Export	Import	Third-country trade	Domestic trade	Total
Mitsubishi Corporation	17.3	29.1	6.5	47.1	100.0
Mitsui & Co.	21.5	20.4	7.2	50.9	100.0
Marubeni Corporation	26.1	17.3	12.9	43.7	100.0
C. Itoh & Co.	20.3	19.1	10.9	49.7	100.0
Sumitomo Shoji	21.4	14.2	5.7	58.7	100.0
Nissho-Iwai Co.	23.1	19.4	10.6	46.9	100.0
Toyomenka	22.7	17.3	18.4	41.6	100.0
Kanematsu Gosho	18.0	26.0	8.0	48.0	100.0
Ataka & Co.	20.2	17.5	5.5	56.8	100.0
Nichimen Company	27.8	24.5	7.4	40.3	100.0
Total	21.3	20.9	9.0	48.8	100.0

Source: Financial statements of the firms, March 31, 1977.

Table 2.4 Profits of the Ten General Trading Companies, FY 1976

	Operating profit (million Yen)	Profit after tax (million Yen)	Annual profit/ equity rate (percent)	Annual dividend rate (percent)
Mitsubishi Corporation	60,311	17,945 ($6.1 million)	40.0	13.5
Mitsui & Co.	38,037	13,325 ($4.6 million)	37.5	14.0
Marubeni Corporation	50,565	8,151	22.9	12.0
C. Itoh & Co.	37,133	5,354	15.3	12.0
Sumitomo Shoji	38,182	7,542	48.1	14.0
Nissho-Iwai Co.	26,955	4,402	20.4	12.0
Toyomenka	17,394	1,574	15.0	12.0
Kanematsu Gosho	12,478	829	9.5	10.0
Ataka & Co.	△8,551[a]	△132,991	–	–
Nichimen Company	13,294	815	3.2	12.0
Total	285,798	△73,054[a]		

Source: Financial statements of the firms, March 31, 1977.

[a] △ signifies deficit.

Mitsui & Co., Ltd.) stand out prominently in terms of annual profit/own capital rate over all the others. All firms, except Ataka & Co., Ltd., and Kanematsu Gosho, Ltd., paid dividends to stockholders at similar annual rates of between 12 and 14 percent.

Historical and Business Background

Despite the common origins described above, the ten largest *sogo shosha* differ considerably from each other in their historical, business, and entrepreneurial backgrounds. Many contemporary differences among the ten firms in character, management and operational style, size of transactions, commodities structure, and group ties result from dissimilarities in their individual company histories.

Most of the firms have been much transformed through mergers, dissolutions, and regroupings. Nissho-Iwai Co., Ltd., formed through the merger of Nissho Co. and Iwai Sangyo in 1968, can trace its origin to 1862 when the original Iwai Shoten was established. Mitsui & Co., Ltd., was set up in 1876 as a successor to Senshu Kaisha, a firm established in the early 1870s to reduce the foreign traders' near monopoly control over Japan's international trade. The Mitsubishi Corporation can trace its origin to 1870, when Yataro Iwasaki, founder of the Mitsubishi *zaibatsu*, opened Tosa Kaisai Shosha.[2] In 1873, Iwasaki renamed it Mitsubishi Shokai and actively embarked on shipping and trading business. It was established as a separate legal entity in 1918 when the Mitsubishi *zaibatsu*'s holding company spun off its commerce department. Marubeni Corporation and C. Itoh & Co., Ltd., can claim 1897 as the year of founding since their common ancestor, Benichu, was established in that year as a cotton and textile trader. However, they did not establish themselves as separate corporations until 1949 when Taiken Industries, a wartime amalgamation of firms, was dissolved in a four-way split. Nichimen Company, Limited, was founded in 1892 as a cotton importer and textile exporter.

Ataka & Co., Ltd., was set up in 1904 as an importer of pulp, lumber, and sugar, but switched its main business in 1927 to trading in steel. Kanematsu Gosho, Ltd., formed in 1967 through the merger of Kanematsu and Gosho, can trace its origin to 1905 when Gosho was established as a cotton importer and textile exporter. Toyomenka Kaisha, Ltd., was Mitsui & Co.'s cotton department until it was separated in 1920 to serve as the Mitsui *zaibatsu* manufacturers' cotton importer and textile marketing channel at home and abroad. Sumimoto Shoji Kaisha, Ltd., is the youngest general trading company among the big ten. Originally set up as a real estate and construction company in 1919, it was reestablished as a trading company in 1945 to serve Sumimoto group firms.

Today, the big ten, with their extensive and highly diversified businesses, are truly general trading companies. This has not always been the case, however. Only two firms among today's big ten and their predecessors—Mitsui & Co., Ltd., and the Mitsubishi Trading Company (the predecessor of today's Mitsubishi Corporation)—developed into general trading firms before World War II. All the rest, except these two firms and Sumimoto Shoji Kaisha, Ltd., which did not come into existence until 1945 or assume its present name until 1952, remained specialized traders with strength in one or two product groups throughout the pre-World War II period. The Marubeni Corporation, C. Itoh & Co., Ltd., Toyomenka Kaisha, Ltd., Kanematsu Gosho Ltd., Itohman, and Chori Co., Ltd., started as and remained cotton importers and textile exporters. Nissho-Iwai Co., Ltd., Ataka & Co., Ltd., Okura & Co., Ltd., and Kinsho Mataichi Corp. specialized in metals and machinery trade. Toshoku Ltd. and Nozaki & Co. started as and remained traders specializing in foodstuffs.

Diversification of the specialized traders did not commence until after World War II and did not shift to high gear until the 1960s. The character of these specialized traders' original business, however, left a lasting imprint on the character and style of their business well into the 1970s. The quadrupling of oil prices following the Middle East crisis of October 1973 and the strong thrust of the big ten into the energy business have had a dramatic impact on the firms' commodities structure. However, traces of the firms' original business remain. This is true even for Sumitomo Shoji Kaisha, Ltd., which was established after the war to serve as the supply and marketing agent of the Sumitomo group manufacturers, known for their considerable strength in metals and in chemical and machinery industries. The success of Marubeni Corporation's and Nichimen Company, Limited's diversification is striking. C. Itoh & Co., too, has achieved remarkable results, but textiles remain its second most important product group. Textiles also remain the most important component of two former textile trades, Toyomenka Kaisha, Ltd., and Kanematsu Gosho, Ltd.

Zaibatsu Background

Their ties to and, in some cases, origins in the pre–World War II *zaibatsu* have had an enormous influence on the companies that today are the ten largest *sogo shosha*. No discussion of the general trading companies can be complete without a brief description of this complex relationship, but we emphasize that no short discussion can do justice to the intricacies of this important part of Japanese business history.

Three of today's big ten had close ties with powerful pre–World War II *zaibatsu* groups. Mitsui & Co., Ltd., had ties with the Mitsui *zaibatsu*. The Mitsubishi Corporation had ties with the Mitsubishi *zaibatsu*. Toyomenka served as the Mitsui *zaibatsu's* cotton importer and textile exporter after it was spun off by Mitsui & Co. in 1920. The other giant prewar *zaibatsu*, Sumitomo, did not have its own independent group trading company because of its desire to concentrate on copper production and other manufacturing industries and because of its aversion to pure commercialism. Six of today's *sogo shosha* (namely, Marubeni Corporation, C. Itoh & Co., Ltd., Nissho-Iwai Co., Ltd., Kanematsu Gosho, Ltd., Nichimen Company, Limited, and Ataka & Co., Ltd.) had no *zaibatsu* ties.

Mitsui & Co., Ltd., and Mitsubishi Trading Company operated as the respective *zaibatsu* group's purchasing and sales channels. However, their roles were far more significant than that of mere group distribution agents. Each played a leadership role in the expansion and solidification of its *zaibatsu* group. This was especially true for Mitsui & Co., Ltd. It not only operated as one of the three nuclear Mitsui corporations (the others were the Mitsui Bank and the Mitsui Mining Co.) but also periodically controlled the Mitsui holding company and other group firms when its top management became top officers of the holding company.

Prewar *zaibatsu* groups were unique and powerful Japanese business institutions. They took the form of Western corporations, but were run like traditional family institutions with emphasis on the authority of the head of the family, on a firm's position in the group hierarchy, and on group loyalties and obligations. While the Mitsui family can trace its origins back to 1630, the Sumitomo family to 1673, and the Mitsubishi family to the early 1870s, the formation of the *zaibatsu* groups did not commence until after the inauguration of the Meiji government in 1868. The *zaibatsu* had their start in the close political and financial ties that Yataro Iwasaki, founder of the new Mitsubishi enterprise, and members and top officers of the already established business families (such as Mitsui and Sumitomo) were able to forge with leaders of the new government. With active government financial assistance and cooperation, they acquired a pivotal role in the nation's industrialization program, moving into banking, shipbuilding, mining, trade, and other industries. Propelled by new business opportunities during World War I, the three largest groups evolved into financial, industrial, and trading combines of considerable strength.

Each group expanded its empire like an octopus, establishing at least one big firm per industry. By the end of World War I, each had under its control nearly all the major industries of the day: financial institutions (commercial bank, trust bank, life and marine insurance companies), trade and other service industries (trading company, shipping company, warehousing company, etc.), a broad range of manufacturing industries (steel and other metals, shipbuilding, mining, heavy machinery, light machinery, oil, chemicals, paper, etc.), and even real estate businesses.

Ownership was in the hands of the Iwasaki, Mitsui, and Sumitomo families, although stocks of selected group enterprises were opened for sales on a limited scale to the Japanese public in the mid-1930s. Each of the three *zaibatsu* groups maintained strong control and coordination of group enterprises through a holding company. The Iwasaki family exerted strong management control over the Mitsubishi group until the start of World War II. The Mitsui family controlled the Mitsui holding company (Mitsui Gomei, established in 1909) through total ownership of capital and filling the top positions (president, vice-president, etc.). Day-to-day management of the Mitsui holding company and of the subordinate enterprises, however, was vested in professional managers. The Sumitomo *zaibatsu*, too, was run largely by professional managers.[3]

In addition to serving as the *zaibatsu* supply and marketing agent, the group trading company seemed to have played the role of manipulating internal transfer prices among group firms and setting prices in transactions with nongroup firms. Different prices were charged in transactions with the outside world, pegged so as to maximize group profit rather than the earnings of individual enterprises, and to maximize the monopoly power of the group.[4]

The *zaibatsu* groups had immense power in the pre-World War II Japanese economy. They forged strong ties with the ascendant Japanese military in the mid-1930s and during World War II, partly as a means of self-defense and partly from nationalistic sentiments. After the war, Occupation authorities issued orders directing the *zaibatsu* families to dispose of their entire stock ownership in the holding companies and in major group enterprises. The holding companies were prohibited by law. Of even greater impact on the trading companies was the Occupation edict issued in 1946 ordering the dissolution of the two giant *zaibatsu* trading firms. Mitsui & Co. was split into 170 separate companies and Mitsubishi Shoji into 139 new entities. They were forbidden to use the well-known Mitsui and Mitsubishi trade marks and any offices that had been in use for ten years or longer.

The complete breakup of the two giant trading companies ushered in a period when hundreds of new and old, medium- and small-sized firms competed for the very small amount of foreign trade that slowly reopened under Occupation control. Golden opportunities for expanding and diversifying into other lines of business developed for older and more experienced trading firms such as Marubeni Corporation, C. Itoh & Co., Ltd., Nichimen Company, Limited, Toyomenka Kaisha, Ltd., and Gosho, which until then had been no match for the two giant *zaibatsu* firms. Of the 300 or so trading companies that split away from the two *zaibatsu* firms, only Daiichi Tsusho made the list of top ten trading companies in 1951.

The Big Six and the Post-World War II Bank-Centered Conglomerate Groups

The postwar Occupation of Japan officially ended in the spring of 1952. The regaining of sovereignty by Japan gave former *zaibatsu* firms a big impetus to regroup. Feelings of kinship, common loyalties and mutual obligations, common corporate cultures and experiences, and close business relations built over many prewar years made it natural for the former *zaibatsu* firms to draw to each other not only for socializing but to reap the benefits of close cooperation in capital, management transactions, and new business ventures.

What was new and unique in the postwar period was the formation of the so-called "bank-centered" conglomerate groups. As the name indicates, these were new groups formed in the mid-1950s and accelerated in the mid-1960s with the active backing of, and often under pressure from, three banks not belonging to the big three prewar *zaibatsus*, namely, the Fuji Bank (formerly the Yasuda Bank belonging to the smaller prewar Yasuda *zaibatsu*), the Daiichi Kangyo Bank, and the Sanwa Bank. Financial institutions acquired considerable clout in the postwar Japanese economy because of their exemption from the Occupation's dissolution order and antitrust law. The practice of giving preferential loans at a lower rate to selected firms, the perennial shortage of capital in the rapidly growing Japanese economy, and the underdevelopment of Japan's critical market led to increased dependence of firms on financial institutions and caused the highly leveraged capital structure of Japanese corporations.

The 1953 revision of Japan's antitrust law raised the limit of stock investment by a financial institution in a given domestic corporation from 5 to 10 percent of the institution's own capital. This further assisted the financial institutions' expansion of power. Taking advantage of the greater competitive opportunities created by the dissolution of the most powerful *zaibatsu* groups, and wishing to create new groups under their control and to compete against the regrouped *zaibatsu* groups, the financial institutions actively prodded the firms under their influence to form the Fuyo group, the Daiichi Kangyo Bank group, and the Sanwa Bank group.

The trading companies also regrouped. Former Mitsubishi Shoji (Mitsubishi Trading Company) firms first merged into four firms (Kowa Jitsugyo, Fuji Shoji, Tozai Koeki, and Tokyo Boeki). Finally, in July 1954, they formed the new Mitsubishi Trading Company. Former Mitsui & Co. firms took considerably longer because of various conflicts of interests, but finally achieved reunification in 1959.

Many other enterprise groupings of various types also emerged in the more competitive post–World War II Japanese economic environment. Among them were the Nippon Steel group, the Kobe Steel group, the Toyota group, the Nissan group, the Matsushita group, and the Toshiba group. Some are members of the six groups mentioned above, although they maintain their own independent groupings. However, today the six *zaibatsu* and bank-centered groups are the mightiest conglomerate groups as measured by their weight in the Japanese economy and in terms of their direct bearing on the *sogo shosha*.

The big six conglomerate groups, as of March 31, 1974, consisted of 187 financial, industrial, and trading giants of Japan, according to the Japan Fair Trade commission (FTC). The number of group firms varied, ranging from the Sumitomo group's sixteen to the Daiichi Kangyo Bank group's fifty-seven. The list reads like a *Who's Who* of Japanese and even world industry. They were all members of the powerful President Clubs of the respective groups, consisting of the presidents of group enterprises. In March 1974 the 187 mammoth firms had a share of approximately 22 percent of the total capital stock of Japanese enterprises (public utilities excluded) and a 23 percent share of their total assets.

Each of the big six *sogo shosha* has been the core trading company and coordinator-secretariat of joint projects of the conglomerate group to which it belongs. The Mitsubishi Corporation has been the core supply and distribution channel and coordinator-secretariat of the Mitsubishi group, Mitsui & Co., Ltd., that of the Mitsui group, the Marubeni Corporation, that of the Fuyo group, C. Itoh & Co., Ltd., that of the Daiichi Kangyo Bank group, Sumitomo Shoji Kaisha, Ltd., that of the Sumitomo group, and Nissho-Iwai Co., Ltd., that of the Sanwa Bank group.

Table 2.5 Share of Six Conglomerate Groups in the Total Capital Stock and Total Asset of Japanese Enterprises (Public Utilities Excluded), March 31, 1974

	Mitsubishi group	Mitsui group	Sumitomo group	Fuyo group	Subtotal	Daiichi Kangyo Bank group	Sanwa Bank group	Grand total
Members of the six President Clubs only:								
Number of firms	27	22	16	29	94	57	36	187
Percent in total capital stock	4.4	3.0	2.5	4.8	14.7	3.4	5.0	21.9
Percent in total asset	4.4	3.3	3.4	4.1	15.2	4.0	4.1	22.9
Affiliates (stock ownership 50% to 100%) added:								
Number of firms	399	486	260	606	1,751	674	842	3,095
Percent in total capital stock	5.2	3.7	2.3	5.8	17.0	4.1	6.0	26.1
Percent in total asset	4.8	3.7	3.6	4.7	16.8	4.4	4.8	25.3
Affiliates (stock ownership 25% to 49%) added:								
Number of firms	1,070	975	578	1,206	3,829	1,180	1,548	6,302
Percent in total capital stock	7.0	4.7	4.3	6.8	22.8	5.2	7.2	33.5
Percent in total asset	5.4	4.1	4.0	5.2	18.7	4.9	5.2	28.2
Affiliates (stock ownership 10% to 24%) added:								
Number of firms	1,460	1,367	781	1,581	5,189	1,623	2,003	8,476
Percent in total capital stock	8.3	6.6	5.0	8.1	28.0	6.5	9.0	41.0
Percent in total asset	5.9	4.7	4.3	5.6	20.5	5.4	5.8	30.9

Source: Japan Fair Trade Commission, *Sogo shosha ni kansuru dainikai chosa hokoku* (Report on the Second Investigation of the General Trading Companies), January 22, 1975, p. 17.

Table 2.6 Members of the President Clubs of the Six Conglomerate Groups, March 31, 1974

	Mitsubishi group	Mitsui group	Sumitomo group	Fuyo group	Daiichi Kangyo Bank group	Sanwa Bank group
Financial	Mitsubishi Bank; Mitsubishi Trust & Banking; Tokyo Marine & Fire Insurance; Meiji Mutual Life Insurance	Mitsui Bank; Mitsui Trust & Banking; Taisho Marine & Fire Insurance; Mitsui Mutual Life Insurance	Sumitomo Bank; Sumitomo Trust & Banking; Sumitomo Marine & Fire Insurance; Sumitomo Mutual Life Insurance	Fuji Bank; Yasuda Trust & Banking; Yasuda Fire & Marine Insurance; Yasuda Mutual Life Insurance	Daiichi Kangyo Bank; Nissan Fire & Marine Insurance; Taisei Fire & Marine Insurance; Fukoku Mutual Life Insurance; Asahi Mutual Life Insurance; Nippon Kangyo Kakumaru	Sanwa Bank; Toyo Trust & Banking; Nippon Mutual Life Insurance
Agriculture and forestry					Furukawa Forestry	
Mining		Mitsui Mining; Hokkaido Colliery & Steamship	Sumitomo Metal Mining; Sumitomo Coal Mining		Furukawa Mining	
Construction		Mitsui Construction; Sanki Engineering		Taisei Construction		Ohbayashi Gumi; Toyo Construction
Manufacturing						
Foods	Kirin Brewery	Nippon Flour Mills		Sapporo Breweries; Nissin Flour Milling; Nippon Reizo		
Textiles	Mitsubishi Rayon	Toray Industries		Nisshin Spinning		Teijin; Unitika
Chemicals	Mitsubishi Chemical Industry; Mitsubishi Petrochemical; Mitsubishi Gas Chemical; Mitsubishi Plastics Industry; Mitsubishi Monsanto	Mitsui Toatsu Chemicals; Mitsui Petrochemical Industries	Sumitomo Chemical	Showa Denko; Kureha Chemical Industry; Nippon Oil & Fats	Asahi Denka; Electro Chemical Industrial; Toa Paint; C. I. Chemical; Sanyo; Nippon Noyaku; Shiseido	Ube Industries; Tokuyama Soda; Kansai Paint; Sekisui Chemical; Hitachi Chemical; Tanabe Seiyaku; Fujisawa Pharmaceutical

Table 2.6 (cont.)

	Mitsubishi group	Mitsui group	Sumitomo group	Fuyo group	Daiichi Kangyo Bank group	Sanwa Bank group
Glass and Cement	Asahi Glass; Mitsubishi Mining Cement		Nippon Glass; Sumitomo Cement	Nippon Cement		Osaka Cement
Steel	Mitsubishi Steel	Nippon Seiko Sho	Sumitomo Metal Industries	Nippon Kokan	Kawasaki Steel	Kobe Steel; Nakayama Steel Works
Nonferrous metals	Mitsubishi Steel	Mitsui Kinzoku			Nikkei Kin; Furukawa Magnesium	
Metal products	Mitsubishi Aluminium				Furukawa Electric; Furukawa Aluminium; Nikkei Aluminium; Nippon Seihaku; Tokai Kinzoku; Furukawa Specialty Metals; Furukawa Metal Industries; Furukawa Founding	Hitachi Metals; Hitachi Cable
Machinery	Mitsubishi Kakoki		Sumitomo Shipbuilding & Machinery	Kubota Tekko; Nippon Seiko	Niigata Engineering;	Toyo Bearing Manufacturing
Electric machinery	Mitsubishi Electric	Tokyo Shibaura Electric	Sumitomo Electric Industries; Nippon Electric Co.	Hitachi Manufacturing; Oki Electric Industry; Yokogawa Electric Works	Fuji Electric; Yasukawa Electric Manufacturing; Fujitsu; Fuji Electrochemical; Kurokawa Communication; Furukawa Battery; Nippon Columbia; Supersonic Industry; Fujitsu FACOM; Fujitsu Electric Industries; Fujitsu FANUC; Fujitsu Ten; Fujitsu Kiden	Hitachi Manufacturing; Sharp; Iwasaki Tsushinki

Category						
Transportation equipment	Mitsubishi Heavy Industries; Mitsubishi Motor	Mitsui Shipbuilding & Engineering		Nissan Motor	Kawasaki Heavy Industries; Fuji Diesel	Daihatsu; Shin Meiwa Industry; Hitachi Shipbuilding & Engineering
Others	Mitsubishi Oil; Nippon Kogaku			Toa Nenryo; Canon Camera	Yokahama Rubber; Kanemachi Rubber; Nippon Jeon	Maruzen Oil; Toyo Rubber
Wholesale	Mitsubishi Corporation	Mitsui & Co.	Shumitomo Shoji Kaisha	Marubeni Corporation	C. Itoh & Co.; Kanematsu Gosho; Furukawa Sangyo; Nikkei Shoji	Nissho-Iwai Co.; Nichimen Company; Iwatani Sangyo
Retail		Mitsukoshi			Seibu Department Store	Takashimaya
Real Estate	Mitsubishi Estate	Mitsui Real Estate	Sumitomo Real Estate	Tokyo Tatemono	Daiichi Kaihatsu	
Transportation and communication	Nippon Yusen Kaisha; Mitsubishi Warehouse	Mitsui O.S.K. Lines; Mitsui Warehouse	Sumitomo Warehouse	Keihin Express; Tobu Railway; Showa Shipping	Nippon Express; Kawasaki Kisen; Shibusawa Warehouse	Nippon Express Hankyu Electric Railway; Shimo Shin Nippon Shipping
Service					Dentsu; Korakuen Stadium	Orient Lease

Source: Japan Fair Trade Commission, *Sogo shosha ni kansuru dainikai chosa hokoku* (Report on the Second Investigation of the General Trading Comapnies), January 22, 1975, pp. 31-32; and Keizai Chosa Kyokai, *Keiretsu no kenkyu* (A Study of *Keiretsu*) (Tokyo: Kyowa Insatsu, 1973), vol. 1, p. 11.

Note: Toyota Motors joined the Mistui group after the completion of the second study by the Japan Fair Trade Commission. Hitachi, Ltd., is a member of two gorups, Fuyo and Sanwa.

The focus of this study is on the ties between the big six *sogo shosha* and the six conglomerate groups. However, it is interesting to note the group ties of the other trading companies. Toyomenka Kaisha, Ltd., has been the core trading channel of the Tokai Bank group and Kanematsu Gosho, Ltd. that of the Tokyo Bank group. Ataka & Co., Ltd., and Nichimen Company, Limited, have been the second-string trading companies of the Sumitomo group and the Sanwa Bank group.

The big *sogo shosha* possess intimate capital, financial, and business ties with member firms of the respective conglomerate groups. Thus, the big six and group firms had significant mutual stock holdings; that is, they owned each other's stocks. According to the Japan Fair Trade Commission, the Mitsubishi group firms (excluding life insurance company and firms with less than 20 billion Yen paid-up capital) owned 31 percent of the total number of stocks issued by group firms as of March 31, 1974. The mutual stock holdings of the Sumitomo group calculated on the same basis (i.e., total stocks owned by member firms of the respective President Club divided by total number of stocks issued by members of the President Club, exclusive of life insurance companies and firms whose paid-up capital fell below 20 billion Yen) amounted to about 28 percent. Mutual stock holding of other groups ranged between 16 percent (Sanwa Bank group) and 19 percent (Daiichi Kangyo Bank group). The six *sogo shosha* all had similar shares (about 2 percent) so far as the percentage of ownership of stocks of group firms was concerned. Their mutual stock holding share was only less than half that of the group main banks, which averaged between 4 and 5 percent.

Furthermore, while group firms have many sources of funds other than their own group financial institutions, they borrow a significant amount of money from the group main bank, trust banks, and insurance companies. As of March 31, 1973, Sumitomo group financial institutions supplied 31 percent of the total borrowing needs of Sumitomo Shoji Kaisha, Ltd., while the Sanwa Bank group financial institutions were the sources of 24 percent of Nissho-Iwai Co., Ltd's borrowing needs. The Mitsubishi group financial institutions supplied 25 percent of the Mitsubishi Corporation's loan needs, while the Fuyo group institutions provided 24 percent of Marubeni Corporation's. The

Table 2.7 Sources of Loans of the Ten General Trading Companies, March 31, 1973 (Share of loans in percent)

Borrower trading companies	Lending banks			
	First main bank[a]	First main bank's group financial institutions[b]	Second main bank[c]	Second main bank's group financial institutions[d]
Mitsubishi Corporation	Mitsubishi Bank (14.8)	Mitsubishi Bank group financial institutions (25.3)	Bank of Tokyo (9.5)	Bank of Tokyo group financial institutions (———)
Mitsui & Co.	Mitsui Bank (12.2)	Mitsui Bank group financial institutions (19.4)	Fuji Bank (10.9)	Fuji Bank group financial institutions (12.1)
Marubeni Corporation	Fuji Bank (14.1)	Fuji Bank group financial institutions (23.8)	Bank of Tokyo (12.1)	
C. Itoh & Co.	Sumitomo Bank (12.9)	Sumitomo Bank group financial institutions (20.5)	Daiichi Kangyo Bank (10.9)	Daiichi Kangyo Bank group financial institutions (12.1)
Sumitomo Shoji	Sumitomo Bank (15.7)	Sumitomo Bank group financial institutions (31.2)	Bank of Tokyo (7.5)	
Nissho-Iwai Co.	Sanwa Bank (17.8)	Sanwa Bank group financial institutions (24.2)	Daiichi Kangyo Bank (14.5)	Daiichi Kangyo Bank group financial institutions (15.0)
Toyomenka	Tokai Bank (14.3)		Mitsui Bank (10.0)	Mitsui Bank group financial institutions (13.5)
Kanematsu Gosho	Bank of Tokyo (27.6)		Daiichi Kangyo Bank (9.3)	
Ataka & Co.	Sumitomo Bank (15.8)	Sumitomo Bank group financial institutions (29.9)	Kyowa Bank (11.6)	
Nichimen Company	Sanwa Bank (20.0)	Sanwa Bank group financial institutions (27.9)	Bank of Tokyo (9.0)	

Source: "Gendai no kaibutsu—sogo shosha no jitsuryoku tenken" (Modern Monster—An Examination of General Trading Companies' Power), *Toyo Keizai Tokei Geppo*, September 1973, p. 7.

Note: [a] and [c] = percent share of total loans to trading company.
[b] includes [a]'s share; [d] includes [c]'s share.
[b] and [d] do not add up to 100% because of trading company's borrowings from other financial institutions.

Mitsui group financial institutions, however, supplied only 19.4 percent of Mitsui & Co., Ltd.'s borrowing needs. It is striking that the Sumitomo financial institutions supplied a greater share of loans (20.5 percent) to C. Itoh & Co., Ltd., than the Daiichi Kangyo Bank group institutions to which C. Itoh & Co., Ltd., belonged.

Finally, group firms—the three *zaibatsu* group members in particular—have important, though not overwhelming, business relations with the group trading company. According to the FTC, during FY 1973 ended March 31, 1974, the sixty-five firms belonging to the President Clubs of the three *zaibatsu* groups purchased between 5 and 6 percent of the total sales of their three group *sogo shosha* (i.e., the Mitsubishi Corporation, Mitsui & Co., Ltd., and Sumitomo Shoji Kaisha, Ltd.). Sales of the sixty-five enterprises to the three trading companies amounted to approximately 20 percent of the latter's total purchases. Both the sixty-five enterprises' sales to and purchases from the three *sogo shosha* amounted to 30 percent of the sixty-five firms' total sales and purchase transactions. (The dependence of the sixty-five enterprises in the three group trading firms was greater than the latter's dependence on them.) Sales and purchasing relationships between bank-centered group firms and their group *sogo shosha* are much lower: about 10 percent of the total sales and purchases of the bank group manufacturers.[5] The FTC's data refer to average transactions, not to transactions between specific group firms and group trading companies that could be higher or lower than averages provided by the FTC. A good example is transactions between Sumitomo group firms and Sumitomo Shoji Kaisha, Ltd., with sales from the former to the latter ranging between 6 and 68 percent of the former's total sales during the fiscal half year ended March 31, 1973.

The Big Six and Their Affiliates

The conglomerate group is one extremely important component of the *sogo shosha*'s world. Another critical component is the *sogo shosha*'s own affiliates. These are mostly medium- and small-sized firms. Affiliates, according to the FTC's definition, include both subsidiaries (firms in which the parent company has majority stock ownership) and related firms (firms in which the investor company's shareholding is less than 50 and more than 10

Table 2.8 Share of Sumitomo Shoji Kaisha in Total Sales of the Core Sumitomo Group Manufacturers, September 1971-March 1974.

	Total sales,[a] six months ended:		Percent share of sales to Sumitomo Shoji, six months ended:			
	9/72	3/73	9/71	3/72	9/72	3/73
Sumitomo Chemical Co.	128,671	136,053	24.1	28.4	30.3	31.1
Sumitomo Shipbuilding & Machinery	58,209	71,041	62.3	48.4	58.5	43.7
Sumitomo Metal Industry	233,475	279,738	50.7	52.2	53.2	53.7
Sumitomo Metal Mining	49,040	57,750	35.0	32.9	34.9	37.4
Sumitomo Electric Industries	82,227	91,628	25.2	36.9	24.8	21.9
Nippon Sheet Glass	24,305	26,632	1.4	16.6	11.6	12.1
Nippon Electric	127,512	149,121	13.0	15.9	7.9	7.1
Sumitomo Cement	28,950	33,217	7.9	6.5	6.1	6.0
Sumitomo Coal Mining	5,533	5,533	42.6	40.0	65.4	68.2
Total	737,922	850,718	33.7	35.2	34.3	33.5

Source: Kazuo Kinada and Hiroshi Yamamoto, *Nippon no shosha—Sumitomo Shoji* (Japanese Trading Company: Sumitomo Shoji) (Tokyo: Mainichi Shimbun, 1973), p. 114.

[a] In million Yen.

percent but which enjoy close and continual business ties). Japanese businesses, fond of using family analogies, call subsidiaries *kogaisha* (children firms) and related firms *keiretsu kigyo* (relations or relatives).

One could say, for example, that the universe of Sumitomo Shoji Kaisha, Ltd., consists of two principal worlds: the world of "we" and the world of "they." The "we" world comprises (1) Sumitomo Shoji Kaisha, Ltd., itself; (2) such rich "older brother" firms as the Sumitomo Bank, Sumitomo Trust & Banking, Sumitomo Metal Industries, and Sumitomo Chemical Co., and powerful "brothers" such as Nippon Sheet Glass Co., Ltd., Sumitomo Shipbuilding and Machinery Co., and Nippon Electric Co., and other group firms; (3) hundreds of "children" firms; and (4) hundreds of related firms, some of which are subsidiaries of other large group enterprises. The "they" world consists of those outside the "we" of the big Sumitomo world.

As of March 1974 the six *sogo shosha* had more than 600 subsidiaries; two-thirds in Japan and one-third abroad. Approximately half of their subsidiaries were in commerce (sales companies, distribution centers, transportation companies, etc.), and about one-third were in a broad range of manufacturing industries. Mitsui & Co., Ltd., had the largest number of subsidiaries (135), followed by C. Itoh & Co., Ltd., (121), Marubeni Corporation (115), Mitsubishi Corporation (94), Nissho-Iwai Co., Ltd. (78), and Sumitomo Shoji Kaisha, Ltd. (73). It is not surprising that Mitsui & Co., Ltd., had many subsidiaries in foodstuffs, chemicals, agriculture and fishing, and warehousing. However, the two former textile traders' possession of a large number of subsidiaries in nontextile industries is striking. The Marubeni Corporation has numerous subsidiaries in foodstuffs, metal products, machinery, and warehousing, and C. Itoh & Co., Ltd., has many subsidiaries in agriculture and fishing, foodstuffs, chemicals, and real estate.

According to the FTC, 43 percent of the six trading companies' subsidiaries depended on the parent companies for both supplies of raw and other materials and sales of manufactures, while 40 percent of the subsidiaries relied on the parent firms for either supplies or sales of manufactured products.

Table 2.9 Subsidiaries (Stock Ownership Exceeding 50 Percent) of Six General Trading Companies Classified by Industries, March 31, 1974

	Mitsubishi Corporation		Mitsui & Co.		Marubeni Corporation		C. Itoh & Co.		Sumitomo Shoji		Nissho-Iwai	
	(D)	(F)	(D)	(F)	(D)	(F)	(D)	(F)	(D)	(F)	(D)	(F)
Manufacturing												
Food	6		7	1	12		8	4	2		7	1
Textile	4	1	3	1	2		4				4	
Wood			2		1		2	1				
Paper and pulp			1		3		1	2				
Chemical	1	1	5	3			7	1	1		3	
Glass and cement	1		4	1					1		1	
Steel	7		3		2			3	3			
Nonferrous metals	3		1						2			
Metal products	4	1	5		8		1	1			6	
Machinery	1		3		7	1	3					1
Other mfg.												
Agriculture, forestry, fishery	1	3	4	2		1	3	3		2		
Mining		4	1	3			1	1		2		
Construction			1		3							
Commerce	26	17	31	30	26	25	31	14	29	14	27	14
Financial and insurance					1				1		1	
Real estate	1		2		1	3	6	2	5	1	1	
Transportation, communication	1	1	1		1		2	2			1	
Warehousing	3		9	1	8		1	1	1	1	3	
Electricity and gas												
Service	4		7		2	1	4		3	3	4	
Others	1	2	3		7		9	3	2		3	
Total	64	30	93	42	84	31	83	38	50	23	61	17

Source: Japan Fair Trade Commission, *Sogo shosha ni kansuru dainikai chosa hokoku* (Report on the Second Investigation of the General Trading Companies), January 22, 1975, p. 30.

Note: D = domestic subsidiaries; F = foreign subsidiaries.

Benefits of Ties with Group Enterprises and Affiliates

A general trading company must be viewed and evaluated in the totality of the several worlds in which it operates and not by itself. Judging General Motors by itself or IBM by itself on the basis of their financial statements may be possible, but this is not feasible in the group- and rank-conscious world of Japanese business where intangible ties, some well-hidden from the public, remain of considerable importance.

The *sogo shosha* do not limit their business dealings to group firms and affiliates. However, their intimate stock, financial, and business ties with "kinship" firms are clearly valuable assets in normal circumstances. Ties with group financial institutions give them assured, though not exclusive, access at preferred rates to the sources of major funds required for domestic and international transactions and investments. Group manufacturing firms provide them assured, it not captive, customers for raw materials, equipment, and technology, and are stable sources of manufactured goods and other supplies for sale. Group financial and manufacturing firms make ready and reliable partners for joint undertaking of huge domestic and overseas projects and can share high risks accompanying new ventures. Mutual stock holdings promote group solidarity and business stability (including some internal transfer pricing and unspoken business agreements) and prevent inroads by outside elements, especially foreign speculators, which might upset group and government relations or disrupt the Japanese management system. The system of mutual stock holding can also increase group profits. Today's *sogo shosha*, however, do not have the clout to manipulate transfer prices to maximize total group earnings as their prewar *zaibatsu* predecessors did.

Ties with their own subsidiaries and related firms enable the *sogo shosha* to conduct their core business of selling and buying and of scrving as trade intermediaries and to generate new business. Subsidiaries, which pay lower wages and benefits and have more flexible employment systems than big *sogo shosha* and manufacturing concerns, enable the trading companies to serve as intermediaries between large manufacturers and numerous small producers, supplying the former with parts and components made by the latter at lower, competitive prices and distributing to the latter intermediate products (such as steel, chemical fiber, and ethylene) and equipment produced by the former. Subsidiaries enable the *sogo shosha* to rationalize and, more important, to integrate their expanding supply and distribution networks. One suspects that the tightly controlled subsidiaries now allow the parent company, like the major multinational oil companies, to minimize the tax bill by allocating prices and profits among worldwide subsidiaries.[6] They give the big trading concerns the flexibility and speed they need to conduct global, multitype, highly diversified business in a fast-changing world.

Loose Oligopolies, Not Monopolies

Japan's ten largest trading companies are definitely not monopolies, nor are they oligopolies if oligopoly is strictly defined as "a market situation where sellers are so few that any one of them can affect the market price...."[7] Neither the big six, nor for that matter the big two, are oligopolies in that sense. None of the post–World War II conglomerate groups to which the big six belong has the manufacturing and market power of the biggest prewar *zaibatsu*, Mitsui, or of the Mitsubishi or Sumitomo *zaibatsu*.

In addition, none of the conglomerate groups has the power to impose strong supply and marketing controls on member firms and to make the group trading company the exclusive group supply and marketing agent. The six President Clubs play some role in control and coordination, but their power cannot match that of the *zaibatsu* holding companies, which, in the prewar period, owned and exercised monolithic control of *zaibatsu* firms with respect to stocks, management, production, marketing (including transfer pricing among *zaibatsu* firms), and other areas. The President Clubs are only a little more than social clubs, group officials claim, where the presidents of member firms gather to wine and dine. In reality, they are, of course, more than that. They serve as forums for discussing common plans for and management of new joint ventures. They provide a place to exchange views on appropriate responses to the changing structure of Japanese industry and to settle periodic disputes among member firms. To be sure, group firms possess intimate stock, financial, and trade relations. There is also the intangible bond of group loyalty and close personal relations. But the postwar groups, and their single central control and coordination mechanisms, the President Clubs, remain informal institutions and not legal entities. They lack the most important requirement: legal authority to control the stock, finance, management, and operations of group firms. That power is denied by a postwar antitrust law prohibiting holding companies.[1]

As noted earlier, during fiscal 1976 ended March 31, 1977, the market share of the ten largest *sogo shosha* was considerable: 18 percent of domestic trade (or approximately 25 percent of the domestic wholesale trade during fiscal 1973), 56.4 percent of Japanese exports, and 55.6 percent of Japanese imports. During fiscal 1975 the big three's market share was about 9 percent of domestic trade, 27.5 percent of Japan's export total, and 30.5 percent of Japan's total import. The market share of the big ten is, however, considerably larger in a few product groups (not individual products). During fiscal 1975 their share in Japanese exports was 82 percent in metals, 65 percent in chemicals, 61 percent in textiles, and 47 percent in machinery, but less than 35 percent in the export total of all other product groups. Their share in Japanese imports was 81 percent of foodstuffs, 78 percent of chemicals, 74 percent of textiles, 54 percent of metal ores and fuel, and 33 percent in all other commodity groups.

The share of the big ten in Japan's domestic trade, and in exports and imports, is of considerable magnitude but hardly makes them monopolies or even partial monopolies. A partial monopoly is a market situation in which the largest firm has a 50 percent share and the big five together more than 90 percent of the market. Nor do the figures above show them to be concentrated oligopolies, a market situation where the largest firm has more than a 30 percent share and the top five combined a share of more than 70 percent.

This is not to suggest, of course, that the market power of the ten firms is insignificant. An important reason for their inability to develop into partial monopolies or even concentrated oligopolies is the easier entry of new firms into distribution industries than into manufacturing industries. The latter, compared with the service industries, require much larger equity, technology, and equipment and entail much greater risk. Despite their considerable market power, the big ten *sogo shosha* remain loose oligopolies.

Who Owns and Controls the Big Ten?

The Occupation order of 1946 directing the powerful families to dispose of their shareholdings in the *zaibatsu* holding companies and other giant group enterprises led to a management revolution in Japan's world of big business: the separation of ownership and management. The eleven Mitsui families lost most of their wealth and all of their economic power. Hachiroemon Takakimi Mitsui, former head of the clan and of the Mitsui empire, and his brother Takasumi, head of the Mitsui Foundation, retired to become directors of private schools.[8] The brothers' magnificent former residence, truly fit for a king, is now the Mitsui Club where Mitsui group firms entertain their guests.

The major owners of the large trading companies today are not private citizens but Japan's giant corporations. Tables 2.10 and 2.11 are highly revealing. As of March 1975, leading financial institutions (other than securities brokerage firms), commercial banks in particular, owned nearly 50 percent or more of the big ten's stocks. Other large nonfinancial corporations owned most of the rest. These two groups alone owned 85 percent of the Mitsubishi Corporation's total stocks issued, 91 percent of Marubeni Corporation's, and 93.4 percent of Nichimen Company's. Private citizens owned only about 14 percent of the Mitsubishi Corporation's shares and even fewer shares in the Marubeni Corporation (8 percent) and Nichimen Company (6 percent). Breakdowns of stock ownership by number of shares owned is even more revealing. The overwhelming majority (87 percent) of the Mitsubishi Corporation's shareholders (about 30,000 persons) owned only 6.5 percent of Mitsubishi Corporation stocks.

Financial statements indicate that group firms are the largest shareholders of the respective group *sogo shosha*. Group banks, trust banks, and insurance companies (marine, fire, and life) are the most important in terms of ownership share. Sumitomo Shoji

Table 2.10 Stocks of Three General Trading Companies Analyzed by Shareholders, March 31, 1975

	Government and public institutions	Financial institutions	Security companies	Other corporations	Foreign corporations	Private individuals and others	Total
Mitsubishi Corporation							
No. of shareholders	1	72	28	549	83	33,675	34,408
Percent share of total stocks issued	0.0	48.47	0.61	36.02	1.08	13.82	100.0
Marubeni Corporation							
No. of shareholders	1	64	46	477	27	17,245	17,860
Percent share of total stocks issued	0.03	61.56	0.52	29.47	0.21	8.21	100.0
Toyomenka Kaisha							
No. of shareholders	0	54	19	448	14	4,473	5,003
Percent share of total stocks issued	0.0	47.62	0.87	45.74	0.04	5.73	100.0

Source: Financial statements of the firms, March 31, 1975.

Table 2.11 Stocks of Three General Trading Companies Analyzed by Number of Shares, March 31, 1975

	1,000,000 and over	500,000 and over	100,000 and over	50,000 and over	10,000 and over	5,000 and over	500 and over	Less than 500	Total
Mitsubishi Corporation									
No. of shareholders	84	50	168	130	1,198	2,792	24,635	5,351	34,408
Percent share of total shareholders	0.24	0.15	0.49	0.38	3.48	8.11	71.60	15.55	100.0
Percent share of total stocks issues	76.89	4.86	4.84	1.20	3.15	2.55	6.36	0.15	100.0
Marubeni Corporation									
No. of shareholders	78	52	122	92	803	1,693	12,093	2,927	17,860
Percent share of total shareholders	0.43	0.29	0.68	0.52	4.50	9.48	67.71	16.39	100.0
Percent share of total stocks issued	82.33	5.46	4.08	0.95	2.18	1.67	3.25	0.08	100.0
Toyomenka Kaisha									
No. of shareholders	43	22	79	28	314	417	2,676	1,424	5,003
Percent share of total shareholders	0.86	0.44	1.58	0.56	6.28	8.33	53.49	28.46	100.0
Percent share of total stocks issued	77.69	6.88	7.99	0.94	3.00	1.24	2.18	0.08	100.0

Source: Financial statements of the firms, March 31, 1975.

Table 2.12 Major Shareholders of Six General Trading Companies and Their Weight, 1973

Mitsubishi Corporation		Mitsui & Co.		Marubeni Corporation	
Shareholders	Percent share	Shareholders	Percent share	Shareholders	Percent share
Mitsubishi Bank	7.84	Mitsui Bank	6.49	Fuji Bank	8.09
Tokyo Marine & Fire Insurance	7.90	Fuji Bank	4.91	Yasuda Fire & Marine Insurance	5.45
Mitsubishi Heavy Industries	5.14	Bank of Tokyo	4.22	Nissan Motor	4.55
Meiji Life Insurance	4.82	Taisho Marine & Fire Insurance	3.67	Kobe Bank	3.67
Mitsubishi Trust & Banking	3.50	Mitsui Life Insurance	3.30	Tokyo Marine & Fire Insurance	3.63
Daiichi Kangyo Bank	2.69	Toyo Trust & Banking	3.03	Sumitomo Bank	3.29
Nippon Yusen	2.43	Mitsui Trust & Banking	2.89	Nippon Fire & Marine Insurance	2.91
Bank of Tokyo	2.37	Mitsui O.K. Life	1.73	Yasuda Trust & Banking	2.91
Mitsubishi Electric	2.05	Toray	1.62	Bank of Tokyo	2.51
Sanwa Bank	1.58	Daihyaku Life Insurance	1.51	Daiwa Bank	2.49
Tokai Bank	1.58				
Total share	41.90	Total share	33.37	Total share	39.50

Sumitomo Shoji		C. Itoh & Co.		Nissho-Iwai Co.	
Shareholders	Percent share	Shareholders	Percent share	Shareholders	Percent share
Sumitomo Bank	8.40	Sumitomo Bank	8.72	Sanwa Bank	7.47
Sumitomo Chemical Co.	6.26	Daiichi Kangyo Bank	8.72	Daiichi Kangyo Bank	7.31
Sumitomo Life Insurance	4.81	Bank of Tokyo	5.23	Daiwa Bank	3.78
Sumitomo Metal Industry	4.78	Nippon Life Insurance	3.50	Tokyo Marine & Fire Insurance	3.57
Sumitomo Trust & Banking	3.82	Fuji Bank	3.43	Kobe Steel	3.22
Nippon Electric	3.34	Tokyo Marine & Fire Insurance	3.36	Bank of Tokyo	3.13
Sumitomo Marine & Fire	3.28	Nippon Fire & Marine Insurance	3.20	Nippon Fire & Marine Insurance	2.23
Sumitomo Metal Mining	3.01	Sanko Steamship	2.85	Asahi Life Insurance	2.14
Nippon Life	2.63	Sumitomo Marine & Fire Insurance	2.84	Nippon Life Insurance	2.14
Sumitomo Electric Industry	2.44	Asahi Life Insurance	2.74	Nissin Fire & Marine Insurance	1.97
Total share	42.77	Total share	44.59	Total share	36.96

Source: Keizai Chosakyokai, *Keiretsu no kenkyu* (A study of *Keiretsu*) (Tokyo: Kyowa Insatsu, 1973).

Kaisha's largest investors (2.44 percent have one share or more) are all Sumitomo group enterprises.[9]

The identities of the *sogo shosha*'s largest individual shareholders are unknown. The firms' financial statements indicate, however, that their top executives own a substantial number of shares. As of March 31, 1975, thirty-six directors of Nissho-Iwai Co., Ltd., each owned between 2,000 and 100,000 shares. President Yoshio Tsuji was the largest owner with 100,000 shares. Each of the thirty-eight directors of Mitsui & Co., Ltd., owned between 8,700 and 163,000 Mitsui shares; President Yoshizo Ikeda owned 163,000 shares. The pattern was similar in other trading firms. Chairman Hisashi Tsuda, with 266,000 shares, was Sumitomo Shoji Kaisha's largest shareholder among directors. Chairman Chujiro Fujino and President Bunichiro Tanabe of the Mitsubishi Corporation owned 520,000 and 300,000 shares respectively. Chairman Masakazu Echigo had 477,000 and President Seiki Tozaki had 41,000 of C. Itoh & Co.'s stocks.

Day-to-day control of the big ten *sogo shosha* is in the hands of professional managers. None of the top executives named above is a Mitsui or an Iwasaki or a Sumitomo. The large corporate shareholders receive considerable benefits in dividends and close business relationships but do not participate in the management of the big ten's daily operations. Stockholders' meetings, unlike their counterparts in the United States, are mostly pro forma gatherings called to ratify decisions already made by the firm's boards of directors, who are internal permanent professional managers. During major business crises, however, the main banks exert considerable influence through financial clout and dispatch of officers. The President Clubs also exert some informal influence through prominent group elder statesmen such as Chairman Hosai Hyuga of Sumitomo Metal Industries and Chairman Norishige Hasegawa of Sumitomo Chemical Co. for Sumitomo Shoji Kaisha, Ltd. However, they rarely intrude directly into the daily operations of the trading company. In a narrow sense, it is not far from the truth to say that it is the top executives, middle-level managers, and other employees of the trading companies, all hired for life, who own and control Japan's ten largest *sogo shosha*.

Notes

1. Kiyoshi Matsui, ed., *Nihon boeki tokuhon*, 3d edition (Tokyo: Toyo Keizai Shimposha, 1971), p. 213.

2. The significance of the *zaibatsu* origins of some of the *sogo shosha* is discussed in the next section.

3. For information on prewar *zaibatsu*, see Kazuo Noda, *Zaibatsu*, 11th edition (Tokyo: Chuo Koronsha, 1967). Also see Eleanor M. Hadley, *Antitrust in Japan* (Princeton, N.J.: Princeton University Press, 1970); and T. A. Bisson, *Zaibatsu Dissolution in Japan* (Berkeley: University of California Press, 1954).

4. Richard E. Caves and Masu Uekusa, *Industrial Organization of Japan* (Washington, D.C.: The Brookings Institution, 1976), pp. 61-62.

5. Nihon Boekikai, "Kosei Torihiki Iinkai no 'sogo shosha ni kansuru dainikai chosa' ni tsuite" (On the Fair Trade Commission's Second Investigation of General Trading Companies), February 6, 1975, p. 18.

6. *The New York Times*, August 21, 1977, Business and Finance Section, p. 1.

7. H. S. Sloan and A. J. Zurder, *Dictionary of Economics* (New York: Barnes & Noble Books, 1970).

8. John G. Roberts, *Mitsui—Three Centuries of Japanese Business* (New York: John Weatherhill, 1974), p. 290.

9. There are a number of interesting variations. In addition to being the largest shareholder of the group trading company, financial institutions invest heavily in other nongroup trading companies. However, the Mitsubishi Bank has not invested in Mitsui & Co., Ltd., and the Mitsui Bank has no investment in the Mitsubishi Corporation. The Daiichi Kangyo Bank (C. Itoh & Co.'s group bank) and the Sumitomo Bank (Sumitomo Shoji Kaisha's group bank) are both the largest shareholders of C. Itoh & Co., Ltd., each with an 8.72 percent share.

3
Services and Resources for Conducting Business

Chapters 1 and 2 analyzed the nature of the *sogo shosha*'s core business, described their great product diversity and multitype enterprise, and distinguished them as trading conglomerates from both manufacturing conglomerates and from other Japanese and Western trading companies. The ten leading *sogo shosha* were examined at close range through a sketch of their individual and shared historical origins and by a description of the complex world of group enterprises and affiliates in which they operate.

Additional legitimate questions of immense interest to the Western business community remain about what the *sogo shosha* are and about what they do. How do the ten *sogo shosha* conduct their business? How did they come to be traders with annual sales of $171 billion, the equivalent of about 30 percent of Japan's gross national product? Specifically, how do they go about selling, buying, and generating new business?

The answers to these questions have two parts. The first set of answers, presented in this chapter, addresses the ways in which the *sogo shosha* go about supplying highly valuable services to their customers. The second set of answers, presented in Chapters 4, 7, and 8, involves the adoption by the *sogo shosha* of appropriate business strategies to fit their changing domestic and foreign environment.

Long before World War II the trading companies, to facilitate and expand their business, began supplying their customers with as many services as they could. Major traditional services included financial, information, risk reduction, paperwork, insurance, warehousing, and transportation services. Since the late 1960s, the *sogo shosha* have been providing large-scale organization and coordination services.

Financial Services

The *sogo shosha* provide four important financial services to clients: extension of credit, loans, loan guarantees, and venture capital. The extension of credit, primarily to a large number of small and medium-sized manufacturing firms, is accomplished by (1) receiving long-term maturity notes and deferred payments from customers for sales of commodities and (2) issuing short-term maturity bills or making advance payments by the big ten to suppliers for purchasers. The six largest *sogo shosha* alone had a staggering 34 percent share of the total commercial credit extended by Japan's major corporations (452 firms) during fiscal 1973 ended March 31, 1974.[1] The two forms of credit result in huge receivables and payables carried by the trading companies. The receivables (caused by credit extension) always exceed the payables by a substantial margin.

The trading companies also provide many loans and loan guarantees to a large number of buyers and sellers: short-term loans to help meet the needs of their current operations, and long-term loans to meet their investment requirements for equipment, plant construction, and even real estate. Loan guarantees are given to many small and medium-size customers and suppliers, but a not insignificant number of loan guarantees also go to well-known, large firms that wish to secure sizable loans from commercial banks.

In supplying credit, loans, and loan guarantees, the *sogo shosha* act as important financial intermediaries between the giant commercial banks (commonly called "city banks" in Japan) and their own customers and suppliers in Japan and abroad. The *sogo shosha* borrow heavily from their own main banks and from other banks and make small loans (although some single credit extensions are of substantial size) to numerous clients. In this process they perform another valuable service as a risk buffer for commercial banks. The last financial service of the trading companies, described in detail below, is the extension of

Table 3.1 Commercial Credit Created by the Ten General Trading Companies, Fiscal Six Months Ended March 31, 1974[a]

	(A) Total assets	(B) Bills receivable	(C) Sales credit	(D) Advance payment	(E) Bills payable	(F) Accounts payable	$\frac{B+C}{A} \times 100$	$\frac{B+C+D}{A} \times 100$	$\frac{E+F}{A} \times 100$
Mitsubishi Corporation	32,013	12,522	9,805	1,555	13,637	5,155	69.7%	74.6%	58.7%
Mitsui & Co.	34,260	11,189	10,365	1,946	11,387	5,770	62.9	68.6	50.1
Marubeni Corporation	20,460	6,287	5,500	1,458	8,878	1,997	57.6	64.7	53.1
C. Itoh & Co.	18,834	5,333	5,074	1,492	6,853	2,505	55.3	63.2	49.7
Sumitomo Shoji	14,586	4,351	4,219	1,887	5,945	1,738	58.7	71.7	52.7
Nissho-Iwai Co.	12,928	4,371	4,242	786	5,896	2,302	66.8	72.7	63.4
Toyomenka	10,054	3,735	2,393	450	4,174	1,054	61.0	65.4	52.0
Kanematsu Gosho	7,298	2,636	1,874	337	3,712	793	61.8	66.4	61.7
Ataka & Co.	9,086	3,201	1,929	420	3,651	830	56.5	61.1	49.3
Nichimen Company	6,616	1,849	1,895	482	2,607	789	56.6	63.9	51.3

Source: Compiled from financial statements of the ten general trading companies for fiscal six months ended March 31, 1974.

[a] In hundred million Yen.

Table 3.2 Short-Term and Long-Term Loans Extended by the Ten General Trading Companies, March 31, 1974[a]

	Short-term loans			Long-term loans		
	To non-affiliates	To affiliates	Total	To non-affiliates	To affiliates	Total
Mitsubishi Corporation	319	41	360	1,089	162	1,251
Mitsui & Co.	272	48	320	2,105	454	2,559
Marubeni Corporation	18	22	40	176	380	556
C. Itoh & Co.	154	170	324	295	348	643
Sumitomo Shoji	97	43	140	165	65	230
Nissho-Iwai Co.	95	71	166	202	122	324
Toyomenka	77	12	89	149	20	169
Kanematsu Gosho	30	27	57	53	173	226
Ataka & Co.	111	52	163	168	50	218
Nichimen Company	24	15	39	80	75	155

Source: Financial statements of the ten general trading companies for fiscal six months ended March 31, 1974.

[a] In hundred million Yen.

venture capital to group and nongroup clients in many kinds of enterprises, notably huge natural resources development projects abroad.

Information Services

Supplying up-to-date information to clients about thousands of product markets from Japan to Africa, Asia, and Latin America is another vital service provided by the ten largest *sogo shosha* to large, medium, and small firms whose information and research and development capabilities may be inadequate for collecting detailed information on a global scale. The *sogo shosha* supply domestic manufacturer customers the detailed information required for inventory control, production planning, and capital investment. These include data about the sources and capacity of

Services and Resources 61

Table 3.3 Bank Loan Guarantees Made by the Ten General Trading Companies, Fiscal Six Months Ended March 31, 1974[a]

Company	Loan Guarantee
Mitsubishi Corporation	1,931
Mitsui & Co.	6,244
Marubeni Corporation	2,273
C. Itoh & Co.	2,027
Sumitomo Shoji	1,161
Nissho-Iwai Co.	275
Toyomenka	480
Kanematsu Gosho	354
Ataka & Co.	606
Nichimen Company	246
Total	15,597

Source: Financial statements of the ten general trading companies for fiscal six months ended March 31, 1974.

[a] In hundred million Yen.

raw materials and equipment supply, domestic and overseas demand, product trends (such as French and American fashion trends), and the upward and downward movement of prices that will have an immediate impact on production.

For firms interested in expanding into export business, they supply information on the size of potential markets; competitive manufacturers in the export country; current prices and profit potential; foreign exchange rates and likely financial fluctuations; distribution channels; the credit standing of potential wholesale and retail distributors; current attitudes of industrial users, consumers, competitors, labor unions, or government officials toward the proposed export products; foreign import regulations and other tariff and nontariff barriers; and the various export permits required by the Japanese government. To domestic manufacturers that depend on advanced technology, the big ten provide information on current scientific and technological advances in the U.S. and Western Europe, on the latest equipment available, on market potential, and on technology licensing or joint venture requirements.

The information services of the *sogo shosha* are not limited to economic and business information of immediate practical value; they extend to global political-legal data (e.g., antitrust law decisions), demographic data, and the sociocultural environment (e.g., antibusiness attitudes, consumer movements, antipollution sentiments, the youth culture, and the like), and trends that are likely to have an impact on the Japanese economy. Recent observers, for example, have been impressed by the great competitive efforts of *sogo shosha* officials stationed in New York to acquire information about President Carter's far-reaching energy policy even before it was officially announced in April 1977, so it could be passed on to their automobile and oil industry clients whose short-term and middle-term fortunes will be greatly affected by the new energy-related policies.

The valuable information services are extended not only to Japanese customers but to foreign clients as well. Information on the structure of various Japanese industries, on the complex distribution channels, on potential joint venture partners, on government policies, laws, and regulations, and on negotiation strategies are provided to foreign firms interested in exporting to the Japanese market or in establishing production and assembly plants in Japan.

Risk Reduction Services

In serving as financial intermediaries between large commercial banks and thousands of small clients, the *sogo shosha* serve the banks as important risk buffers. Banks prefer to lend large sums to several well-established *sogo shosha* rather than to lend small sums to thousands of small producers. The small loans require large staffs and may involve as much time as very large loans to process and handle. By using the *sogo shosha* as intermediaries, the banks avoid the high costs associated with small loans. Perhaps even more important, the *sogo shosha* have day-to-day contacts with the management of the small firms. They are in an excellent position to realistically assess the risks involved in extending credit to small producers and are thus less likely to suffer from loan defaults than are the banks.

The information services noted above are also invaluable in

reducing risks for firms that move into international trade, whether or not they use the trading companies as export-import agents. Risk is unavoidable in any business venture, domestic or international. The number and degree of risks taken in international business, however, increase substantially because the transactions are across national boundaries. International business involves a wide variety of new problems: different languages, customs, and economic and political systems; varied government economic policies; unfamiliar antitrust regulations and import and export controls; sudden economic swings and shifts in commodity prices; the floating of major world currencies; and exposure to customers and suppliers of widely varied credit standings and reputations. Risks can range from simple delays to costly litigations on uncollectable losses amounting to tens of millions of dollars because of the bankruptcy of a foreign customer. Such risks could clearly be reduced if the exporter had a better knowledge of the customer's financial health.

A good example of the value of the quick information provided to regular clients occurred in September 1974. The Mitsubishi Corporation's local information source in Zambia alerted Triland Metal, Ltd. (a joint metals trading venture established by Mitsubishi, American and British concerns, and a member of the London Metal Exchange), of a 20 percent reduction in copper production only half an hour before it was officially announced by the Zambian government. Triland promptly relayed the information by direct telex line to the Mitsubishi Corporation's Copper Metals Section, which wasted no time in advising its own officials and customers. In turn, this enabled the latter to quickly take the necessary actions before the world copper price rose by $70 a ton. The compensatory actions were completed just twenty minutes after the Zambian announcement was made and avoided substantial losses for the firms involved.

The floating of major world currencies in the spring of 1973 presented another major risk to international traders. Foreign exchange risks can be staggering, a fact large Japanese shipbuilders discovered when the U.S. dollar, the currency of long-term payment, was officially devalued in the winter of 1971. Japanese exporters are exposed if the customer country's currency is used for account settlement. Their customer is affected if the Japanese Yen is used. Both assume risks if a third country's currency, such as the U.S. dollar or the British pound sterling, is used.

Trading companies enjoy considerable capacity for hedging risks from foreign exchange rate fluctuations. Extensive involvements in both exports and imports encompassing numerous commodities and markets ("marrying" exports and imports, as trading company officials in Japan say) enable them to offset export losses caused by sharp Yen appreciation (which results in sharply reduced dollar returns) with import gains resulting from sharp drops in payments to foreign suppliers because of dollar and other foreign currency devaluations. If they expect the U.S. dollar or the British pound to depreciate, they will either "lead" American and British customers to pay their bills quickly or sell export bills to foreign exchange banks at discounts as soon as they received bills of lading from shippers, thus receiving prompt export payments in Yen and avoiding losses from future dollar or pound depreciation. On the other hand, when they are importers they will try to "lag" their payments to American and British suppliers as long as payment deadlines will allow in the expectation that the dollar and pound will drop in value against the Yen and result in reduced payments. Trading companies also seek hedges in the foreign exchange futures market, signing contracts to sell—at certain exchange rates at given future dates to foreign exchange banks—predetermined amounts of dollars, pounds, or other foreign currencies (usually equal to the value of export goods) that they expect will depreciate in the future. Another device used by many trading companies is heavy borrowings in depreciating foreign currencies, even when interest rates abroad are higher than those in Japan. This method enables the borrower to enjoy sizable reductions in (or even negative) debt servicing cost when the foreign currencies drop sharply in value. All these hedging techniques are risky and not to be used lightly by inexperienced manufacturers. General trading companies can advise manufacturer clients on various risk-hedging methods or share foreign exchange risks when they serve as manufacturers' foreign trade agents.

Organization and Coordination Services

The *sogo shosha*'s organization and coordination services have increased in importance since the late 1960s because of the tremendous rise in the number of large-scale overseas natural resource development projects. (These are discussed in detail in Chapter 6). Projects include mining iron ore in Australia and drilling for natural gas and oil in Indonesia to meet the rising demands of Japan's heavy industries and of her petrochemical industry. The rise in plant export has also increased the demand for organization and coordination services. Demands for these services involving the oil-producing countries of the Middle East since the oil crisis, for example, have been phenomenal.

Natural resource development projects and plant exports are systems enterprises. They differ radically from simple commodity exports in number, scale, and complexity of financing, equipment, technology, processes, and stages. For example, a resource development project requires the participation of many trading, financial, development, engineering, and manufacturing firms. These firms, both Japanese and foreign, must be so organized as to effectively and efficiently pool their capital, technical, and other resources. They do more than share the high risks of the resource development project. Their activities must be integrated and coordinated beginning with feasibility studies through the construction of whatever infrastructure is needed (railroads, harbors, roads), actual project construction, the production phase, and distribution and marketing of the final product. Similar high-level coordinating and integrative activities are required in the export of large industrial plants. The magnitude and complexity of these resource development and plant export projects are immense. The *sogo shosha*, with their tremendous arsenal of financial, information, human, and group resources, are able to organize and coordinate such gigantic enterprises.

Auxiliary Services: Paperwork, Insurance, Warehousing, Transportation

The general trading companies also provide their customers

with many valuable auxiliary services. One is handling much of the paperwork required in business transactions. This service can be of immense value in international business in saving time, money, and headaches, especially for those in the initial stage of the export business. For a small commission, a trading company will handle the tedious paperwork and documentation required, including export declarations, commercial and consular invoices, ocean bills of lading, insurance certificates, export letters of credit, and documents related to collection problems (such as arbitration and legal action). Another auxiliary service is insurance; all the *sogo shosha* are licensed insurance agents. Thus, the Marubeni Corporation can, for example, in the course of handling export of the group firm Hitachi, Ltd.'s electric machinery to Kenya, obtain insurance coverage from Yasuda Fire & Marine Insurance Co., its group insurance firm.

Two related auxiliary services are warehousing and transportation. The big trading companies own many warehousing subsidiaries, including rolled steel warehouses, grain elevators, and refrigerated warehouses. They also own large ore carriers, log carriers, and general cargo ships. Firms such as Nippon Kokan K. K., Nisshin Flour Milling Co., and Sapporo Breweries Ltd., to use the Fuyo group as an illustration, can often employ group railways such as Keihin Electric Express Railway Co., or Tobu Railway Co., Marubeni Corporation warehouses such as Marubeni Reizo K. K. at the Tokyo harbor, and Marubeni-owned cargo boats or transports operated by group member Showa Shipping Co.

Economies of Scale and Cost Reduction Services

The financial, information, organization-coordination, and auxiliary services discussed above, and the strong emphasis the *sogo shosha* place on volume trade on low margins rather than on profit maximization, give them the ability to provide economies of scale services and cost reduction benefits to customers and suppliers.

The *sogo shosha* borrow large sums from commercial banks at prime lending rates. Their customers and suppliers, to whom the trading companies extend financial services in the form of credit, loans, or advance payments, can in turn borrow money at lower cost than they could by direct borrowing from commercial banks. The trading companies collect an enormous amount of business intelligence from all over the world and then disseminate it, usually free of charge, to their customers. The savings in information costs are not insignificant. The trading concerns provide organization and coordination services for huge overseas natural resource development, plant export, and other projects to participating financial institutions and manufacturers. They serve as project secretariat, provide valuable information, spend much staff time, and incur huge expenses. When a project becomes operational, they receive agents' rights to sell equipment to the project and to handle the volume sales of raw materials and products. They do not charge the high consulting and organization fees imposed by U.S. and Western European engineering consulting firms. The savings to participating firms can be substantial.

The *sogo shosha*'s global office and communications networks also save money for their clients. These networks are required and made possible by global training in 20,000 individual products, multiple types of business, and multiseason trade. Even a large single-product manufacturer, not to speak of small single-product or multiproduct manufacturers, would find the cost of maintaining offices in a number of foreign countries prohibitive if the markets were not sizable. Large manufacturers just moving into a new foreign market, and small and medium-sized producers unable to establish their own overseas offices, can engage in profitable exports at substantial cost savings when they use the trading companies' global commercial networks.

Greater Capital Efficiency Services

The financial, information, risk reduction, organization-coordination, economies of scale, and auxiliary services described above lead to substantial cost reductions for the manufacturer customers of the trading companies. This leads in turn to a sizable increase in the total amount of capital employed. The increase in capital occurs because without the financial and other services the *sogo shosha* provide, some small manufacturers would find it difficult to obtain credit and long-term financing. Even large manufacturers would have to allocate a substantial amount of capital to provide or purchase these services independently at a higher cost. This increased capital was of immense value to Japanese manufacturing firms of all sizes during the era of rapid economic growth of the 1960s and early 1970s when all were searching and competing for scarce capital.

The services provided by the *sogo shosha* also lead to more efficient use of capital. Instead of having substantial capital tied down in financing sales and distribution and for higher cost transportation and insurance, nearly all the capital can be invested in plants and equipment to expand production and the manufacturer's market share. This can be critical for manufacturers whose price competitiveness depends on reduced production cost generated by economies of scale. For them, not to increase the scale of capital investment in a rapid growth economy results not only in reduced competitiveness but, eventually, in loss of their market share.

Human Resources

To provide the valuable financial, information, risk reduction, organization-coordination, economy of scale, greater capital efficiency, and auxiliary services that the *sogo shosha*'s customers require and to facilitate and expand their businesses, the ten big *sogo shosha* have acquired immense human, financial, organizational, and communications resources. Manpower is the most critical of these resources. Although the *sogo shosha* have invested heavily in communications equipment and computers, which we will examine shortly, and also in plants and equipment of subsidiaries, these are not as critical as the special skills of their staffs. Communications equipment and computers are mere tools, but manpower is the very heart of this knowledge-intensive service industry. Since their core business is global selling and buying and not manufacturing, the intelligence, diligence, dedication, creativity, alertness, adaptability, human relations skills, language facility, and organizational capabilities of the *sogo shosha*'s managers are critical. For this reason all the firms devote immense efforts to the hiring and training of employees.

Services and Resources

Table 3.4 Employees of the Ten General Trading Companies, September 1976

	Number of employees	Average age
Mitsubishi Corporation	10,171	32
Mitsui & Co.	11,262	34
Marubeni Corporation	8,242	33
C. Itoh & Co.	7,638	32
Sumitomo Shoji	6,250	32
Nissho-Iwai Co.	7,046	34
Toyomenka	3,940	35
Kanematsu Gosho	4,079	33
Ataka & Co.	3,188	33
Nichimen Company	3,948	35
Total	60,764	33

Source: Compiled from Toyo Keizai Shinposha, *Kaisha Shikiho* (Quarterly Directory of Corporations), January 1977 issue (Tokyo: Toyo Keizai Shinposha, December 1976), pp. 629-654.

Note: Figures exclude directors, temporary employees, employees of subsidiaries, and locally hired non-Japanese employees working at overseas offices.

In September 1976 the ten largest *sogo shosha* had on their payrolls approximately 61,000 full-time Japanese employees. These figures would increase substantially if members of the boards of directors, temporary employees, and locally hired non-Japanese personnel working at numerous overseas offices (about 600 for the smallest and about 2,700 for the largest among the big ten) are added. Mitsui & Co. alone hired 11,262 Japanese, the largest employer among the big ten, exceeding the employment figure of the Mitsubishi Corporation by nearly 1,100. Male employees, constituting about three-fifths of trading company personnel, are hired for life for managerial tasks. Most are hired immediately following college graduation and form the nucleus of the trading companies' human resources. The majority of female employees are hired as secretaries. After several years, they usually leave the firms to get married.

Large *sogo shosha* such as the Mitsubishi Corporation, Mitsui

& Co., and Sumitomo Shoji Kaisha each year hire 200 to 300 management trainees (almost all males) fresh out of Japan's most prestigious government universities (Tokyo, Kyoto, Hitotsubashi, Nagoya, Yokohama, Osaka, and Kobe City University) and private institutions of higher education (including Waseda, Keio, and Kansai universities). Hiring is highly selective because the large trading companies have great appeal to college seniors searching for lifelong employment. Despite public criticism of the firms between 1972 and 1975, they still attract fifteen to twenty applicants for each opening for a new recruit.

The trading companies attach extraordinary importance to the training of personnel in general and of new recruits in particular. Sumitomo Shoji Kaisha, for example, which hires an average of 200 college graduates out of 4,000 applicants a year, devotes considerable time and expenditure to this effort, according to Executive Vice President Sumio Okahashi, former head of Sumitomo's personnel division. Freshmen employees attend a special training program at the Osaka head office for two weeks after joining the firm. They are then placed temporarily in various staff and line divisions for on-the-job training. They attend another training program three months later. Top officials, rather than low-ranking officers, take charge of these training sessions. Formal job assignment is made six months after joining Sumitomo. At this time, each new employee is assigned to a guide (*shidonin*) who will give him personal advice and care in all aspects of his work and life, ranging from human relations within the firm to sickness at home and to marriage. For the next three years, the guide and the chief of his own section will be his counselors and mentors as he tries to become a good Sumitomo-man.

Training focuses on the nature and objectives of the firm's business, the company's values (most firms emphasize harmony, loyalty, and corporate interests), and the company's organizational structure (emphasizing proper procedures and obeying orders once they are made and come through the hierarchy). New recruits are socialized at training centers. New colleagues, guides, and superiors mold the new recruits into skilled and trustworthy employees by the end of their third year in the firms. Once trained, these men become valuable permanent company assets. They are hired for life and promoted by seniority, although merit has been given greater consideration in recent years. Their reflexes will lead them to act and react automatically to attain company objectives, whether they are at work at a company office or traveling alone to a Brazilian jungle to investigate or negotiate a new business venture. It does not take long before new employees learn that work does not cease at 5 P.M. and that hundreds of company officials work into the night drafting project reports, dispatching telex messages to overseas customers, and entertaining customers.

In addition to on-the-job training, the big ten provide their young managers with opportunities to attend business seminars in Tokyo and to pursue advanced studies abroad at the leading American business schools or other well-known training centers of management and commerce. In March 1976 the big four alone had 240 Japanese managers studying at various foreign institutions. The large trading companies also conduct training programs for non-Japanese managers working at their overseas offices. The Mitsubishi Corporation, as part of its internationalization program, has sponsored an annual international seminar for foreign managers since 1974. In addition, English-language seminars for Japanese managers at Tokyo headquarters have been conducted since 1974 by language education specialists. In June 1977 Mitsubishi flew nearly fifty non-Japanese managers from twenty-six countries to Tokyo to attend its fourth international seminar. Afterwards, some of them were placed in various specialized departments for six months' on-the-job training and exposure to operations at the home office.

Financial Resources

To extend vital credit, loan, loan guarantee, and venture capital services to customers and suppliers, the *sogo shosha* amass a phenomenal amount of capital, both their own and borrowed. The ten largest firms employed a total capital (total liabilities and net worth) of 16,614 billion Yen or $55,379 million as of March 31, 1974. Mitsui & Co. and the Mitsubishi Corporation employed larger capitals (3,426 billion and 3,201 billion Yen, respectively) than Nippon Steel Corp. (2,271 billion Yen), the world's largest

Table 3.5 Capital Structure of the Ten General Trading Companies, March 31, 1974[a]

	(A) Total capital	(B) Liabilities	Net worth	Capital stock	$\frac{B}{A} \times 100$
Mitsubishi Corporation	32,013	31,192	821	335	97.4%
Mitsui & Co.	34,260	33,258	1,002	332	97.1
Marubeni Corporation	20,460	19,879	581	305	97.2
C. Itoh & Co.	18,834	18,015	819	269	95.6
Sumitomo Shoji	14,586	14,153	433	157	97.0
Nissho-Iwai Co.	12,929	12,570	358	173	97.2
Toyomenka	10,054	9,803	252	100	97.5
Kanematsu Gosho	7,298	7,105	193	73	97.4
Ataka & Co.	9,086	8,895	191	100	97.9
Nichimen Company	6,616	6,376	239	100	96.4

Source: Compiled from Toyo Keizai Shinposha, *Kaisha shikiho* (Quarterly Directory of Corporations), Autumn 1974 issue (Tokyo: Toyo Keizai Shinposha, 1974), pp. 640-666.

[a] In hundred million Yen.

steel producer and Japan's largest industrial corporation. They were respectively Japan's largest and second-largest corporations in terms of total capital employed. Nippon Steel, Mitsubishi Heavy Industries, and Nippon Kokan, the three giant steel makers, each had larger capital employed than the next four largest *sogo shosha*, namely, the Marubeni Corporation, C. Itoh & Co., Sumitomo Shoji Kaisha, and Nissho-Iwai Co. These four trading companies, however, had larger amounts of capital at their disposal than Japan's other industrial giants, such as Hitachi, Ltd., Toyota Motor, Nissan Motor, Matsushita Electric, Sumitomo Metal Industries, Tokyo Shibaura Electric, and Kansai Steel.

An overwhelming share, about 97 percent, of the *sogo shosha*'s total capital employed is liabilities. This indicates that the trading companies borrowed abnormally heavily from financial institutions to provide the manifold financial services required by their domestic and international businesses. As of March 31, 1974, Mitsui & Co. borrowed $11,086 million (an approximate translation from the Japanese Yen because of currency float) or

Table 3.6 Top Five Financial Institutions Lending to Six General Trading Companies, March 31, 1974

	No. 1 bank		No. 2 bank		No. 3 bank		No. 4 bank		No. 5 bank	
	Bank	Amount[a]	Bank	Amount[a]	Bank	Amount[a]	Bank	Amount[a]	Bank	Amount[a]
Mitsubishi Corporation	Mitsubishi Bank	1,470	Bank of Tokyo	981	Daiichi Kangyo Bank	812	Mitsubishi Trust & Banking	758	Sanwa Bank	613
Mitsui & Co.	Mitsui Bank	1,607	Fuji Bank	1,383	Bank of Tokyo	1,347	Mitsui Trust & Banking	670	Sumitomo Bank	558
Marubeni Corporation	Fuji Bank	889	Bank of Tokyo	813	Yasuda Trust & Banking	460	Taiyo Kobe Bank	383	Kogyo Bank	248
C. Itoh & Co.	Bank of Tokyo	787	Sumitomo Bank	780	Daiichi Kangyo Bank	624	Sumitomo Trust & Banking	473	Nippon Long-Term Trust & Banking	374
Sumitomo Shoji	Sumitomo Bank	686	Sumitomo Trust & Banking	463	Bank of Tokyo	340	Nippon Fudosan Bank	273	Nippon Long-Term Trust & Banking	244
Nissho-Iwai Co.	Sanwa Bank	607	Daiichi Kangyo Bank	448	Bank of Tokyo	315	Daiwa Bank	282	Toyo Trust & Banking	204

Source: The Japan Foreign Trade Council, Inc., *Kosei Torihiki linkai no "sogo shosha ni kansuru dainikai chosa hokoku" ni tsuite* (On the Fair Trade Commission's Second Investigation of General Trading Companies), 1975, p. 17.

[a] In hundred million Yen.

97.2 percent out of a total employed capital of $11,420 million. The Mitsubishi Corporation borrowed $10,397 million, or 97.4 percent of total capital employed, amounting to $10,671 million. They borrow heavily but not exclusively from group financial institutions, as Table 3.6 suggests.

Western financiers without previous experience with the *sogo shosha* all shudder in disbelief when they read the trading concerns' financial statements and discover the high-leverage capital structure and the 1:1 current ratio (i.e., the ratio of total current assets to total current liabilities). They question if the *sogo shosha* can meet current payment obligations and even wonder if they are bankrupt. The truth is that borrowing up to 97 percent or more of total capital and maintaining a 1:1 current ration has been the *sogo shosha*'s accepted method of business in the post–World War II years. The method started in the early 1950s and developed into an accepted business behavior during the high-flying years of the Japanese economy, the 1960s and early 1970s. This pattern of business has had the backing and even encouragement of financial institutions, which in turn had the strong backing of the Bank of Japan. Although horrifying to the Western businessman, the practice has enabled the *sogo shosha* to provide vital financial services to their customers.

Global Commercial Network

Another critical asset of the ten general trading companies is their network of global offices. In addition to strengthening their domestic commercial network, the *sogo shosha* have made special endeavors to expand their already extensive overseas office networks. As a result, in March 1976 each of the big six *soga shosha* had between 100 and 140 offices abroad—in all the major cities of Asia, the Middle East, Western Europe, Africa, North and South America, Eastern Europe, and the Soviet Union. These include overseas branch offices of the Japanese head office and offices that are locally incorporated but are in reality branch offices. For example, in the United States alone, Nissho-Iwai Co. had offices in New York, Chicago, Houston, Detroit, San Francisco, Los Angeles, Portland, Seattle, St. Louis, and Anchorage in March 1976. It has since established

Services and Resources

established a new office in Atlanta, Georgia, to take advantage of the expanding economy in the sunbelt. The Nissho-Iwai Co. thus has a far more extensive office network in the U.S. than many medium-size American firms. Its network in Africa and the Middle East includes branch offices, among others, in Nairobi (Kenya), Addis Ababa (Ethiopia), Kinshasa (Zaire), Algiers (Algeria), Tripoli (Libya), Cairo (Egypt), Khartoum (the Sudan), Beirut (Lebanon), Baghdad (Iraq), Kuwait (Kuwait), Qatar (Qatar), Abu Dhubai, and Riyadh (Saudi Arabia). Each of the six largest firms employed from about 2,000 to 3,400 people overseas, of whom about 600 to 1,050 were officials dispatched from the Japan head office.

The *sogo shosha* also strive for efficient and flexible control and coordination of their worldwide commercial network, a difficult task because their business involves so great a variety of products, so wide a geographic spread, and so many types of trading. With minor differences, the *sogo shosha*'s head offices are generally organized into corporate staff divisions and worldwide product divisions. Corporate staff divisions include control, general affairs, personnel, planning and development, marketing, finance, and area control divisions. Product divisions, vertically organized, usually include energy, ferrous metals, nonferrous metals, machinery, chemicals, food, textile, wood and paper, and construction divisions. Each product division exercises global control over business transactions related to the division and forms an independent profit center. The sole exception is Mitsui & Co., where each area office is a profit center.

Each product division generally has a divisional staff that has a role similar to that of the corporate staff. The corporate staff assumes overall companywide product and project control and coordination through systems of multiple responsibilities and multiple reporting relationships. Members of product division staffs report not only to their own division heads but also to the corporate staff. There is also expanded use of project teams and task forces. Area coordination for North, Central, and South America, for Western Europe, for the Middle East and Africa, and for Oceania is increasingly assumed by regional headquarters established in the early 1970s. Responsibilities of area coordination for East and Southeast Asia and for the communist bloc

Figure 3.1 Organizational structure of Sumitomo Shoji Kaisha, March 1974

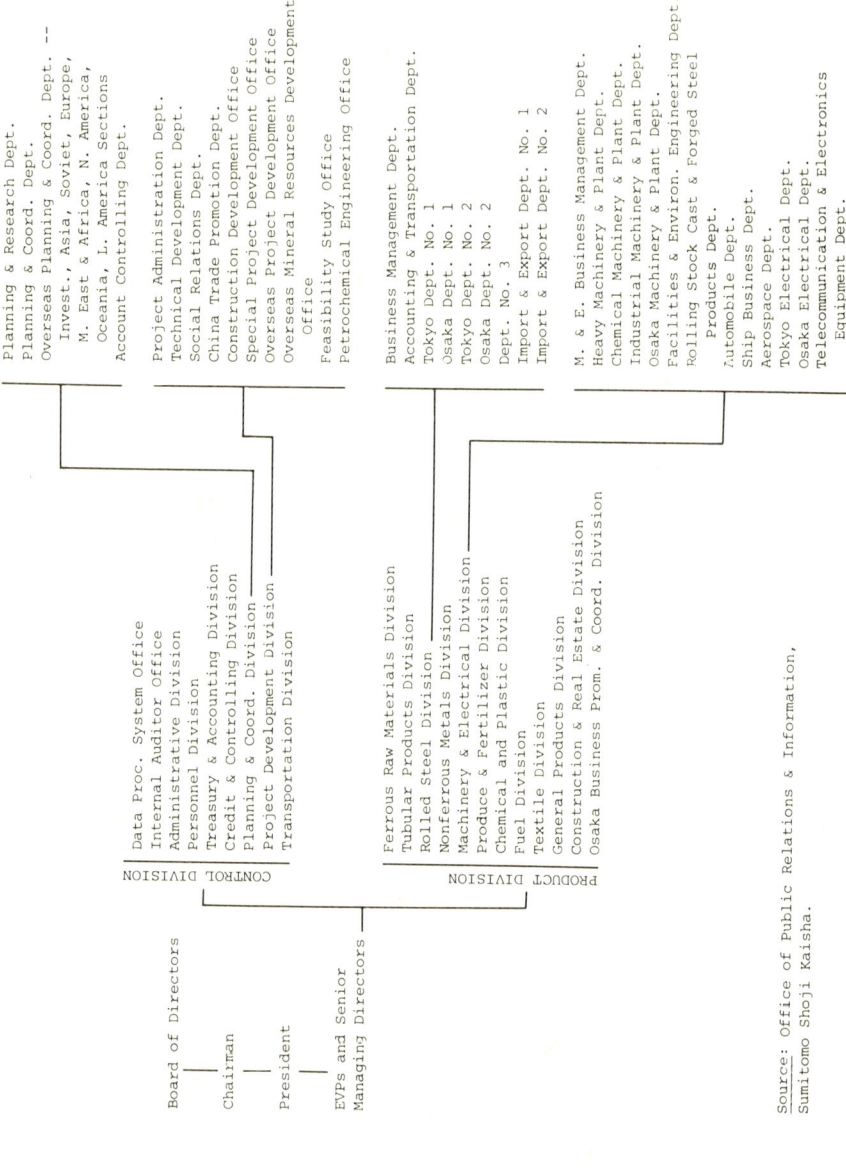

Source: Office of Public Relations & Information, Sumitomo Shoji Kaisha.

countries are generally assumed by the head offices in Japan.

Each *sogo shosha* is organized military-style in a highly regimented way from the chairman (the commander-in-chief) through chiefs of divisions (division commanders) and of departments or offices (regiment commanders) to heads of sections (platoon leaders). But unlike the military, each *sogo shosha* is extraordinarily flexible, mobile, and adaptive. This is a marked contrast to the bulkiness and inflexibility of many large manufacturers.

Global Communications Systems

The *sogo shosha* have spent enormous amounts of money to strengthen their communications systems, both to provide information services to clients and to expand their own business. It is no exaggeration to say that information is the lifeblood of the giant traders. Data on where the buyers, suppliers, and joint venture partners are; on commodities prices; on trends in production, supply, and demand; and on changes in government trade policies abroad are critical. Furthermore, information, once obtained, must be communicated quickly to the relevant head office managers and to customers throughout the world. Speedy information can save millions of dollars; news obtained ten minutes too late can mean financial disasters. The Zambian copper case mentioned earlier is only one example. Inquiries from overseas businessmen about possible sales to or purchases from Japan demand speedy action and reply if the deals are not to be lost to competitors. Accurate, detailed information and quick communication can increase or reduce a trading concern's competitiveness and substantially affect its transactions and profits.

The expenditure of the *sogo shosha* on information gathering and global communications systems is staggering. During fiscal 1975 ended March 31, 1976, the top six firms alone spent 57.5 billion Yen (approximately $192 million) on expenditures related to information and communication. Mitsui & Co., for example, in late 1973 employed three telegraph communication systems for global communications: a privately leased channel (PLC), telex, and public telegraph. The PLC, responsible for about 95 percent

Figure 3.2 Mitsui global communications network (September 1, 1973)

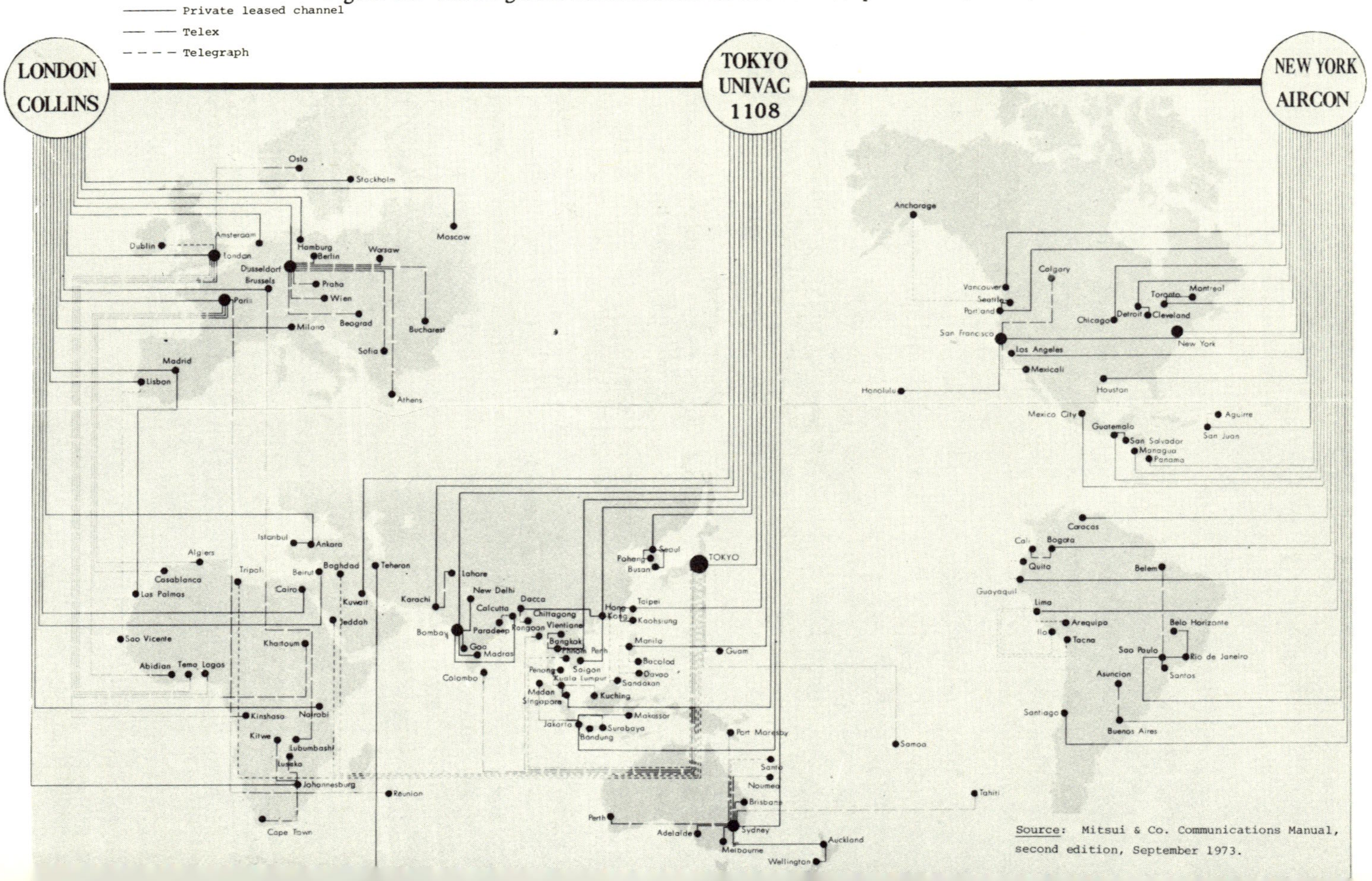

——— Private leased channel
——— Telex
- - - Telegraph

Source: Mitsui & Co. Communications Manual, second edition, September 1973.

of the firm's global telecommunications, handled about 20,000 Mitsui messages daily. Messages were automatically switched and transmitted around the clock by computers at three global communication centers. The PLC system, with more than 200 telex lines, links the Tokyo head office with 44 domestic branch offices and 112 overseas branch offices on an "on line" 24-hour basis. All telegraph messages flow through the UNIVAC 1108 computer in Tokyo and are then automatically transmitted either to domestic or overseas offices. Messages going overseas are transmitted directly to branch offices in Asia and Oceania; to the AIRCON computer in New York for retransmission to offices in North, Central, and South America and Iran; or to the Collins computer in London for automatic switching to offices in Western Europe, Africa, and the Middle East (except Iran).

Communication is almost instantaneous. A message going to even the remotest branch office in Africa takes at most a few minutes. The number of messages handled is so large and the load so heavy that optical character readers (OCR), with the capacity to process 2,000 letters a second (equal to the capacity of 300 well trained telex operators), had to be developed and employed. According to Mitsui officials, as of late 1973 the U.S. Department of Defense was the only other institution in the world using this system. A single message can be sent to multiple destinations all over the world. Thus, the Mitsui branch office in Taipei, Taiwan, can send quotations on Taiwan's sports goods and receive offers from several offices in the United States or Western Europe in a few days. In late 1973 Mitsui was spending 100 million Yen ($330,000) a month for the operation of the PLC.

Notes

1. Information and Research Department, Mitsui & Co., "Nihon keizai ni okeru shosha no yakuwari: genjo to tenbo" (The Role of Trading Companies in the Japanese Economy: Current State and Future Prospects), 1976, p. 28. Major corporations are those firms that are included in the Bank of Japan's periodic management study.

Part 2
Evolution and Roles

4
Growth Trends and Business Strategies: 1960-1973

The ten trading companies did not become *sogo shosha*, $171-billion-a-year global traders, overnight. It took many years of toil and trial and error for their sales, their business, and their modes of operation to evolve and crystallize. This evolution reflects both the firms' efforts to satisfy the changing needs of the Japanese people and economy and their various strategic moves in response to the changing domestic and international environment.

Although the present study focuses on the trading companies in recent years, a brief survey of the firms' growth trends and business strategies between fiscal 1960 and fiscal 1973 (ended March 31, 1974) will enhance our understanding of the *sogo shosha*'s evolution and modes of operation. The dramatic shift in strategy after the Middle East oil crisis of October 1973 will be analyzed in Chapter 7.

Transactions Trends

The *sogo shosha* grew by leaps and bounds after the mid-1950s. The big ten's combined annual sales expanded by nearly nine and one-half times between fiscal 1960 and fiscal 1973. Although mergers, inflation, and revaluations of the Yen following President Nixon's new economic policy of August 1971 contributed to the expansion, their growth nonetheless can only be characterized as phenomenal. Total sales of the big ten rose from 3,994 billion to 37,214 billion Yen a year. In thirteen years the Mitsubishi Corporation's sales grew from 644 billion to 7,484 billion Yen a year. Even the smallest firm, Nichimen Company, grew from 306 billion to 1,589 billion Yen.

The ten firms grew at strikingly different paces, however. The three former *zaibatsu* firms (the Mitsubishi Corporation, Mitsui & Co., and Sumitomo Shoji Kaisha) and the two former iron and steel traders (Nissho-Iwai Co. and Ataka & Co.) achieved faster growth than the ten firms' average, while the five former textile traders (the Marubeni Corporation, C. Itoh & Co., Toyomenka Kaisha, Kanematsu Gosho, and Nichimen Company) grew at a much "slower" pace of from five to eight times the average. The most impressive was Sumitomo Shoji Kaisha, the youngest *sogo shosha*, whose traditional strength lies in iron and steel trade. It grew by nearly twenty times in slightly over a decade.

The different growth paces experienced by the various firms led to a significant shift in the sales ranking of the big ten, the most important Japanese yardstick in determining the standing of the firms. Between 1954, the year the Mitsubishi Corporation achieved its final merger, and 1974, the ranking among the top four firms remained remarkably stable. The Mitsubishi Corporation was consistently number 1, except for a couple of terms in the mid-1960s when it was overtaken by the newly merged Mitsui & Co. The Marubeni Corporation was number 3 and C. Itoh & Co. number 4 throughout the entire period.

Rankings below the top four underwent radical shifts, however. Nichimen Company, number 5 in 1960, dropped to number 10 by 1972. Toyomenka Kaisha, number 7 in 1955, rose to number 6 by 1960 and to number 5 by 1965 but dropped back to number 7 by 1970 and has remained there since. Nissho Co., number 6 in 1955, dropped steadily to number 7 by 1960 and number 8 by 1965. Iwai Sangyo was highly erratic: number 9 in 1955, number 12 by 1960, and number 9 by 1965. Nissho and Iwai merged in 1968, becoming the number 5 firm. However, it dropped to number 6 by 1972 because of the phenomenal growth of Sumitomo Shoji Kaisha. Sumitomo was the only firm below the top four that rose steadily without experiencing a single drop in ranking. Number 11 in 1955, Sumitomo Shoji Kaisha rose to number 8 by 1958, number 7 by 1961, number 6 by 1967, and number 5 by 1971, overtaking the newly merged Nissho-Iwai Co. By 1974, Sumitomo Shoji Kaisha was within striking distance of C. Itoh & Co. Despite the numerous mergers, most of which

Table 4.1 Annual Sales of the Ten General Trading Companies, FY 1960–FY 1976 (fiscal year ended March 31)[a]

	FY 1960	FY 1964	FY 1966	FY 1969	FY 1971	FY 1972	FY 1973	FY 1974	FY 1975	FY 1976
Mitsubishi Corporation	644,413	1,318,283	1,729,197	3,242,009	4,529,833	5,181,920	7,484,192	9,407,680	9,140,648	9,609,009
Mitsui & Co.	639,528	1,207,636	1,775,598	3,090,183	4,135,025	4,955,481	6,967,730	8,627,216	7,885,170	9,024,958
Marubeni Corporation	612,738	1,135,093	1,379,614	2,164,153	2,910,005	3,399,751	4,441,105	5,556,495	5,762,570	6,438,242
C. Itoh & Co.	544,596	1,106,614	1,246,425	2,056,428	2,773,268	3,173,698	4,228,797	5,229,503	5,630,673	6,332,657
Sumitomo Shoji	196,623	451,921	629,054	1,308,221	1,976,646	2,414,929	3,850,455	5,117,789	5,509,561	5,825,444
Nissho-Iwai Co.	333,600	734,621	995,584	1,508,252	1,925,079	2,392,536	3,382,831	4,005,096	3,959,844	4,527,070
Toyomenka	277,798	n.a.	738,912	1,185,306	1,393,159	1,551,017	1,834,334	2,444,449	2,394,810	2,521,751
Kanematsu Gosho	294,200	n.a.	569,949	715,536	970,672	1,192,741	1,821,228	2,320,649	2,308,101	2,335,713
Ataka & Co.	144,700	n.a.	298,496	658,373	944,428	1,165,651	1,616,469	2,094,832	1,998,937	1,490,174
Nichimen Company	305,587	n.a.	591,757	777,819	916,734	1,163,675	1,586,800	2,068,679	1,688,074	1,810,546
Total	3,993,783		9,994,591	16,706,280	22,474,849	26,591,399	37,213,941	46,872,388	46,278,388	49,915,564

Source: Financial statements of the firms.
Note: n.a. = not available. Sales total for Nissho-Iwai Co. before 1969 combines sales of Nissho Co. and Iwai Sangyo.
[a] In million Yen.

involved absorption of small and medium-size firms by big traders, and despite the spectacular growth in sales, the share of the ten *sogo shosha* in Japan's foreign trade during the decade between FY 1964 and FY 1973 changed remarkably little.

As a result of the vastly different growth paces among the firms, the ten *sogo shosha*, already highly stratified in 1961, became even more stratified by 1974. By 1974, the Mitsubishi Corporation was almost five times the size of the Nichimen Company in terms of the scale of transactions; it had been only about twice that of the Nichimen Company back in 1961. The gap between the six largest firms (serving Japan's six giant conglomerate groups) and the bottom four also widened, although by a smaller margin. Their share of Japan's exports in FY 1973 was approximately 53 percent, a rise of only 1 percent over FY 1964, while their percentage share in Japan's import total in FY 1973 was 63 percent, only 1 percent less than a decade earlier. Moreover, the weight of the big ten declined steadily for four years between FY 1966 and FY 1969, while imports also experienced a drop for two years during FY 1968 and FY 1969.

The share decline until FY 1969 and rise after FY 1970 reflect important changes in the Japanese economy and business and also strategic shifts made by the *sogo shosha*. These changes and shifts will be analyzed shortly.

The structure of the *sogo shosha*'s business in terms of the four major types of trade shows two significant trends between March 1955 and March 1974. The first is a substantial rise in the weight of domestic sales in the mid-1950s. As of March 1955, domestic sales of most of today's six largest trading companies were below 50 percent of total sales. Prime Minister Hatoyama's five-year economic plan for 1956-1960, aiming at economic independence and full employment through the rapid growth of the heavy and chemical industries, had a big impact on the firms. All saw their domestic business increase dramatically. By March 1960 there was not a single firm whose domestic sales fell below 50 percent. Domestic sales of the Marubeni Corporation, C. Itoh & Co., and Sumitomo Shoji Kaisha exceeded 60 percent of their total sales. The weight of foreign trade, especially of imports, in the firms' total sales transactions fell accordingly.

The second trend was a gradual expansion of third-country

Table 4.2 Share of the Ten General Trading Companies in Japan's Foreign Trade, FY 1963–FY 1976 (customs clearance basis)

Fiscal year	Export (million Yen)			Import (million Yen)		
	(A) Japan's total	(B) Ten firms' total	Share of B in A (percent)	(A) Japan's total	(B) Ten firms' total	Share of B in A (percent)
1963	2,029,108	1,027,510	50.6	2,608,949	1,635,247	62.7
1964	2,587,290	1,347,899	52.1	2,851,560	1,806,404	63.3
1965	3,140,608	1,654,226	52.7	3,030,017	1,951,135	64.4
1966	3,584,929	1,857,529	51.8	3,606,985	2,337,756	64.8
1967	3,878,485	1,972,648	50.9	4,342,018	2,825,149	65.1
1968	4,921,549	2,383,379	48.4	4,784,361	3,015,756	63.0
1969	6,047,208	2,856,558	47.2	5,761,204	3,598,636	62.5
1970	7,290,125	3,508,481	48.1	6,967,080	4,365,110	62.7
1971	8,470,606	4,316,935	51.0	6,822,595	4,134,418	60.6
1972	9,070,923	4,550,051	50.2	7,659,410	4,797,401	62.6
1973	10,877,202	5,732,800	52.7	12,369,133	7,925,656	64.1
1974	17,079,634	9,577,444	56.1	18,276,314	10,462,932	57.2
1975	17,029,943	9,599,884	56.4	17,396,283	9,674,440	55.6
1976	20,671,000	10,655,800	51.5	19,709,700	10,408,400	52.8

Source: Data provided by Yoshishige Murakami of the Japan Foreign Trade Council, Inc., and by Information and Research Department, Mitsui & Co.

Table 4.3 Share of Domestic, Foreign, and Overseas (Third-Country) Trade in Sales of Six General Trading Companies, 1955-1977 (fiscal six months ended March 31)[a]

	1953	1960	1965	1970	1973	1974	1975	1976	1977
Mitsubishi Corporation									
Domestic	32.8[b]	51.5	50.7	58.1	57.4	54.2	45.1	47.3	47.1
Export	23.9	18.6	18.9	15.7	16.1	13.8	20.2	17.0	17.3
Import	43.4	29.2	28.2	23.1	19.0	26.0	27.6	28.4	29.1
Overseas	0.0	0.8	2.2	3.1	7.5	6.0	7.1	7.4	6.5
Total	100.0	100.0	100.0	100.0	100.0	100.0	100.0	100.0	100.0
Mitsui & Co.									
Domestic	42.7[b]	53.8	53.8	55.5	56.8	56.0	45.6	51.2	50.9
Export	22.1	21.0	21.1	19.1	17.9	14.9	21.9	20.4	21.5
Import	34.8	21.6	21.5	23.8	18.8	22.1	22.2	20.9	20.4
Overseas	0.3	3.6	3.6	1.6	6.5	7.0	10.3	7.5	7.2
Total	100.0	100.0	100.0	100.0	100.0	100.0	100.0	100.0	100.0
Marubeni Corporation									
Domestic	45.3	62.3	61.4	60.1	59.9	55.8	45.6	44.2	43.7
Export	22.8	13.7	16.1	18.0	19.8	18.0	26.2	26.4	26.1
Import	31.9	22.2	18.8	19.3	15.0	20.9	20.6	18.5	17.3
Overseas	0.0	1.8	3.7	2.6	5.3	5.6	7.6	10.9	12.9
Total	100.0	100.0	100.0	100.0	100.0	100.0	100.0	100.0	100.0

C. Itoh & Co.								
Domestic	53.2	61.3	62.8	60.5	57.7	54.5	48.9	52.7	49.7
Export	19.8	16.8	14.3	14.9	16.3	15.4	21.0	19.9	20.3
Import	27.0	20.4	18.8	19.0	19.1	24.6	22.9	20.2	19.1
Overseas	0.0	1.5	4.1	5.6	6.9	5.5	7.2	7.2	10.9
Total	100.0	100.0	100.0	100.0	100.0	100.0	100.0	100.0	100.0
Sumitomo Shoji								
Domestic	62.7	63.3	62.7	63.2	61.6	58.6	52.3	53.4	58.7
Export	22.6	19.4	16.5	17.8	17.3	14.5	23.7	21.9	21.4
Import	14.8	17.3	18.0	16.1	14.1	16.2	15.0	14.5	14.2
Overseas	0.0	0.0	2.8	2.9	7.0	10.7	9.0	10.2	5.7
Total	100.0	100.0	100.0	100.0	100.0	100.0	100.0	100.0	100.0
Nissho-Iwai Co.								
Domestic	47.0c	56.0	50.0	54.0	52.0	51.0	46.0	46.2	46.9
Export	22.0	13.0	20.0	16.0	16.0	15.0	22.0	23.8	23.1
Import	31.0	30.0	26.0	24.0	21.0	24.0	23.0	20.3	19.4
Overseas	0.0	1.0	4.0	6.0	11.0	10.0	9.0	9.7	10.6
Total	100.0	100.0	100.0	100.0	100.0	100.0	100.0	100.0	100.0

Source: Compiled from financial statements of the firms.
[a]In percent. [b]Data for fiscal six months ended September 30. [c]Data for October 1954–September 1955.

trade after 1965. Today's big six had *no* third-country trade in the fiscal year ended March 1955. By March 1965, however, third-country trade expanded to between 2 percent and 4 percent of total sales. It rose even more noticeably between March 1972 and March 1974. The third-country trade of Sumitomo Shoji Kaisha rose to 11 percent and that of Nissho-Iwai Co. to 10 percent by March 1974. The result of this trend for most firms was a drop in the share of domestic business and imports during fiscal 1972 and a drop in the weight of domestic sales and exports during fiscal 1973. This critical trend is analyzed in detail in Chapter 7.

The product structure of the *sogo shosha* underwent an even more dramatic transformation between 1955 and 1974. The changes of the big six are shown in Table 4.4. The transformation pattern of the other three former textile traders (Toyomenka Kaisha, Kanematsu Gosho, and Nichimen Company) is similar to that of the Marubeni Corporation and C. Itoh & Co.; that of Ataka & Co., the former iron and steel trading company, is similar to Sumitomo Shoji Kaisha's.

Only the Mitsubishi Corporation could be considered a well-developed general trading company in 1955, using our definition of a *sogo shosha* as a huge highly diversified trading company. Nissho Co., too, was a *sogo shosha*, but was not highly diversified. The Ministry of International Trade and Industry defines a specialized trader as one who specializes in one product group whose share in total sales is 50 percent or more. On this definition, all the other trading companies were still specialized traders in 1955. Mitsui & Co. did not become a *sogo shosha* until the final merger of former Mitsui firms in 1959; the Marubeni Corporation and C. Itoh & Co. did not become general trading companies until the mid-1960s; and Sumitomo Shoji Kaisha remained a metals trader until 1971.

While the transformation the former metals traders made with respect to their product structure was massive, the change the former textile traders made was revolutionary. Metals were 62.4 percent of Sumitomo Shoji Kaisha's total sales in fiscal six months ended March 1955; by March 1974 this share was down to 36 percent. The share of textiles in the Marubeni Corporation's sales total during fiscal six months ended March 1955 was 67 percent, and that of C. Itoh & Co.'s was 71 percent. The share was

Table 4.4 Share of Various Products in Sales of Six General Trading Companies, 1955–1977 (percent)

	1955	1961	1965	1970	1972	1974	1975	1976	1977
Mitsubishi Corporation									
Metals	23.00*	25.4	26.9	39.2	33.3	30.1	30.0	30.1	33.4
Machinery	15.77	22.5	22.1	18.5	21.2	14.1	14.5	17.9	15.0
Fuel	7.49				8.1	13.9	17.7	18.8	18.5
Chemicals		9.8	18.4	15.7	7.7	8.4	8.8	8.0	8.4
Foodstuffs	32.08	18.7	16.8	12.4	14.0	13.4	15.0	13.9	12.9
Textile	12.88	11.7	9.2	8.0	9.3	9.1	5.7	5.5	5.4
Materials	8.57	11.9	6.5	6.0	6.1	6.4	5.2		
Development and construction	0.21		0.1	0.2	0.3	3.6	3.1	5.8	6.4
Total	100.00	100.0	100.0	100.0	100.0	100.0	100.0	100.0	100.0
Mitsui & Co.									
Ferrous metals	15.2*	28.0	29.1	38.3	30.8	33.7	34.2	30.7	31.7
Nonferrous metals									
Machinery	6.7	15.3	14.6	18.5	20.4	15.6	15.4	18.4	18.2
Chemicals	4.9	17.0	14.9	12.0	11.6	12.0	11.9	11.9	12.0
Fuel								7.4	7.3
Textile	8.3	10.7	10.3	7.7	9.0	9.2	6.8	7.1	6.7
Foodstuffs	53.2	21.4	18.9	10.8	13.3	15.1	18.1	15.7	13.9
Materials and others	11.7	7.6	12.2	12.7	14.9	14.4	13.6	8.8	10.2
Total	100.0	100.0	100.0	100.0	100.0	100.0	100.0	100.0	100.0
Marubeni Corporation									
Metals	7.77*	13.6	15.1	30.5	24.2	27.0	26.9	25.1	24.5
Fuel	1.23								
Machinery and construction	3.20	10.4	16.7	18.8	26.3	19.9	22.3	24.6	24.3
Chemicals and fuel		3.3	9.2	7.3	7.6	9.9	12.3	13.1	14.4
Textile	66.85	47.2	49.2	22.2	20.3	19.7	15.4	14.6	14.2
Foodstuffs	14.89	14.6	14.2	10.8	12.1	12.8	14.9	14.4	14.1
Others	6.06	10.8	10.7	10.4	9.5	10.7	8.2	8.2	8.5
Total	100.00	100.0	100.0	100.0	100.0	100.0	100.0	100.0	100.0

(Table 4.4 continues)

Table 4.4 (cont.)

	1955	1961	1965	1970	1972	1974	1975	1976	1977
C. Itoh & Co.									
Machinery and construction	2.4*	7.8	10.7	14.1	17.4	15.8	16.4	17.9	18.0
Chemicals		8.6	10.5	11.4	12.3	17.8	22.9	27.0	27.6
Textile	71.0	53.8	41.5	35.7	31.9	30.4	20.8	21.0	19.8
Foodstuffs	13.2	11.8	15.0	13.2	14.2	12.4	15.7	13.5	13.3
Lumber, materials, etc.	9.1	6.9	9.2	8.4	10.4	8.3	6.0	5.7	6.3
Metals	4.3	11.1	13.1	17.2	13.8	15.3	18.2	14.9	15.0
Total	100.0	100.0	100.0	100.0	100.0	100.0	100.0	100.0	100.0
Sumitomo Shoji									
Metals	62.4	57.5	51.5	50.6	39.4	36.0	38.2	35.2	33.9
Machinery	13.5	18.0	15.1	19.3	22.0	18.2	20.4	22.0	23.4
Chemicals and fuel	4.5	8.4	6.7	12.2	13.8	16.7	21.0	21.4	20.7
Textile	4.0	3.4	2.6	3.3	6.2	8.2	7.6	6.2	5.3
Foodstuffs	15.2	6.6	12.6	4.9	9.4	12.1	6.7	7.7	8.7
Materials and construction	0.5	6.1	11.4	9.8	9.2	8.8	6.1	7.5	8.0
Total	100.0	100.0	100.0	100.0	100.0	100.0	100.0	100.0	100.0
Nissho-Iwai Co.									
Metals	46.0*	48.0	30.3	34.7	42.0	39.0	38.0	35.1	38.3
Machinery	7.0	11.0	24.4	37.7	22.0	19.0	22.0	25.7	21.8
Textile	23.0	17.0	34.1	14.4	9.0	10.0	7.0	7.8	8.6
Foodstuffs	15.0	7.0	3.0	2.2	9.0	11.0	14.0	11.3	11.3
Materials	9.0	17.0	8.2	11.0	18.0	21.0	19.0	20.1	20.6
Total	100.0	100.0	100.0	100.0	100.0	100.0	100.0	100.0	100.0

Source: Financial statements of the firms.
Note: Data for 1955 through 1975 are for fiscal six months ending March 31 unless otherwise noted by asterisk (*); data with an asterisk are for fiscal six months ending September 30. Data for 1976 and 1977 are for the fiscal twelve months ending March 31. See footnote 3 on p. 20 and note 2 in Chapter 2 on the various commodities classification standards used by the general trading companies.

down to about 20 percent for Marubeni Corporation by March 1974 and to 30 percent for C. Itoh & Co. The weight of chemicals (including fuel) and textiles in Sumitomo Shoji Kaisha's sales increased tremendously as the share of metals declined. It was exactly the opposite with the Marubeni Corporation and C. Itoh & Co.; the weight of metals, machinery, and chemicals rose dramatically in direct proportion to the extraordinary share-drop in textiles. C. Itoh & Co., for example, in March 1955 had *no* sales of chemicals. By March 1974, C. Itoh & Co.'s share of chemicals in total sales was about 18 percent. In March 1955, the weight of metals in C. Itoh & Co.'s sales was only 4.3 percent and that of machinery just 2.4 percent. By March 1974, the former had risen to 15.3 percent and the latter to about 16 percent.

The capital structure of the *sogo shosha* changed little during the two decades before 1974. The share of the firms' own capital (i.e., equity = capital stock + retained earnings + various reserves) in total capital employed remained extremely small throughout the whole period: 2 to 6.6 percent for individual firms, 3 to 5.4 percent for the top six firms combined. The own capital/total capital rate peaked in the mid-1960s and dropped steadily thereafter through the fiscal six months ended March 1972. It rose for a majority of the big six during the March 1973 period but dropped again during fiscal 1973 to the lowest rate in a decade for the six firms, except for C. Itoh & Co.

The *sogo shosha*'s highly leveraged capital structure during the post–World War II period was a radical departure from the prewar pattern. The average own capital/total capital rate during fiscal 1939 of Japanese wholesalers and retailers that engaged in foreign trade was 41.3 percent instead of 2 to 6 percent.

Net profits (six months only) of the big six more than doubled between March 1967 and March 1974. The Mitsubishi Corporation's net profits rose from 2.7 billion to 6.9 billion Yen and those of Mitsui & Co. from 3.5 billion to 7 billion Yen. The increase of 5.6 times in net profits of the Marubeni Corporation was mainly a result of the exceptionally small profit of the March 1964 period. Sumitomo Shoji Kaisha's net profits more than tripled.

Net profits of the big six, however, grew only half as fast as sales. While net profits of the Mitsubishi Corporation and Mitsui & Co. doubled in seven years (March 1967 to March 1974), sales of

Table 4.5 Own Capital as Percentage of Total Capital Employed, Six General Trading Companies, 1939-1974

	FY 1939 ended March 1940	FY 1952 ended March 1953	1966[c]	1968[d]	1970[d]	1972[d]	1973[d]	1974[d]
Mitsubishi Corporation			6.4	4.7	3.8	3.3	3.2	2.6
Mitsui & Co.			3.3	2.9	2.9	2.5	3.3	2.9
Marubeni Corporation			4.9	4.0	2.9	3.9	3.4	2.8
C. Itoh & Co.			6.6	5.3	3.9	3.3	4.0	4.4
Sumitomo Shoji			4.8	4.8	3.0	2.8	3.1	3.0
Nissho-Iwai Co. (Nissho Co. only before 1969)			6.3	5.0	2.0	2.8	3.2	2.5
Japanese wholesalers and retailers	41.3[a]	3.5[b]	5.4[e]	4.5[e]	3.1[e]	3.1[e]	3.4[e]	3.0[e]

Source: Compiled from Tsusho Sangyosho (MITI), *1953 Boeki gyotai tokeihyo* (1953 Foreign Trade Statistics by Industries) (Tokyo: Tsusho Sangyo Chosakai, 1954), p. 29, and various semiannual issues of *Kigyo keiei no bunseki* (Analysis of Management Record of Japanese Firms) published by Mitsubishi Keizai Kenkyusho.

[a] Average of wholesalers and retailers.
[b] Average of wholesalers engaged in foreign trade.
[c] Data are for fiscal six months ending September 30.
[d] Data are for fiscal six months ending March 31.
[e] Six firms' average.

the two firms quadrupled. The same was true for Sumitomo Shoji Kaisha; net profits tripled, while sales increased six times.

Between 1966 and 1973 over 50 percent of current profits (profits before nonoperating costs and taxes) of most of the six firms were from investment and other sources unrelated to operations. Throughout the entire period an extraordinarily large portion of Mitsui & Co.'s and C. Itoh & Co.'s current profits came from outside their trading operations; between 62 percent and 69 percent for Mitsui & Co. and between 59 percent and 67 percent for C. Itoh & Co. Sumitomo Shoji Kaisha was the only firm that almost consistently received more than 50 percent of its current profits from trading activities. The proportion of profit from investment and other nonoperating sources in total current profits suddenly dropped below 50 percent, however, during the fiscal six months ended March 1974 for all the firms except Mitsui & Co.

Investment earning (both direct and indirect investment) was the most important single source (over 95 percent) of nonoperating current profit for the big six between 1966 and 1974. It accounted for 99 percent of Mitsui & Co.'s nonoperating current profits throughout the period. Only the Mitsubishi Corporation and C. Itoh & Co. had earnings from investments falling below 95 percent; March 1972 and March 1973 for Mitsubishi, and after March 1972 for C. Itoh & Co.

Because the *sogo shosha* place extraordinary emphasis on large-scale transactions on low profit margins and on large-scale borrowings from banks to provide various vital financial services to clients, the low net profit/total capital rates between 1966 and 1974 are not surprising. Even so, the extremely small net profit/total capital rate of about 0.5 percent during fiscal 1973 is striking, especially to those unacquainted with the modes of operations of the *sogo shosha*.

The net profit/total capital rate of the big six (except the Marubeni Corporation) during the latter half of the 1960s was about 1 percent. It deteriorated suddenly during the March 1971 and March 1972 accounting periods, dropping below the 0.5 percent mark. It rose slightly during the March 1973 period but declined again during the March 1974 period. Despite the extremely low net profit/total capital rate, the six *sogo shosha*,

Table 4.6 Net Profit Rates of Six General Trading Companies, 1966-1974

	1966[b]	1967[a]	1968[a]	1969[a]	1970[a]	1971[a]	1972[a]	1973[a]	1974[a]	1974[b]
Mitsubishi Corporation										
Net profit (million Yen)	2,242	2,656	3,779	4,282	7,889	4,209	4,283	6,438	6,941	6,986
Net profit/total capital rate (%)	0.85	0.93	1.03	0.94	1.27	0.52	0.45	0.60	0.47	0.43
Net profit/own capital rate (%)	12.98	15.04	20.33	21.48	33.62	15.31	14.34	18.46	17.43	15.66
Mitsui & Co.										
Net profit (million Yen)	2,682	3,546	4,276	4,569	6,758	3,706	3,751	5,058	7,326	7,052
Net profit/total capital rate (%)	0.78	1.01	1.02	0.91	1.00	0.44	0.36	0.41	0.47	0.41
Net profit/own capital rate (%)	24.64	30.66	33.31	32.22	37.04	15.79	14.46	14.05	15.24	13.69
Marubeni Corporation										
Net profit (million Yen)	188	904	2,665	1,243	2,182	2,012	2,018	4,023	5,058	4,912
Net profit/total capital rate (%)	0.09	0.40	1.01	0.41	0.57	0.41	0.35	0.58	0.53	0.47
Net profit/own capital rate (%)	1.68	8.13	23.70	10.88	18.54	11.65	9.84	16.18	17.90	16.40

C. Itoh & Co.										
Net profit (million Yen)	1,422	2,631	2,663	2,269	2,845	2,304	2,173	5,835	5,653	3,159
Net profit/total capital rate (%)	0.79	1.41	1.18	0.86	0.86	0.53	0.40	0.88	0.64	0.34
Net profit/own capital rate (%)	12.05	21.82	20.99	17.36	20.59	13.83	12.11	21.25	14.14	7.64
Sumitomo Shoji										
Net profit (million Yen)	1,004	1,145	1,125	1,915	2,404	1,635	1,476	2,538	3,751	3,649
Net profit/total capital rate (%)	0.92	0.97	0.76	1.12	1.02	0.51	0.40	0.56	0.56	0.49
Net profit/own capital rate (%)	18.81	20.82	14.74	23.86	27.94	16.80	14.37	17.36	17.90	16.40
Nissho-Iwai Co.										
Net profit (million Yen)	692	817	860	1,081	1,637	1,312	1,146	2,131	3,036	2,808
Net profit/total capital rate (%)	0.89	0.96	0.84	0.56	0.69	0.44	0.35	0.51	0.51	0.43
Net profit/own capital rate (%)	13.83	16.01	16.04	12.55	20.02	14.98	12.65	14.83	17.88	15.31

Source: Mitsubishi Keizai Kenkyusho, Kigyo keiei no bunseki (Analysis of Management Record of Japanese Firms), various semiannual issues.

Note: Net profit/total capital rate = net profit ÷ total capital × 100.

[a] Data for fiscal six months ended March 31.

[b] Data for fiscal six months ended September 30.

except the Marubeni Corporation, maintained very high net profit/own capital rates from 1967 to 1970; between 15 and 37 percent. Average rates for all six firms were even higher for the three years between 1968 and 1970. This proves that the big six gained substantial profits during those three years.

As can be inferred from the sharp decline in net profit/total capital rate, net profit/own capital rate also saw sudden and substantial drop during the March 1971 fiscal six months accounting period. The Mitsubishi Corporation's rate dropped from 34 to 15 percent; that for Mitsui & Co. from 37 to 16 percent; for Nissho-Iwai Co. from 20 to 15 percent. The rate declined again during the March 1972 accounting period, although not as sharply. The six firms' rates, except for Mitsui & Co., made a noticeable improvement during the next fiscal year, although not to the pre-1970 level.

The big six were able to achieve net profit/own capital rates of between 14 and 18 percent during fiscal 1973 ended March 1974, slightly smaller than the previous fiscal year but large enough to issue respectable dividends of from 12 to 15 percent to stockholders.

The Changing Japanese Economic Environment: 1955-1970

The transactions, trade and product structure, and capital and profit trends described above reflect several basic changes that occurred in the Japanese economic environment during the two decades between 1955 and 1974. They also reflect business strategies the *sogo shosha* were compelled to adopt given the vastly altered environment. A brief description of five of the changes in the Japanese economic milieu that directly affected the trading companies enlarges our understanding of the trading companies' business strategies. These changes, occurring between 1955 and 1970, included rapid economic growth, the radical transformation of Japan's industrial structure, a thrust by manufacturers into direct marketing, the emergence of a mass consumer society and the growth of mass merchandise stores, and liberalization of the restrictions on foreign investment.

Rapid Economic Growth

Rapid economic growth was the first and foremost change. The

Japanese economy took off in 1955, signaling the end of the postwar era of defeat, Occupation, and gradual recovery. The Japanese government led the drive for maximum growth of the heavy and chemical industries with a series of middle-term and long-term economic plans to achieve larger national objectives. Two of the most important long-term economic plans were Prime Minister Hatoyama's five-year economic plan for 1956-1960, aimed at Japan's economic independence and full employment, and Prime Minister Ikeda's double national income plan for 1961-1970, aimed at maximum economic growth, an improved standard of living, and full employment. Both plans exceeded their original objectives by wide margins. The Japanese economy grew by an annual average of 9.1 percent in real terms between 1956 and 1960, rather than the projected 5 percent, and by 10.9 percent between 1961 and 1970, instead of 7.2 percent as planned. The industrial sectors scored even higher growth rates than the official projection: 15.6 vs. 7.4 percent between 1956 and 1960, and 13.8 vs. 10.5 percent between 1961 and 1970. The result was spectacular industrial development at a pace previously unknown in the annals of economic history. In one decade, from 1956 to 1965, steel production expanded by 4.4 times, shipbuilding by 11 times, and automobile and television production by an unbelievable 35 times.

Radical Transformation of Japan's Industrial and Export Structures

Rapid development of the heavy industries (steel, shipbuilding, automobile, etc.) and chemical and petrochemical industries was at the heart of the Japanese government's economic plans. The rapid development of these critical growth industries in turn fueled rapid general economic growth.

The result was a radical transformation of Japan's industrial and export structures. In 1955 the weight of heavy and chemical industries in the Japanese manufacturing industry was the smallest (about 48 percent) among Japan, the United States, West Germany, and Britain. By 1970 Japan's proportion was the largest (60 percent) among the industrialized countries. The transformation of Japan's export structure was especially dramatic. In

1955 the weight of heavy and chemical industrial products in Japanese export was only about 38 percent, much smaller than that of West Germany (67 percent), Britain (58 percent), and the United States (51 percent). It almost doubled (72 percent), however, by 1970, becoming only slightly smaller than that of West Germany and far larger than that of Britain and the U.S.[1] In 1970, the most important Japanese export commodities in terms of absolute value were steel, ships, chemicals, motor vehicles, metal products, electronic equipment, synthetic fibers, clothing, and motorcycles, rather than cotton textile products or sundry goods as in 1955.

Manufacturers' Thrust into Direct Marketing

Japan's steel, shipbuilding, chemical, and machinery industries grew substantially in strength as a result of the concerted drive for rapid industrial growth. Earnings and capital accumulation of major firms rose substantially, leading to a vastly strengthened capital structure in terms of the weight of own capital in total capital employed. Many of the manufacturers, especially steel makers and shipbuilders, continued to rely on the trading companies to market their products at home and abroad. An increased number of large manufacturers, however, began to make their own purchases of supplies and, more important, to independently market their own products. The trend toward direct purchases and sales first appeared in the early 1950s and increased in tempo in the mid-1960s among electronics, automobile, and other manufacturers of consumer durables, all industrial sectors that require engineering expertise, sales promotion, and after-sales service to customers.

The trend toward direct purchases and sales by manufacturers was especially pronounced in foreign trade. The result was a substantial rise in the manufacturers' share of both Japanese import and export and a proportionate decline for all trading companies, not just the top ten. During fiscal 1952 the weight of the manufacturers in Japanese exports and imports was 9 and 11 percent respectively, while that of the trading companies was 91 and 89 percent. Twenty-one years later (fiscal 1973) the manufacturers' share in Japanese export was 32 percent, a three-and-one-half times increase, while their share in Japanese

Table 4.7 Shifts in Trading Companies' and Manufacturers' Share of Japanese Exports and Imports, FY 1952–FY 1973 (MITI double accounting system basis, in percent)

	Wholesalers and retailers	Department stores	Manufacturers	Others	Total
FY 1952					
Export	90.7			9.3	100.0
Import	88.9			11.1	100.0
FY 1953					
Export	84.4			15.6	100.0
Import	86.1			13.9	100.0
FY 1954					
Export	82.5			17.5	100.0
Import	86.6			13.4	100.0
FY 1955					
Export	86.0			14.0	100.0
Import	82.4			17.6	100.0
FY 1956					
Export	83.0			17.0	100.0
Import	85.2			14.8	100.0
FY 1957					
Export	82.0			18.0	100.0
Import	86.7			13.3	100.0
FY 1958					
Export	78.9			21.1	100.0
Import	82.7			17.3	100.0
FY 1959					
Export	80.2			19.8	100.0
Import	84.2			15.8	100.0
FY 1960					
Export	82.7			17.3	100.0
Import	83.8			16.2	100.0
FY 1961					
Export	79.7			20.3	100.0
Import	83.4			16.6	100.0
FY 1962					
Export	78.1			21.9	100.0
Import	81.3			18.7	100.0
FY 1963					
Export	75.2			24.8	100.0
Import	82.2			17.8	100.0

(Table 4.7 continues)

Table 4.7 (continued)

	Wholesalers and retailers	Department stores	Manufacturers	Others	Total
FY 1964					
Export	75.0		25.0		100.0
Import	81.9		18.1		100.0
FY 1965					
Export	72.3	0.1	26.6	1.0	100.0
Import	80.9	—	18.7	0.4	100.0
FY 1966					
Export	71.6	—	26.7	1.7	100.0
Import	81.4	—	18.1	0.5	100.0
FY 1967					
Export	70.8	0.1	27.4	1.7	100.0
Import	81.2	0.1	18.1	0.6	100.0
FY 1968					
Export	70.5	0.1	28.0	1.4	100.0
Import	82.1	0.1	17.3	0.5	100.0
FY 1969					
Export	69.2	0.1	28.8	1.9	100.0
Import	80.9	0.1	18.0	1.0	100.0
FY 1970					
Export	68.8	0.1	29.8	1.2	100.0
Import	80.7	0.1	17.8	1.4	100.0
FY 1971					
Export	69.4	0.1	30.0	0.5	100.0
Import	79.5	0.1	19.1	1.3	100.0
FY 1972					
Export	67.1	—	32.4	0.5	100.0
Import	78.6	0.2	19.6	1.6	100.0
FY 1973					
Export	67.1	—	32.2	0.7	100.0
Import	77.5	0.2	21.7	0.6	100.0

Source: Compiled from Tsusho Sangyosho (MITI), *Boeki gyotai tokeihyo* (Foreign Trade Statistics by Industries), annual volumes, 1953-1975.

Note: FY 1952 and FY 1953 start October 1 and end September 30 of the following year. After FY 1954, fiscal year starts April 1 and ends March 31 of the following year. MITI statistics do not give detailed breakdowns until FY 1965. See footnote 3 on p. 21 on the double accounting system of Japan's foreign trade transactions used in MITI's *Boeki gyotai tokeihyo.*

Table 4.8 Gross National Product of Japan, 1955-1972

Calendar year	Nominal terms		Real terms (1965 price)	
	Value (hundred million Yen)	Annual growth rate (%)	Value (hundred million Yen)	Annual growth rate (%)
1955	86,236	10.1	117,827	–
1960	154,992	19.9	196,987	14.1
1961	191,255	23.4	227,659	15.6
1962	211,992	10.8	242,281	6.4
1963	244,640	15.4	267,853	10.6
1964	289,317	18.3	304,656	13.7
1965	319,555	10.5	318,790	4.6
1966	368,294	15.3	351,334	10.2
1967	435,845	18.3	398,783	13.5
1968	516,772	18.6	455,576	14.2
1969	603,038	16.7	510,591	12.1
1970	710,078	17.8	563,366	10.3
1971	793,068	11.7	601,870	6.8
1972	906,939	14.4	655,140	8.9

Source: Economic Planning Agency, *1974 Keizai yoran* (1974 Economic Handbook) (Tokyo: Ministry of Finance Printing Office, 1974), p. 2.

imports increased two times. In contrast, the trading companies' shares in Japanese export and import were down respectively to 67 and 78 percent.

The Emergence of a Mass Consumer Society and the Growth of Mass Merchandise Stores

Japan's GNP in nominal terms grew slightly over four and one-half times between 1960 and 1970: from 15,499 billion Yen ($43,053 million) to 71,008 billion Yen ($197,243 million). This rapid economic growth led to a tremendous rise in the income of the Japanese people. This expanded personal income in turn led to rising consumer expectations, to the transformation of the structure of family expenditures (i.e., a drop in food expenditures and a rise in service and leisure expenditures), and to the emergence of the first mass consumer society in Asia. Manufacturers of consumer durables (such as appliances, electronic

Table 4.9 Structure of Japanese Household Expenditure, 1955–1972 (cities with a population of 50,000 and over)

	Average number in household	Expenditure (Yen)						Share (percent)				
		Total	Food	Dwelling	Light and heating	Clothing	Miscellaneous	Food	Dwelling	Light and heating	Clothing	Miscellaneous
1955	4.84	23,211	10,891	1,331	1,216	2,717	7,056	46.9	5.8	5.2	11.7	30.4
1960	4.51	31,276	13,000	2,790	1,597	3,755	10,134	41.6	8.9	5.1	12.0	32.4
1961	4.35	34,329	13,842	3,399	1,731	4,326	11,031	40.3	9.9	5.1	12.6	32.1
1962	4.29	38,587	15,063	3,951	1,906	4,933	12,734	39.0	10.2	4.9	12.8	33.1
1963	4.30	43,616	16,793	4,131	1,989	5,423	15,279	38.5	10.1	4.6	12.4	34.4
1964	4.28	47,834	18,139	4,474	2,123	5,683	17,415	37.9	9.8	4.5	11.9	35.9
1965	4.24	51,832	19,738	5,787	2,317	5,916	19,073	38.1	9.9	4.6	11.4	36.0
1966	4.17	56,097	20,836	4,228	2,456	6,206	21,371	37.1	10.1	4.6	11.1	37.1
1967	4.13	61,091	22,355	5,779	2,580	6,725	23,653	36.6	10.5	4.5	11.0	37.4
1968	4.05	66,441	23,666	6,834	2,675	7,340	25,927	35.6	11.5	4.3	11.0	37.5
1969	3.97	73,497	25,426	7,970	2,845	7,988	29,268	34.6	10.8	3.9	10.9	39.8
1970	3.95	82,792	28,307	8,864	3,169	8,968	33,484	34.2	10.7	3.8	10.8	40.4
1971	3.93	90,742	30,319	10,047	3,542	9,868	36,965	33.4	11.1	3.9	10.9	40.7
1972	3.90	98,640	32,453	10,804	3,673	10,794	40,915	32.9	11.0	3.7	10.9	41.5

Source: Economic Planning Agency, *1974 Keizai yoran* (1974 Economic Handbook) (Tokyo: Ministry of Finance Printing Office, 1974), pp. 268-269.

equipment, cameras, and automobiles) and soft goods (foods, cosmetics, etc.) expanded their output to meet the rising demand.

Supermarkets and mass merchandise retail stores appeared in response to the growing mass consumer society. They thrived on high volume, self-service sales on small profit margins; their number and sales expanded between 1964 and 1970. In six short years their share in Japan's retail sales almost doubled (from 4.7 to 9 percent). The number of retail stores operated by the various chains rose to 9,403, their employees to more than 173,000 and their sales to 1,612.5 billion Yen (or $4,479 million). Their weight in Japan's retail sales was only slightly lower than that of the much older department stores that emphasized customer service rather than self-service.

Manufacturers' thrusts into direct marketing and the growth of mass merchandise stores during the 1960s were two revolutionary developments in the Japanese marketing system.[2]

Foreign Investment Liberalization

Japan joined the Organization for Economic Cooperation and Development (OECD) in 1964. Three years later the Japanese government, under foreign pressure, moved to liberalize foreign investment (direct and indirect) in Japanese industry by stages. Despite the greatly increased international competitiveness of Japanese industry, the new policy aroused strong mixed reactions in the country's business establishment. Some called it Japan's second opening (the first was in 1854 when the Tokugawa *shogunate* was compelled by Commodore Perry to sign the Treaty of Kanagawa after almost two and one-half centuries of isolation) and believed it would lead to the absorption of advanced foreign technological and management know-how and to even greater rationalization and growth of the Japanese industry. Others called it the second coming of "black ships" (i.e., Commodore Perry's warships that knocked forcefully on Japan's door in 1853) and feared domination of "weak" Japanese industries and disruption of Japan's economic order, management system, and business cycle adjustment mechanisms by such giant U.S. firms as GM, Ford, GE, ITT, du Pont, and IBM.[3]

The Big Ten's Strategic Response: Transformation into *Sogo Shosha*

The radical changes in the Japanese economic environment between 1955 and 1974 required the trading companies to adopt appropriate strategies to ensure their survival and growth. Many business strategies were pursued by the ten trading companies: growth, diversification, creation of demand and supply, the organization of new growth industries, consumer market penetration, and the consolidation of affiliates. These six strategies are closely interrelated and can be summarized in one word: *sogoka* (integration). They will be considered individually for clarity and because none of the firms has yet succeeded in pursuing a total integration strategy. This examination covers all ten trading companies, but more references will be made to C. Itoh & Co., Sumitomo Shoji Kaisha, and Nissho Co. because of the availability of company histories of each.[4]

The Growth Strategy

There was not a single trading company of significance that did not vigorously pursue growth as a strategy during the 1950s and 1960s. Expansion of sales was on the mind of every trader, encouraged by the trade policy of the Japanese government in the early 1950s. The government based the allocation of scarce foreign exchanges to trading companies for import of food, industrial raw materials, and equipment on the size of their exports. Furthermore, it issued permission to remit money for the support of personnel manning newly reopened and expanding overseas offices only to firms with a sizable foreign trade record. Obtaining valuable foreign exchanges and expanding overseas offices, both indispensable for future growth, thus required expanded transactions.

The basic reason for the pursuit of this strategy, however, was the rapid growth of the Japanese economy. In a fast-growing economy, a minimum requirement is that a firm grow at the same rate as the economy grows if it is to maintain its market share. Faster growth enables a firm to capture competitors' markets and leads to even greater market expansion, a snowballing effect. Failure to grow means shrinkage in market share, loss of competitiveness, and possibly even eventual demise.

Many methods were employed to expand sales. Merging with other firms, discussed below, was one. Another was expanded business dealings with group firms, pursued vigorously by the Mitsubishi Corporation and Sumitomo Shoji Kaisha. Sumitomo Shoji Kaisha spared no efforts in expanding transactions with Sumitomo Metal Industries and Sumitomo Chemical Company. Getting big manufacturers in the growth industries (steel, automobile, shipbuilding, and chemicals) to become one's customers or clients was another. As soon as private trade was reopened in 1951, Nissho Co. lost no time in pushing sales of iron ore and scrap iron to Kobe Steel, Kawasaki Steel, Sumitomo Metal Industry, and Nippon Kokan. Its ship department exported tankers of Hitachi Shipbuilding & Engineering, Harima Shipbuilding, and Mitsui Shipbuilding & Engineering. Fanning a fiercely competitive spirit among company employees was another method used. Recapturing the number 1 ranking from the Mitsubishi Corporation was the goal set for the Mitsui & Co. men throughout the late 1960s and early 1970s. Passing Nissho-Iwai Co. and beating C. Itoh & Co. and the Marubeni Corporation was the goal set by Sumitomo Shoji Kaisha's top management in the late 1960s. "Becoming a big three is the goal of every Sumitomo employee," declared Yukio Shibayama when he became president of the firm on November 26, 1970.[5]

The most important method, however, was the introduction of three-year economic plans in the early 1960s by most of the firms, spurred by the Ikeda cabinet's ambitious long-term economic plan. In 1961 Sumitomo's top management conference began an annual examination of three-year sales estimates compiled by its staff. In 1965 it adopted three-year plans that set goals for growth of sales and earnings and targets for domestic sales/foreign trade ratio and hard goods/soft goods ratios. The plans, compiled and examined annually, were formulated on the basis of various macroeconomic indices, the economic plans of major customers, and such internal data as the firm's past growth rates and the plans of various divisions and branch offices.

The Diversification Strategy

The trading companies pursued the diversification strategy as a logical response to the radical transformation of Japan's industrial and export structures. The two long-term government economic plans of 1955 and 1960 projected a substantial rise in the weight of the steel, shipbuilding, automobile, electronics, heavy machinery, petrochemical, and synthetic fiber industries. The general trading companies also foresaw that the food and other consumer products industries would grow substantially as a result of the rising personal incomes of the Japanese people. Furthermore, bitter past experiences had impressed on them the highly cyclical nature and risks of metals (ferrous and nonferrous) and textile businesses, and the speculative nature and risks of the grain trade. There was only one way to ensure growth and safety: become a *sogo shosha* through diversification. The task was especially urgent for textile traders such as the Marubeni Corporation and C. Itoh & Co., whose main business of textiles was clearly marked for gradual decline. Nondiversification, and thus not embarking on the road to becoming *soga shosha*, would lead to certain loss of their market shares and to their eventual demise.

Many techniques were employed: expansion into businesses outside one's traditional trade; thrusts into growth industries such as the importing of passenger planes from Boeing, Lockheed, and McDonnell Douglas and nuclear plants from General Electric and Westinghouse; and the establishment of subsidiaries, including sales companies, to handle more specialized products. The most important method during the 1950s and 1960s, however, was merger with other trading companies. Mergers ensured both growth and diversification, and thus facilitated the transformation into *sogo shosha*.

The two *zaibatsu* firms achieved diversification and the status of *sogo shosha* by a simple amalgamation of the many firms created by the Occupation's *zaibatsu* dissolution order. In 1947 the two *zaibatsu* trading companies split into firms along product lines (department or section) or by branch offices, resulting in the creation of many specialized product traders. Major new firms that split from Mitsui & Co. and their product specialization were: Daiichi Bussan (materials and grains); Daiichi Tsusho (materials); Muromachi Bussan (metals); Sanshin Seni (textiles); Tokyo Shokuhin (foodstuffs); Nippon Kikai Boeki (machinery); Kyokuto Boeki (machinery); and Taiyo Shosha (transportation). Mitsui & Co.'s Osaka branch became Goyo Boeki. Thus a simple merger of these dissolved firms, many of which had grown considerably by the mid-1950s, ensured diversification and *sogo shosha* status. Those split from Mitsubishi Trading Company merged into three firms (Fuji Shoji, Tozai Koeki, and Tokyo Boeki) in 1952 as soon as the Occupation ended. Finally, they merged with Kowa Jitsugyo in July 1954 to establish the new Mitsubishi Trading Company. Merger of firms that split from Mitsui & Co. took considerably longer because of conflicting interests among the firms and clashes of views and personalities among strong-willed leaders, but *sogo shosha* Mitsui Bussan (Mitsui & Co.) was finally born in 1959.

The other eight trading companies effected mergers by absorbing smaller trading companies, some of them well known and of significant size. Thus, Nissho Co., a metals trader, absorbed Shinko Menka, a cotton trader, in 1954, and Hakuyo Boeki, an importer and exporter of foodstuffs and textiles, in 1956. Marubeni, a cotton and textile trader, absorbed Takashimaya Iida, a well-known metals trading company, in 1955. It absorbed Totsu, a strong iron and steel trader, in 1966. C. Itoh & Co., a cotton and textile trader, absorbed Taiyo Bussan in 1955 with diversification clearly in mind. C. Itoh & Co. took an even more important step in 1961 by absorbing Morioka Kogyo, a well-known wholesale steel trader.

The Creation of Demand and Supply

The increased power of financial institutions and manufacturers in the postwar period caused considerable concern among officials of the trading companies. They saw the role of trading companies often reduced to that of manufacturers' commission merchants during the 1950s. The rising trend toward direct marketing by large manufacturers deepened their anxieties. Some predicted during the early 1960s that the role of the trading companies would steadily decline as manufacturers eliminated intermediaries and resorted to direct marketing. It became apparent to the trading companies that diversification alone was insufficient, and that they must discover a new strategy to induce producers and consumers to continue to rely on them.

The trading firms discovered and have pursued vigorously since the 1960s a strategy of creating demand and supply through upstream integration (prospecting, development, and production) and downstream integration (processing, wholesale distribution, and retail sales). However, total integration remains an ambition and not a reality. Furthermore, it is unlikely the trading companies will ever succeed completely, because much upstream integration is limited to equity participation and not actual development and production by the trading firms, despite their fondness for using production terms. Three courses of action, however, merit our attention: the supply of more specialized services; the organization of new growth industries; and thrusts into the consumer goods industry and market.

One specialized service the trading companies expanded greatly after the mid-1960s was the construction of steel fabrication-distribution centers. This enabled them to strengthen their position as intermediaries between huge steel producers and small manufacturing users of steel products. Nine *sogo shosha* and five steel wholesalers built more than 200 centers by the summer of 1972, about 70 percent of them in Tokyo, Nagoya, Osaka, and Chiba near where the users are concentrated. These centers stock large inventories of steel delivered from steel mills, take fabrication orders from steel users of various types and sizes, provide shearing, sawing, and grinding services according to tight specifications, and make quick deliveries. They also provide important information and financial resources to steel makers and users. (See Chapter 5 for details.)

The Organization of New Industries Strategy

Another strategy designed to actively create demand and supply was to organize and coordinate new industries. As the trading companies grew in the scale of their transactions, the number of their products, global spread, and service capabilities and resources, their officials became aware of one capability in which they were superior to the manufacturing concerns: the ability to organize large, complex projects (such as natural resource development or urban and regional development), plant exports, and complex systems industries (such as ocean resource development). These huge projects, exports, and industries, unlike traditional industries and types of trade, cut across numerous industries, require the participation of many diverse financial, manufacturing, engineering, and trading firms, and need to be organized and operated as an efficient integrated system.

The large trading companies, most of which had become well developed *sogo shosha* by the late 1960s, seized on this discovery. Organization of large enterprises such as natural resource development projects and new industries meant new businesses, investment opportunities, and demands for their services and equipment. Furthermore, such organization meant the development of ample new supplies of—and assured long-term opportunities to sell—iron ore, coking coal, uranium ore, natural gas, and other newly developed products to manufacturers after production started. In a phrase: the creation of both demand and supply.

One domestic project, the Konan food industries complexes operated by Mitsui & Co., illustrates this process. Located at one of the industrial zones at the Kobe harbor, the complex was organized by Mitsui & Co. in 1972. It centralizes at one convenient location in one of the world's largest harbors the unloading, storage, distribution, and processing of large-volume imported grains, meats, and marine products and the distribution of processed foods to food distribution centers, wholesalers, and retail chains. Cargoes carrying wheat, sugar, maize, soybeans, milo, edible fat, corn, marine products, and meats from the United States, Cuba, Thailand, Australia, and other countries (some developed and produced by joint ventures organized by Mitsui & Co.) are unloaded at the Konan Pier. The pier itself is a Mitsui & Co. subsidiary manned by Mitsui managers. It has berthing capacity for cargoes of up to 60,000 tons. Grains from cargoes are moved by conveyors to silos for storage or directly to the many first-stage food processing plants located on the 23,000-square-meter complex. Wheat is sent to Nippon Flour Mills, oil to Yoshihara Oil Mill, raw sugar to Taito Co., Ltd., and corn and milo to Nippon Feed Co. After first stage processing they are sent by conveyors or pipes for further processing to noodle factories (Myojo and others), to dry milk and ice cream factories (Morinaga Milk Industry), and chocolate plants (Cosmopolitan).

By-products and lees are sent to animal feed plants. Marine products and meats are transported first to refrigeration plants and then to fish and meat processing plants. Processed foods are then sent to the food distribution center on the complex for final distribution to wholesalers and retailers. The Konan Utility Co., another Mitsui & Co. subsidiary managed by Mitsui men, although with equity participation by the various companies (mostly Mitsui group firms) on the complex, provides electricity and steam, water disposal service, fire prevention, and management services to the entire complex.

Benefits to the large food processing firms are considerable. Production efficiency and large cost reductions are made possible by an integrated import, processing, distribution, and management system. Only a *sogo shosha* of Mitsui & Co.'s size, resources, and organizational capability could have organized this system. And for Mitsui & Co. the complex means continuing demand from food producers for grains, meats, and marine products it develops or buys abroad as well as assured long-term opportunities for selling processed foods to supermarket and merchandise chains at home or for shipping them abroad.

Thrust into the Consumer Goods Industry and Market

A thrust into the consumer goods industry and market was another *sogo shosha* strategy responding to the emerging mass consumer society and the rapid growth of mass merchandise stores. The *sogo shosha* exerted immense efforts to achieve total integration in this area. The firms' most important upstream integration effort was in the consumer food industry. Various food processors, feed companies, and mass merchandise chains also moved into the production of broiler chickens, eggs, hogs, beef, vegetables, and rice to ensure large-volume supplies and sales. The *sogo shosha*, however, were the most ambitious. They moved into the broiler chicken and hog business in the mid-1960s. They signed contracts with local agricultural cooperatives to supply imported chicks, piglets, and feed to the cooperatives. The cooperatives agreed to raise a definite number of chickens and hogs through farmers under separate contract to them. The trading companies then shipped the chickens and hogs delivered by the cooperatives to their group firms, joint ventures, or subsidiaries for processing, packaging, distribution, and retail sale. In 1968 they became even more ambitious. Some firms eliminated local agricultural cooperatives and began to operate their own chicken and pig farms.

The *sogo shosha* also vigorously pushed downstream integration. This involved the management of their own supermarkets, the construction and leasing of supermarkets and shopping centers, tieups with large retailers, and joint ventures with foreign businesses seeking entry into the Japanese market. Sumitomo Shoji Kaisha pioneered in direct management of supermarkets. In 1963 it established the Summit Store, a joint Sumitomo-Safeway venture, under the management of Takashi Maku, who later became president of Sumitomo Shoji America, Inc. Summit Store was capitalized at 60 million Yen as of September 1970 and had only twenty-eight stores, a very small chain compared with its giant American counterparts such as Safeway and A&P with their thousands of stores each. Summit encountered numerous difficulties in the beginning, including strong opposition from small and medium-size Japanese retailers and from politicians, the pullout of Safeway in 1967, and the initial inexperience of Sumitomomen in retail business. Nevertheless, it was not only a radical departure from the trading firms' past wholesale business but a revolutionary event in Japan's retail business. It became an important training ground in retail business for trading company officials and enabled them to have a better and quicker grasp of consumer needs and to expand business ties with consumer food producers.

A more popular method of entry into the consumer market by the *sogo shosha* was the construction and leasing of supermarkets and shopping centers to supermarkets and mass merchandise chains. The *sogo shosha* earned leasing and consulting fees and, most important, made considerable profits from the right to supply large-volume merchandise on a continuing basis to the retail chains. It was a highly visible method of moving into the consumer market without having to assume day-to-day operating responsibility.[6]

Closely related were tie-ups with large supermarkets and mass merchandise chains. The Marubeni Corporation entered a tie-up with Hoteiya, O.K., Sanko, Daiei, and Fuchu; Sumitomo Shoji

Kaisha with Seiyu and Fuchu; C. Itoh & Co. with Seiyu and Tokyo Voluntary Chain; Mitsui & Co. with Sanko, Fujino Bread, Tokai Super, Uoman Super, Kinokuniya, Seiyu, and the Tokyo Voluntary Chain; and the Mitsubishi Corporation with the Tokyo Voluntary Chain, Akebono Meat Chain, My Mart, and Jasco.

In 1968 the Mitsubishi Corporation took an epoch-making step by signing a five-year contract with Seiyu, the Sears Roebuck of Japan, under which it extended a 20-billion-Yen credit to Seiyu and agreed to mobilize the resources of the entire Mitsubishi group on behalf of the large retail chain, including the supply of raw materials, processing, and packaging, imports of foreign merchandise, merchandise development and information, and leasing stores and equipment. Seiyu agreed to purchase 20 percent of its merchandise needs from the Mitsubishi Corporation. The Mitsubishi Corporation also signed an agreement in 1969 with Jasco, the newly formed retail chain (Japan's third largest) to establish a joint venture, Diamond City Development, to build shopping centers in Osaka and Nagoya.

Last but not least in the *sogo shosha*'s thrust into the consumer goods market was the establishment of joint ventures with foreign firms seeking entry into the Japanese markets after the government liberalized foreign investment policy. Best known in the food sector are the Mitsubishi Corporation's tie-up with Kentucky Fried Chicken (1970) and the Marubeni Corporation's tie-up with Dairy Queen (1973). These provide the huge American fast food chains with easy entry into the Japanese market and gave the trading firms ready and growing opportunities to lease or sell store sites and equipment and, more important, to supply chickens, beef, milk, bread, and the other foodstuffs required by the fast food chains.

The Consolidation Strategy

Japan's admission to the OECD in 1964 and her obligation to liberalize foreign investment spurred a flurry of activities by Japan's financial, manufacturing, and trading establishments. Anticipating greater international competition both on Japan's home front and on the world market and possible domination by giant U.S. multinationals, Japanese corporations announced one merger after another. The number of major mergers in 1964 was double that in 1963. It included the merger of Ishikawajima-Harima Heavy Industries with Nagoya Shipbuilding & Engineering and Nagoya Heavy Industries; that of Mitsubishi Nippon Heavy Industries, New Mitsubishi Heavy Industries, and Mitsubishi Shipbuilding & Engineering into Mitsubishi Heavy Industries; and that of the Daiichi Bank and the Asahi Bank.

The recession of 1965, the Japanese government's announcement of foreign investment liberalization policy in 1966, and the dollar protection measures taken by the U.S. government led to even more frantic merger activities. Automobile companies either merged with each other or entered joint production agreements. Kawasaki Heavy Industries, Kawasaki Locomotives, and Kawasaki Aircraft Industry announced their intention to unite by spring 1969. The most dramatic was the appeal made by Fuji Steel president Shigeo Nagano in 1966, calling for the amalgamation of Japanese steel makers into two steel companies and the subsequent announcement in April 1968 that Japan's two steel giants Yawata Steel and Fuji Steel would merge to form Nippon Steel Corp. in March 1970.

These activities were part of a larger movement, led by the Mitsubishi, Mitsui, Fuji, Daiichi, Kangyo, Sumitomo, Tokyo and Sanwa Banks, to consolidate Japan's major conglomerate enterprise groups by means of expanded mutual stock holdings and transactions among group firms. Each large bank envisioned a greatly consolidated conglomerate group centering around one main bank and one core *sogo shosha* and containing one giant corporation from each major industrial sector.

The Mitsubishi, Mitsui, and Sumitomo groups were already well developed and powerful groups by the mid-1960s. In contrast, the Fuyo Bank, Daiichi Bank, Sanwa Bank, and Bank of Tokyo groups were not as united and powerful. The Daiichi Bank and the Kangyo Bank merged in 1971 to form the Daiichi Kangyo Bank, thus becoming Japan's largest commercial bank and serving as the main bank of a large new group bearing its name and consisting of firms that previously belonged to the Kawasaki and Furukawa groups. With strong support of the Daiichi Kangyo Bank, C. Itoh & Co. emerged as the core *sogo shosha* of the new group.

Trading companies also moved to expand and consolidate their activities, seeking even greater growth, diversification, resources, and trading and service capabilities. In 1965 Mitsui & Co. absorbed Kinoshita Sansho, a sizable iron and steel trading firm. Marubeni absorbed another well-known metals and fuel trading company, Totsu, in 1966. In 1967 Keinematsu, Ltd., the tenth largest trading company, absorbed Gosho, Ltd., the number 12 firm, to seek greater strength and to serve as the main *sogo shosha* of the Bank of Tokyo group. A far more important event was the merger in 1968 of Nissho Co. and Iwai Sangyo, the eighth and ninth largest trading companies during the mid-1960s, into Nissho-Iwai Co. to become the core *sogo shosha* of the Sanwa Bank group. The two mergers forming Kanematsu Gosho, Ltd., and Nissho-Iwai Co. represented far more important mergers than those of the 1950s and early 1960s. Each of these two mergers was between two well-established *sogo shosha* firms, whereas the earlier mergers represented absorptions by large trading companies of small specialized product traders.

At the beginning of Chapter 3, some significant questions were posed. How do the *sogo shosha* conduct their business? How did they go about selling, buying, and generating new business? Chapter 3 described the highly valuable services and resources the *sogo shosha* provide to their customers—the first part of the answer to these questions. Chapter 4 has introduced the second part of the answer by examining the evolution of the general trading companies from 1960 to 1973—their growth trends and their strategic responses to the changing Japanese economic environment (Chapters 7 and 8 will complete the answer). In effect, the two-part answer to these salient questions will tell us how the trading companies became *sogo shosha*.

Notes

1. Tsusho Sangyosho (MITI), *1972 Tsusho hakusho* (1972 International Trade White Paper) (Tokyo: Sangyo Chosakai, 1972), vol. 1, p. 123.

2. For more on Japan's marketing system, see Tsusho Sangyosho Kigyokyoku, ed., *Ryutsu kindaika no tenbo to kadai* (An Overview of the Task of Modernizing the Distribution System) (Tokyo: Okurasho

Insatsukyoku, 1968); Keizai Shingi Ryutsu Kenkyu Iinkai, ed., *Korekara no ryutsu* (Tomorrow's Distribution System) (Tokyo: Nihon Keizai Shimbunsha, 1972); and M. Y. Yoshino, *The Japanese Marketing System* (Cambridge: M.I.T. Press, 1971).

3. For the projected impact of foreign investment on Japanese industry, see Tsusho Sangyosho (MITI), *1968 Tsusho hakusho* (1968 International Trade White Paper), vol. 1, pp. 259-269.

4. Itoh Chu Shoji Kabushiki Kaisha, *Itoh Chu Shoji 100 nen* (100 Years of C. Itoh & Co.) (Osaka: Dai-Nippon Insatsu, 1969); Sumitomo Shoji Kabushiki Kaisha, *Sumitomo Shoji Kabushiki Kaishashi* (History of Sumitomo Shoji Kaisha, Ltd.) (Osaka: Dai-Nippon Insatsu, 1972); Nissho Kabushiki Kaisha, *Nissho yonjyunen no ayumi* (The Forty-Year History of Nissho Co.) (Nara: Kyodo Seihan, 1968).

5. Sumitomo Shoji Kabushiki Kaisha, *Sumitomo Shoji Kabushiki Kaishashi* (Osaka: Dai-Nippon Insatsu, 1972), p. 426.

6. M. Y. Yoshino, *The Japanese Marketing System*, p. 213.

5
Roles in the Post-World War II Japanese Economy

The *sogo shosha* played substantial roles in the phenomenal growth of the Japanese economy in the post-World War II period through their global business, the vital services they provided to manufacturers and consumers, and the strategic moves described in Chapter 4. They served Japan and the Japanese people well as the primary importers of foodstuffs, industrial raw materials, equipment, and, to a lesser extent, advanced foreign technology; as the advance guard of Japan's export drive; as a force in the modernization of Japan's domestic production and distribution systems; and as the chief organizers of Japan's overseas natural resource development projects. This chapter examines each of these roles in turn.

Service to the nation has been a distinct business objective of the large trading companies from their inception. It is more than an incidental result of their business, services, and strategic moves. Senshu Co. (Mitsui & Co.'s predecessor) and others were established in the early 1870s to break the domination of Japan's foreign trade by European and American businessmen and to support the Meiji government's policy of building a rich and powerful Japan. Mitsui & Co. from the very beginning stressed the subordination of private profit to service to the nation as its basic business principle. The late Chairman Koyata Iwasaki adopted *shoki hoko* (service to the nation) as the firm's business objective and *ritsugyo boeki* (foreign trade) as the firm's main business in 1934 as two of the Mitsubishi Trading Co.'s three basic business principles.[1] Of course, pursuit of private profits periodically supplanted service to Japan as the main objective, for example, from the late 1890s to the mid-1930s. The spirit of service to the nation, however, surfaced again and was one of the *sogo shosha*'s prime objectives, if not the overriding one, in the post–World War II period.

Importers of Foodstuffs

The *sogo shosha*'s first role in the post–World War II Japanese economy was to import foodstuffs, industrial raw materials, equipment, and foreign technology. One trading official likened the import of foodstuffs to the existence of air and water: basic, yet taken for granted until unavailable. The analogy is a little exaggerated, but there is no question about the significance of the trading firms in the daily life of the Japanese.

Japan would suffer a food crisis if the ten *sogo shosha* stopped importing grains and other foodstuffs. Bakery stores in Tokyo would run out of bread; 92 percent of wheat is imported. Housewives from Hokkaido in northern Japan to Okinawa at the southern tip would riot if local grocery stores ran out of tofu (bean cake) because the trading companies stopped buying soybeans from the U.S. and Brazil. Japan imports 96 percent of its soybeans and relies on the ten *sogo shosha* and a few other Japanese grain traders for about 94 percent of wheat and soybean imports. Many *unagiya* (broiled eel restaurants) and *sushiya* (*sushi* restaurants) all over Japan would have to close their doors if the trading companies ceased importing live eels from Taiwan or shrimps from Mexico. Chicken, hog, and beef farms all over Japan, which produce a substantial (though insufficient) amount of meats for domestic consumption, would have to cease operation if the trading companies stopped importing corn and animal feeds. Few Japanese realize how dependent their island nation is on foreign sources of food and what a critical role the trading companies play. Other Japanese importers could, of course, take over the grains and meats import business from the *sogo shosha*, but food prices in Japan would then rise because the other traders lack the *sogo shosha*'s resources and experience in large-scale trading.[2]

Table 5.1 Breakdown of Wheat Import Contracts by Fifteen Trading Companies and by Countries of Production, FY 1973[a]

Trading Companies	Countries of Wheat Production					
	United States	Canada	Australia	Argentina	South Africa	Total
Kanematsu Gosho	437,584	186,766	50,642	15,240	–	690,232
Mitsui & Co.	462,552	108,929	37,342	15,240	–	624,063
Nichimen Company	397,100	172,110	71,642	–	13,500	654,352
Mitsubishi Corporation	393,642	86,342	21,000	–	–	500,984
Marubeni Corporation	289,442	134,864	14,500	–	–	438,806
Nissho-Iwai Co.	274,500	144,500	14,000	–	–	433,000
Toshoku	272,960	119,482	32,000	–	–	424,442
C. Itoh & Co.	273,342	111,926	29,000	–	–	414,268
Sumitomo Shoji	190,000	102,510	6,000	–	–	298,510
Toyomenka	123,500	21,500	11,600	–	–	156,600
Ataka & Co.	108,394	29,200	4,000	–	–	141,594
Yuasa	112,800	37,600	7,642	–	–	158,042
Kinsho Mataichi	58,000	92,450	9,000	–	–	159,450
Toho Bussan	13,000	63,600	11,300	–	–	87,900
Shin Toa Koeki	28,500	47,700	5,000	–	–	81,200
Sixteen other firms	98,056	242,300	18,400	–	–	358,756
Total	3,533,372	1,701,779	343,068	30,480	13,500	5,622,199

Source: Isao Kato, ed., *1974 Sogo shosha nenkan* (1974 General Trading Company Yearbook) (Tokyo: Seikei Tsushinsha, 1974), p. 388.

[a] In tons.

Supply Agents for Industrial Raw Materials, Equipment, and Advanced Foreign Technology

If the *sogo shosha* stopped importing iron ore, coking coal, scrap iron, copper, bauxite, nickel, chrome, molybdenum, and other metals from the United States, Australia, Indonesia, Zambia, Canada, and elsewhere, Japan's industrial giants such as Nippon Steel, Nippon Kokan, Furukawa Aluminum, Hitachi Shipbuilding & Engineering, and Mitsubishi Heavy Industries would literally grind to a halt in a few weeks. Thus, for example, during fiscal 1973 the ten trading firms handled 81 percent of Japan's metals imports and supplied the six giant steel makers with 79 percent of their iron ore imports and 89 percent of their coking coal imports.

If the steel makers are well aware of how heavily they depend on

Table 5.2 Volume of Iron Ore Imported by Japanese General Trading Companies for Japanese Steel Makers, FY 1973[a]

Trading companies	Steel makers						
	Nippon Steel	Nippon Kokan	Kawasaki Steel	Sumitomo Metal	Kobe Steel	Nisshin Steel	Others	Total
Mitsui & Co.	2,133	246	244	227	215	124	24	3,193
Mitsubishi Corporation	866	466	349	297	110	68	—	2,156
Marubeni Corporation	485	718	77	228	151	16	5	1,680
Nissho-Iwai Co.	652	35	52	25	417	60	8	1,249
C. Itoh & Co.	384	49	258	72	77	13	—	853
Toyomenka	190	173	186	197	33	8	28	815
Sumitomo Shoji	49	3	14	690	1	5	11	773
Nichimen Company	171	65	33	28	15	19	5	336
Kanematsu Gosho	106	13	33	55	34	6	5	252
Ataka & Co.	43	—	3	5	—	5	6	62
Other firms	1,029	322	777	214	155	13	16	2,926
Total	6,108	2,087	2,026	2,027	1,210	338	91	13,887

Source: Isao Kato, ed., *1974 sogo shosha nenkan* (1974 General Trading Company Yearbook) (Tokyo: Seikei Tsushinsha, 1974), p. 131.

[a] In ten thousands of tons.

Table 5.3 Volume of Coking Coal Imports Signed by Trading Companies, 1973[a]

Contracted by	Nippon Steel	Nippon Kokan	Kawasaki Steel	Sumitomo Metal	Kobe Steel	Nisshin Steel	Others	Total
Mitsubishi Corporation	726	368	243	280	140	54	98	1,909
Mitsui & Co.	837	104	112	242	138	56	75	1,564
Marubeni Corporation	173	261	84	24	56	8	105	711
C. Itoh & Co.	168	106	144	91	6	2	39	566
Nissho-Iwai Co.	313	2	—	2	114	44	29	504
Toyomenka	105	96	34	31	16	4	35	321
Sumitomo Shoji	106	11	7	197	3	2	6	332
Nichimen Co.	160	55	42	13	20	14	12	316
Ataka & Co.	115	—	—	20	4	—	28	167
Kanematsu Gosho	19	—	—	—	—	—	—	19
Others	278	108	299	57	9	12	13	776
Total	3,000	1,111	965	957	506	196	440	7,175

Source: Isao Kato, ed., *1974 sogo shosha nenkan* (1974 General Trading Company Yearbook) (Tokyo: Seikei Tsushinsha, 1974), p. 132.

[a] In ten thousands of tons.

the traders for the continuing development and supply of essential industrial raw materials, they are also cognizant of Japan's increasing dependence on overseas raw materials during the 1960s. From fiscal 1960 to fiscal 1972, the proportion of coking coal imported rose from 52 to 82 percent of the total, and that of iron ore from 68 to 90 percent (see Chapter 6, Table 6.2 for details). The trading companies have long regarded supplying overseas raw materials to Japanese industry as one of their most important tasks. When foreign sources of supply found it increasingly difficult to meet the voracious demand of Japanese industry during the mid-1960s, and as the resulting shortages became major constraints on Japan's drive for rapid economic growth, the *sogo shosha* found a new system called "resource development import" to secure long-term, stable supplies of raw materials. (See Chapter 6 for a detailed discussion of this critical system.)

The large-volume supply of raw materials (especially iron ore, coking coal, nonferrous metals ores, and unprocessed logs) at low cost by the *sogo shosha* to Japan's steel, metals, food, lumber, and other industries enables these industries to enjoy economies of scale, reduced unit cost of production, and greater price competitiveness of products. Low-cost supply results not only from the general trading companies' large purchases but from their low commission rates and reduced transportation costs. Commission rates are reported to be from 2 to 3 percent of total import transactions for grains and unprocessed logs, and from about 0.5 to 2 percent for iron ore, coking coal, and nonferrous metal ores.[3] Commission rates for cotton and wool imports are about 1 percent. Rates are negotiable and may be even lower in large transactions involving group manufacturers. The average import gross margin of all trading companies was 2.9 percent in 1955 and 2.7 percent in 1956. Nissho-Iwai Co.'s gross margin for all sales transactions for the six months ended March 31, 1974 was 2.3 percent.[4]

Import of plants and equipment has been another contribution of the *sogo shosha*. They actively searched for and supplied plants and equipment to Japan's steel, petrochemical, and electric power industries when those industries embarked on ambitious plant rationalization and expansion plans during the late 1950s and the 1960s. Several examples may be cited. In 1954 Nissho Co. became the Japanese sales agent of Allis-Chalmers Corp., a U.S. machinery maker, and sold turbines to Chubu Electric Power Company and Tokyo Electric Power Company. In 1956, Nissho Co. pushed the formation of the First Atomic Power Industry Group, consisting of Fuji Electric, Kawasaki Heavy Industries, Kawasaki Aircraft, Kobe Steel, Nissho Co., and other firms, and sold a nuclear reactor, manufactured by the British General Electric, and related equipment to the Tokai Nuclear Power Plant, the first nuclear power plant in Japan. When the steel industry launched an ambitious plant expansion plan in 1955, Sumitomo Shoji Kaisha imported rolling mills from two large West German firms, Sack Maschinenfabrik and Schloemann A.G., on behalf of Sumitomo Metal Industries. When the steel and electric machinery industries embarked on another huge capital investment plan in the autumn of 1966, Sumitomo Shoji Kaisha imported a wirerod mill from Morgan Construction Company of the U.S. on behalf of Sumitomo Electric Industries. Sumitomo Shoji Kaisha imported a mandrel mill from Blaw-Knox Co. of the U.S. on behalf of Kawasaki Steel in 1970, and wirerod mills using Morgan Construction Co.'s technology on behalf of Nippon Steel and Kobe Steel in the early 1970s.[5]

Although manufacturers and non-*sogo shosha* trading companies have also imported machinery, the statistics tend to confirm the *sogo shosha*'s repeated claims that they have played an indispensable role in supplying industrial equipment required by Japan's industrial drive. The *sogo shosha*'s weight in the decade before FY 1965 always exceeded 50 percent of Japan's machinery import total, ranging between 53 and 60 percent, while that of all manufacturers never exceeded 13.7 percent and was only an insignificant 3.7 percent in FY 1960. In the years between FY 1966 and FY 1969, the *sogo shosha*'s share saw a steady decline, while that of the manufacturers increased. The share of both, however, declined after FY 1970, though the *sogo shosha* scored a big gain during FY 1973, rebounding to 46.4 percent. The trading companies apparently continue to play a critical role in importing machinery and equipment.

The *sogo shosha* also played a significant role in discovering and negotiating the import of the advanced foreign technologies

Table 5.4 Machinery Import of General Trading Companies and Manufacturers and Share in Japan's Total Machinery Import, FY 1957–FY 1973

Fiscal year	(A) Japan's machinery import total (million Yen)	(B) General trading companies			(C) Manufacturers	
		No. of firms	Million Yen	Percent of B in A	Million Yen	Percent of C in A
1957	114,099	18	64,942	52.9	11,213	9.8
1958	111,024	16	66,692	60.1	15,184	13.7
1959	120,989	16	67,736	56.0	12,980	9.3
1960	161,497	22	90,185	55.9	5,962	3.7
1961	238,463	31	134,365	56.3	14,755	6.2
1962	299,148	29	178,206	59.6	24,444	8.2
1963	307,884	31	179,694	58.4	26,110	8.5
1964	300,422	29	159,008	52.9	41,185	13.7
1965	251,463	29	135,714	54.0	27,158	10.8
1966	263,643	13	105,608	40.1	39,584	15.0
1967	378,444	12	143,659	38.0	74,119	19.6
1968	—	—	—	—	—	—
1969	554,266	11	255,159	46.0	94,209	17.0
1970	785,946	12	328,025	41.7	145,506	18.5
1971	762,293	11	292,755	38.4	128,348	16.8
1972	780,201	11	282,326	36.2	128,257	16.4
1973	1,003,868	14	466,289	46.4	125,275	12.5

Source: Tsusho Sangyosho (MITI), *Boeki gyotai tokeihyo* (Foreign Trade Statistics by Industries) (Tokyo: Tsusho Sangyo Chosakai, various annual issues 1958-1974.

Note: See footnote 3 on p. 21 on the double accounting system of Japan's foreign trade transactions used in MITI's *Boeki gyotai tokeihyo*.

Table 5.5 Japanese Imports of Foreign Technology, 1950-1970

	1950-1960		1961-1970	
	Number of cases	Share (percent)	Number of cases	Share (percent)
Light industries	226	7.7	1,997	16.5
Food	46	1.6	189	1.6
Textile	88	3.0	910	7.5
Kiln, cement	25	0.9	163	1.3
Plastic products	13	0.4	392	3.2
Heavy and chemical industries	2,388	81.8	8,811	72.9
Metals	488	16.7	1,108	9.2
General machinery	498	17.1	3,552	29.4
Electrical machinery	396	13.6	1,532	12.7
Transportation equipment	121	4.1	428	3.5
Chemical	885	30.3	2,191	18.1
Total[a]	2,920	100.0	12,084	100.0

Source: Science and Technology Agency, *Gijitsu donyu nenji hokoku* (Annual Report on Import of Technology), in MITI, *1972 Tsusho hakusho* (1972 International Trade White Paper) (Tokyo: Tsusho Sangyo Chosakai, 1972), vol. 1 (Soron), p. 224.

[a]Because of partial listing of industries, figures do not add up to totals.

that contributed so much to the sharp rise in the international competitiveness of Japanese industry during the 1960s. The Ministry of International Trade and Industry acknowledged candidly in 1967 that Japan's core industries, such as petrochemicals, electronic equipment, and synthetic fiber industries, owed their growth almost wholly to advanced foreign technologies purchased by Japanese manufacturers.[6]

Japanese manufacturers have played the primary role in the introduction of foreign technologies into Japan. The *sogo shosha*'s role in direct import of foreign technologies seems to have been rather small in recent years: 7 percent during FY 1971 and 6.1 percent during FY 1972. However, *sogo shosha* officials

Table 5.6 Percentage Participation of the General Trading Companies in Japanese Import of Foreign Technology, FY 1971 and FY 1972

	FISCAL 1971						FISCAL 1972					
	Category A		Category B		Total		Category A		Category B		Total	
	No. of cases	Percent	No. of cases	Percent	No. of cases	Percent	No. of cases	Percent	No. of cases	Percent	No. of cases	Percent
Japan total	1,546	100.0	461	100.0	2,007	100.0	1,916	100.0	487	100.0	2,403	100.0
Ten general trading companies	50	3.2	90	19.5	140	7.0	68	3.5	78	16.0	146	6.1
Mitsui & Co.	9	0.6	16	3.5	25	1.2	6	0.3	17	3.5	23	1.0

Source: Information and Research Department, Mitsui & Co.

Note: Category A: technology imports whose contract and payment period exceeds one year. Category B: technology imports whose contract and payment period is less than one year.

insist that their contribution looms considerably larger, if their indirect participation (i.e., finding new foreign technology, providing information to manufacturers, and serving as intermediaries) is taken into consideration.

The Advance Guard of Japan's Export Drive

The *sogo shosha* have been the advance guard of Japan's export drive and the force behind Japan's extraordinary success in selling large volumes of manufactured goods to the industrialized, the less developed, and communist bloc countries. The trading companies' role in export expansion has been, without any doubt, their greatest contribution to the postwar Japanese economy. However, their role in selling consumer durables that require sales promotion and after-sales service to the industrialized countries has declined in recent years.

The Japanese government lost no time after the conclusion of the Allied Occupation in the spring of 1952 in adopting export expansion as one of its top national policies. It established two important councils in 1954: the Export Council (*Yushutsu kaigi*), headed by the prime minister, and the Export Council for Individual Industry (*Sangyobetsu yushutsu kaigi*). The former was given the task of establishing and achieving annual national export goals; the latter's goal was to set up and attain annual export goals for individual industries. The government adopted various measures to promote export expansion. These measures covered financing, tax credit (the overseas market development reserve system, the overseas market development loss write-off system, etc.) insurance (export insurance, overseas investment insurance, foreign exchange insurance, etc.), inspection, and orderly foreign marketing (such as the Export-Import Law).[7]

The trading companies jumped immediately at the opportunity to expand their overseas commercial networks after Japan regained independence. They set up eighty-eight sales offices between October 1952 and September 1953 and dispatched 270 officials to all parts of the world, concentrating on the strategic markets of the U.S. and Southeast Asia.[8] They rapidly expanded worldwide office and sales networks. By 1958, these offices had grown sufficiently to become overseas business headquarters with their own branches. As the overseas offices grew increasingly important in the home office's transactions, they steadily replaced foreign agents and brokers. Their number quadrupled between FY 1954 and FY 1960. Their weight in Japan's exports grew more than fivefold and their share in Japan's imports total rose by 2.7 times in six years. More important, their weight in Japan's foreign trade total during FY 1960 jumped to 77 percent from the 50 percent of the preceding fiscal year.[9] The Ministry of International Trade and Industry correctly paid repeated tributes to the overseas offices' substantial contributions in pushing the expansion of Japan's exports.[10]

The *sogo shosha* also lost little time in developing new overseas markets for Japan's steel, synthetic fiber, petrochemical products, and heavy machinery based on these growth industries' ambitious capital investment and production expansion plans during the mid-1950s and 1960s. In the steel industry, for example, Japan's six steel manufacturing giants (Nippon Steel, Nippon Kokan, Kawaski Steel, Sumitomo Metal Industries, Kobe Steel, and Nisshin Steel) almost completely delegate the marketing of their products to the *sogo shosha* and a number of other steel traders. The trading companies competed to export oil pipes (oil well pipes, oil transport pipes, and boiler pipes) to North and South America before 1955. After 1955 they expanded their steel markets to all parts of the world, including the Middle East and communist bloc countries. They sent officials to strategic cities everywhere and worked hard to cultivate close relationships with and woo auto makers, shipbuilders (including builders of LNG and LPG tankers), manufacturers of electric generators and boilers, and appliance makers. They spared no expense in studying overseas demand and the needs of steel users, dispatching mission after mission in the late 1950s to study overseas markets and distribution systems, especially the steel warehousing, fabrication, and distribution system in the United States. They lavished all kinds of services on customers and prospective customers, from information on new Japanese steel products and steel-making processes to liberal credits to sending engineers from Japanese steel makers to the United States or the Middle East to correct problems that manufacturer-users encountered.

To compete against Western European steel makers in the U.S. and the rest of the world market, which had an edge over the Japanese in shorter distances to markets and thus in lower transportation costs, the trading companies bought their own steel transports and adopted a "full cargo" policy, using large orders from automobile and electric machinery makers as base cargoes. To prevent excess competition and price drops, large Japanese steel makers conducted joint negotiations with customers on large orders, which often were government orders calling for bids from U.S., Western European, and Japanese steel makers, and allocated export shares to various *sogo shosha* when bids were successful. One of the largest export orders the trading companies successfully handled in recent years was the shipment of 460,000 tons of oil pipe to the 800-mile Alaska oil pipeline project completed in 1977.

Catalyst in Japan's Rapid Economic Growth

In expanding Japanese exports the *sogo shosha* earned billions of dollars in valuable foreign exchanges for Japan. This enabled Japan, a resource-poor country, to pay for imports of grains and foodstuffs to feed its people and to finance the purchases of overseas industrial raw materials, capital goods, and advanced technologies required for rapid economic development. The expansion of exports also enabled Japan to maintain its balance of payments through several business cycles in the post–World War II period. The *sogo shosha* increased imports of industrial raw materials, capital goods, and advanced technology during periods of rapid economic growth to meet the requirements of domestic industries. When increased imports as well as recession led to trade and payments deficits, they reduced imports and stepped up exports, while the government imposed stringent monetary and fiscal policies until a favorable balance was restored. This pattern continued until 1962.

Since 1962 the *sogo shosha*'s accelerated export drive has led to enormous trade surpluses. These surpluses enabled the Japanese government to allow imports to rise to meet the greatly increased capital investment demands of domestic industries, spurred by Prime Minister Ikeda's rapid economic growth policy, and still maintain the balance of payments. This also enabled Japan to expand deferred payment plant exports to developing countries and thereby increase capital account deficits. Finally, it allowed the Japanese government to adopt an export drive policy, rather than the stringent monetary and fiscal policy of earlier years, to prop up the economy during the recession of 1965.[11]

Export expansion was the single most important stimulant to the growth of the Japanese economy until the early 1960s. In 1955, for example, export, rather than domestic demand, accounted for more than half of the production growth of primary steel, shipbuilding, nonferrous metals, precision machinery, synthetic fiber, and textiles, and for a substantial portion (although less than 50 percent) of production increases in intermediate textile products and daily sundry goods.[12]

The huge overseas markets developed by the trading companies enabled domestic manufacturers to rationalize and invest heavily in manufacturing equipment and plants, to expand production, and to enjoy the benefits of economies of scale. Since 1962 export as demand has become of primary importance, although domestic demand has also grown substantially. The unprecedented growth of exports (averaging 13.7 percent annual real growth between 1955 and 1963 and 18.2 percent real growth between 1963 and 1970)[13] at much higher growth rates than those of imports and domestic production not only helped Japan maintain its balance of payments, but also removed the one major constraint on economic growth (balance of payments deficits). Export growth thus paved the way for the extraordinarily rapid growth of the Japanese economy in the 1960s.

By contributing to the rapid growth of the Japanese economy, the *sogo shosha* also helped strengthen the competitiveness of Japanese export goods (especially heavy and chemical products) in the world market. A nation's ability to expand exports is determined by four major factors: (1) growth in world imports; (2) ability to expand production scale to meet world market demand; (3) price competitiveness; and (4) nonprice competitiveness. Japan's tremendous export growth has been due (apart from the sizable expansion of world imports since the war, benefits of which were available to all trading nations) to the substantial rise in production scale (responsible for 5 of the 13.7 percent growth

Figure 5.1 Shift in export/production ratio of major commodities, 1954 and 1955

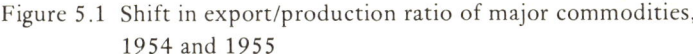

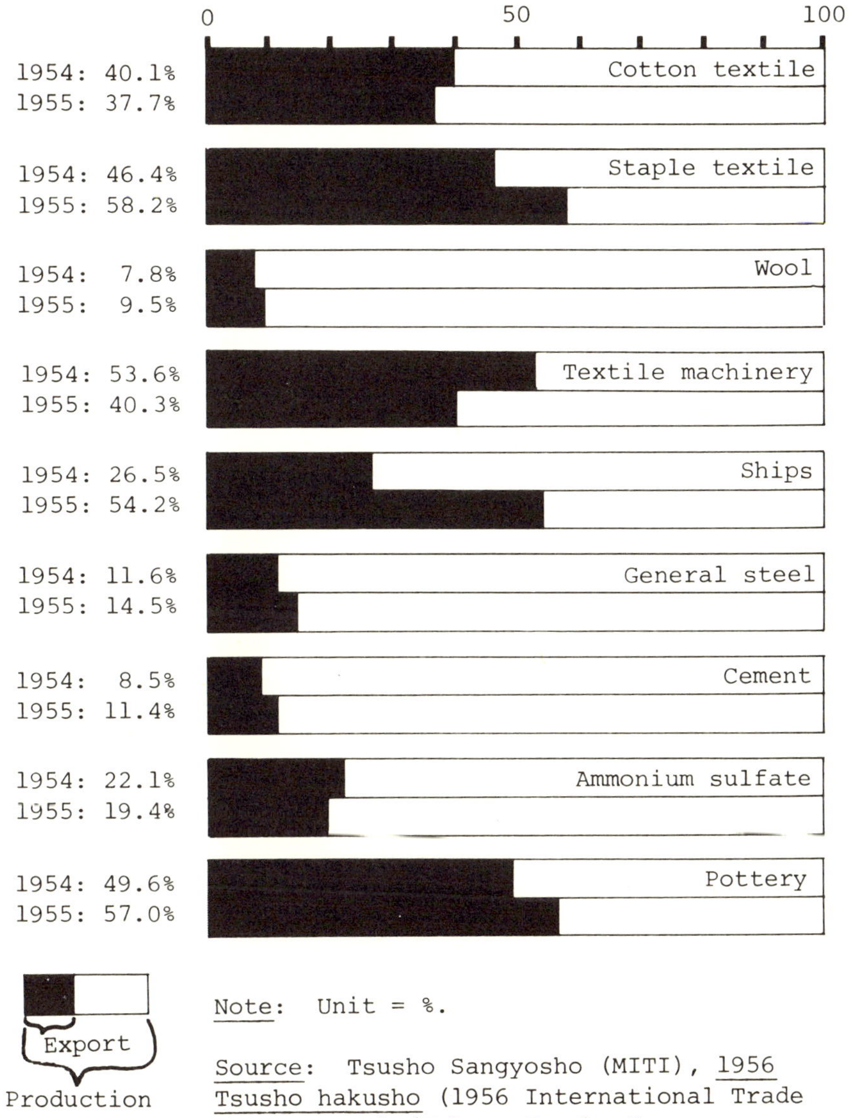

1954: 40.1% 1955: 37.7%	Cotton textile
1954: 46.4% 1955: 58.2%	Staple textile
1954: 7.8% 1955: 9.5%	Wool
1954: 53.6% 1955: 40.3%	Textile machinery
1954: 26.5% 1955: 54.2%	Ships
1954: 11.6% 1955: 14.5%	General steel
1954: 8.5% 1955: 11.4%	Cement
1954: 22.1% 1955: 19.4%	Ammonium sulfate
1954: 49.6% 1955: 57.0%	Pottery

■ Export
□ Production

Note: Unit = %.

Source: Tsusho Sangyosho (MITI), 1956 Tsusho hakusho (1956 International Trade White Paper) (Tokyo: Tsusho Sangyo Chosakai, 1956), p. 5.

Table 5.7 Export Growth Factors of Major Countries, 1955-1970[a]

	1955-1963				1963-1970			
	Real export growth rate	Scale factor	Price factor	Nonprice factor	Real export growth rate	Scale factor	Price factor	Nonprice factor
Japan	13.7	5.0	1.2	2.0	18.2	5.8	0.9	3.1
Canada	3.9	2.1	0.6	-3.4	11.3	2.7	-2.0	3.0
United States	3.7	1.6	-1.6	-1.0	6.5	2.1	-1.6	-1.3
Belgium and Luxemberg	7.5	1.9	1.0	-0.3	11.3	2.5	0.2	1.0
Holland	7.3	2.0	-0.6	1.0	11.9	3.1	0.8	0.3
West Germany	10.0	3.4	1.9	3.5	10.8	2.5	-0.0	0.7
France	6.6	2.9	0.8	-2.0	10.2	3.1	0.4	-0.8
Italy	14.9	3.2	3.0	3.1	13.1	2.8	0.9	1.5
Britain	2.8	1.5	-2.4	-1.0	5.5	1.4	0.5	-3.6
Sweden	7.5	2.2	-0.4	0.8	8.8	2.4	-0.9	-0.1
Denmark	7.2	4.4	0.3	-2.3	7.3	2.5	0.9	-3.4

Source: Tsusho Sangyosho (MITI), 1972 Tsusho hakusho (1972 International Trade White Paper) (Tokyo: Tsusho Sangyo Chosakai, 1972), vol. 1, p. 247.

[a]In percent per year.

between 1955 and 1963, and for 5.8 of the 18.2 percent growth between 1963 and 1970); to price competitiveness (accounting for 1.2 of the 13.7 percent annual growth average during the first period and for 0.9 of the 18.2 percent annual growth average during the second period); and finally to nonprice competitiveness (accounting for 2 of the 13.7 percent annual growth between 1955 and 1963, and for 3.1 of the 18.2 percent annual growth between 1963 and 1970).

While an exact determination is not possible, it can be safely stated that the *sogo shosha*'s role in raising the competitiveness of Japanese exports was substantial. Their large-scale imports at low cost of industrial raw materials and the large overseas markets they developed enabled Japanese manufacturers to concentrate on continuously expanding the scale of production through record high capital investment during the 1960s (over 30 percent annually except 1962, 1963, and 1965). The manufacturers' ability to enjoy the economy of scale enabled them to cut production costs by 20 to 30 percent each time accumulated production experience doubled, according to James Abegglen and William Rapp.[14] This in turn substantially raised the price competitiveness of Japanese exports between 1955 and 1971, although other factors (wages, tariff policies, and currency exchange rates) should not be ignored. The various low-cost services the *sogo shosha* provided to the manufacturers (i.e., export financing, insurance, warehousing, transportation, contract negotiation, and fabrication, processing, and distribution centers) also enabled manufacturers to cut costs and raise the price competitiveness of manufactures.

Equally important is the *sogo shosha*'s role in the nonprice competitiveness of Japanese exports through extensive worldwide sales networks and by providing low-cost (often free) information or advice to manufacturers on advanced technology, market conditions, foreign tariffs, local laws, overseas business customs, human relations, natural resource development, project feasibility, product quality, and sales promotion. While the *sogo shosha* are a long way from providing extensive after-sales services to customers of automobile, electronics, computer, and other high-technology industries that require specialized knowledge and technical training, their role in this area is bound to grow as the price competitiveness of Japanese exports declines because of continuing rises in wages and other costs, and as the weight of nonprice competitiveness, rising steadily since the mid-1960s, gains even more in importance.

Driving Forces to Rationalize the Domestic Production and Distribution Systems

In addition to being the primary importers of foodstuffs and industrial raw materials and the advance guard of Japan's export drive, the *sogo shosha* have played a significant role in Japan's domestic economy during the late 1950s and 1960s by assisting the rationalization of the production and distribution system, supplying production and distribution capital, and aiding small and medium-size firms. These activities, interrelated and inseparable in the real world, will be discussed separately for analytic convenience and clarity.

Three of the *sogo shosha*'s efforts to rationalize the domestic production and distribution system were the construction of steel fabrication and distribution centers, the construction of coastal food industries complexes, and the integration of consumer goods production and distribution systems. As noted in Chapter 4, these efforts reflected strategic moves made in response to the changing domestic economic environment and designed to sustain the firms' continuing growth and profits. They also, however, led to more efficient domestic production and distribution systems.

The construction of steel fabrication and distribution centers provides an example. Japanese steel production expanded from 11 million tons in 1955 to 118 million tons in 1973. Direct sales from producers of crude steel to large users such as the Japanese government (which used steel for public works projects), shipbuilders, and automobile manufacturers amounted to about 20 percent of total production. Shipbuilders and automobile makers prefer purchasing directly from steel makers because they can negotiate lower purchase prices on large orders, avoid commissions to intermediaries, and do fabrication work at their own facilities or at subsidiaries near their shipyards or automobile assembly plants. Eighty percent of Japanese steel production is sold through two groups of primary steel wholesalers (*daiichiji tonya*), the *sogo shosha*, and specialized steel traders, to large end users that do not possess their own fabrication centers. The fabrication work is done at the fabrication and distribution centers of the two primary wholesale groups. Among such end users are appliance manufacturing plants, electronic equipment makers, electric machine makers, construction companies, and construction machine manufacturers. The *sogo shosha* and specialized steel wholesalers also sell to small end users—for example, the local construction companies widely scattered all over Japan—through approximately 4,000 secondary steel wholesalers called *tokuyakuten*.

Large Japanese steel makers, unlike U.S. Steel and other counterparts in the United States, prefer indirect sales. End users of steel, except shipbuilders and automobile makers, also prefer indirect purchases from steel fabrication centers because of the considerable economic benefits provided by these centers, backed up by the *sogo shosha* parent company. These benefits include supply and demand adjustment; financial, transportation, and warehousing inventory; and fabrication services. The supply and demand adjustment service keeps steel makers closely informed about the demand situation, including whether demand is strong or weak, what type of steel is in strong demand, which industrial sectors and users need how much shape steel, rolled steel, steel plates, and steel pipes, when, and at what price. It also involves informing industrial users about steel makers' supply capacities for each type of steel and about future price trends. It is a critical service for the production plans of steel mills and for the purchase and production plans of end users. These centers stock large inventories of steel delivered from steel mills and provide shearing, sawing, and grinding services according to tight specifications of end users. They also make quick deliveries.

Steel manufacturers prefer using these centers to constructing their own fabrication centers because they can receive large orders from and sell large quantities of steel to these centers instead of receiving small orders from hundreds of small firms and making hundreds of small sales that require costly sales personnel and extension of credits. They thus reduce inventories and eliminate the transportation costs of delivering fabricated steel to hundreds of users all over Japan. As a result, steel manufacturers can invest almost all of their manpower and financial resources in and concentrate on large-scale production of steel. The benefits to manufacturer-users include: (1) an assured supply without requiring their own inventories; (2) speedy deliveries after quickly meeting tight shearing, sawing, grinding, and other specifications; (3) reduction in stockpiling and warehousing costs; and (4) saving and more efficiently using capital by eliminating the need to build their own fabrication centers (which, if built, would not enjoy full and large-scale operation). The benefits from the coastal food industries complexes, from integrated food production and distribution systems, and from the tie-ups with large mass merchandise retail chains, while obviously different in detail, in general follow the same pattern.[15]

The benefits to the general trading companies have also been considerable. They are of three kinds. The first involves sales of commodities to producers, fabricators, processors, distributors, mass merchandise stores or consumers on a long-term continuing basis. The second is the profit from providing financing, information, fabrication, processing, inventory, transportation, and other services at various stages of production and processing. Finally, there is the creation of demand and thus the generation of new business opportunities.

It would be misleading to say that the construction of steel fabrication and distribution centers, the organization of the coastal food industries complexes, and the integration of consumer goods production and distribution systems was done purely out of unselfish motives. These responses by the *sogo shosha* to the changing domestic economic environment were made to maintain continuing growth and profits, but the moves also met the growing and diversified needs of producers, industrial users, and the consuming public and contributed to more efficient domestic production and distribution.

Domestic Financing and Assisting the Growth of Small and Medium-Size Firms

Chapter 3 discussed how the *sogo shosha* provide vital financial services to domestic and foreign sellers and buyers through credit, loans, loan guarantees, and venture capital. For instance, the twelve designated primary steel wholesalers (*shitei tonya*) of Nippon Steel (nine general trading companies and three other steel wholesalers) join Nippon Steel in extending four months' credits to buyers. The trading companies extend the period of payment and provide additional loans or loan guarantees and management services when buyers run into financial difficulties during a recession. Monthly credit extended by steel makers and primary wholesalers amounted to about $5.9 billion during FY 1973, an extraordinary sum and a heavy burden and risk to the steel makers and the *sogo shosha*.[16]

The trading companies sell plants and equipment to domestic steel, petrochemical, and heavy machinery industries, energy development industries, and others on a long-term deferred-payment basis. They invest heavily in the fabrication/processing and distribution centers required by steel and petrochemical, oil, and synthetic fiber industries, and thus allow giant producers to concentrate on investing in their own plant and equipment and on large scale production.

There are four major reasons why the *sogo shosha* provide the vital financial services that in the United States and Western Europe are normally provided by commercial and merchant banks. First is the extraordinarily rapid and large-scale growth of the Japanese economy between 1955 and the early 1970s. This caused a tremendous increase in demand for huge capital sums and a chronic shortage of capital for plant and equipment investment and for distribution. Distribution capital was especially limited because the policy of the Japanese government gave top priority to the manufacturing rather than the distribution sector in the allocation of scarce capital. Additional contributing factors were the underdevelopment of the Japanese capital market and the propensity of the Japanese public for saving and for putting large savings in banks rather than using them to purchase securities. The chronic shortage of capital until late 1971 caused Japan's manufacturing giants (most of which were in capital-intensive heavy and chemical industries) to concentrate on rapid heavy investment in plant and equipment, and not on fabrication/processing and distribution, to raise production. Financing of the fabrication/processing and distribution sectors was left largely to the *sogo shosha*, which, for their own growth reasons and business strategies, chose to meet the financial need the manufacturing sectors were unable to meet.

The second reason underlying the *sogo shosha*'s provision of financial services was related to the structural changes of post–World War II Japanese industry and the changing needs of the postwar market. The growth of such process industries as energy, steel, petrochemicals, consumer foods, and synthetic fiber for clothing was revolutionary. Those industries are characterized by (1) high technology and complex production processes and products (crude, intermediate, and finished products) and (2) the need to integrate the various production and distribution processes of more than one stage. Investment in a single production and distribution process is not sufficient. Investment not only in every process but also in the total production-distribution system was required to develop new products and markets. Since large manufacturers suffered a chronic shortage of capital, the *sogo shosha* had to step in to offer financing, especially for distribution and sales, at various stages.

Third, for cost reduction and for sound banking reasons the large commercial banks of Japan preferred lending large sums to and earning interest charges from large, well-established general trading companies rather than lending small sums to thousands of small firms of uneven credit standing whose management they did not monitor on a day-to-day basis over a long period of time. Furthermore, fearing financial losses, they were not always willing to lend to firms starting such new risky businesses as energy development. The *sogo shosha* borrowed huge sums from the financial institutions and lent small sums to small and medium-size firms needing operational and distribution capital and to new ventures needing venture capital. The *sogo shosha* thus concurrently served as the financial institutions' risk buffer.

Fourth and finally, many of the *sogo shosha*'s sellers and buyers had been small and medium-size firms. Many of them lacked strong management and financial resources. They often requested financial support to tide them over or even to help avoid bankruptcies during prolonged economic downturns as the 1974-75 recession. Japan's steel, petrochemical, heavy machinery, automobile, and shipbuilding giants all subcontract the production of components to small and medium-size firms. They rely on fabrication/processing and distribution centers run by medium-size firms for fabrication/processing work. They have used these small and medium-size firms, which pay lower wages and benefits and can produce standardized components or fabricate/process numerous small orders more efficiently, for cost saving. Many of these smaller firms have been either *sogo shosha* subsidiaries or manufacturer–*sogo shosha* joint ventures. (In the 1960s, however, some manufacturers, including automobile and electric equipment makers, began switching gradually to their own subsidiaries.) In addition to assisting these giant producers' subcontractors, which played a critical role in double-structured Japanese industry, the general trading companies have provided financial services to small firms in labor-intensive light industries. The small firms also received information, procurement of raw materials and equipment, and distribution and marketing services. These services made it possible for small and medium-size firms to export their products competitively to many parts of the world that they could not have done independently. The *sogo shosha* thereby contributed significantly not only to the growth of small and medium-size firms but to the expansion and international competitiveness of Japanese exports.

The so-called "tie-over or connection import system" (*tsunagi yunyu hoshiki*) was widely used by the trading companies during the 1960s. Whenever a large domestic producer bought an advanced foreign technology and decided to mass produce a new product, trading companies competed to import the new product and to develop a domestic market. Construction of plant and other preparations may take months. More months may pass before domestic producers attain large-scale production capabilities. Trading companies, however, usually ceased import of the product and switched to procuring from domestic producers as soon as the latter went into mass production. By then a sizable domestic market was already developed. This system benefits both producers and trading companies. It was widely used when domestic production of polyethylene, polystyrene, polypropylene, and nylon got started but is not limited to synthetic fibers, plastics, and other petrochemical products. It has also been used for computers and other high-technology products.

In providing the various vital financial services the *sogo shosha* have been the lubricant of Japan's production and distribution systems. Without this lubricant the Japanese economy could not have operated so smoothly and grown so rapidly. The *sogo shosha* have been an indispensable and integral part of the postwar Japanese economic system (import raw materials from abroad; manufacture and process in Japan; and export manufactured goods abroad), operating on a remarkable system of division of work in which each member of the system plays a specialized role. This system is an important source of Japan's economic strength and lies behind its miraculous post–World War II economic growth. The Japanese government has made short-term and long-term economic policy in close partnership with leaders of the major economic and business organizations. It has given financial support and administrative guidance. The financial institutions have supplied the necessary financial resources. The manufacturers have concentrated on production. The *sogo shosha* have acted as the chief importers of foodstuffs, industrial raw materials, and equipment; as financial intermediaries; as the vanguard of export; as a force to rationalize the domestic production and distribution systems; and as the chief importers-organizers of overseas natural resource development projects.

Notes

1. The other principle is *shoji komei* (fairness and integrity) as the firm's method of business.
2. Grain trade is a highly speculative and risky business. Only large traders such as the *sogo shosha* possess the resources, the diversification, and the skills to balance profits and losses. Wheat, barley, and milo are controlled by the Japanese government, so the trading companies make up the usual losses sustained by low competitive bids submitted to the Ministry of Agriculture through profits from skillful trading in futures. See Yasuo Oki, *Sogo shosha to sekai keizai* (General Trading Companies and the World Economy) (Tokyo: Tokyo Daigaku Shuppankai, 1975), p. 64.
3. Mitsubishi Corporation's reply to questionnaire.
4. See Nissho-Iwai Co.'s financial report for March 1974, p. 27.
5. *Sumitomo Shoji Kabushiki Kaishashi* (History of Sumitomo

Shoji Kaisha, Ltd.) (Osaka: Dai-Nippon Insatsu K.K., 1972), pp. 495-501.

6. Tsusho Sangyosho (MITI), *1967 Tsusho hakusho* (International Trade White Paper) (Tokyo: Tsusho Sangyo Chosakai, 1967), vol. 1, p. 107.

7. For details, see various annual volumes of *Tsusho hakusho* (International Trade White Paper) 1952-75, issued by the Ministry of International Trade and Industry.

8. 1954 *Tsusho hakusho* (International Trade White Paper) vol. 1, p. 264.

9. Tsusho Sangyosho (MITI), *1961 Boeki gyotai tokeihyo* (Foreign Trade Statistics by Industries), p. 17.

10. Ibid., p. 17.

11. For more on Japan's balance of payments, see Patricia Hagan Kuwayama, "Japan's Balance of Payments and Its Changing Role in the World Economy" in Jerome B. Cohen, ed., *Pacific Partnership: United States-Japan Trade* (Lexington, Mass.: D.C. Heath, 1972), pp. 51-79.

12. Tsusho Sangyosho (MITI), *1956 Tsusho hakusho* (International Trade White Paper) (Tokyo: Tsusho Sangyo Chosakai, 1956), p. 5.

13. Tsusho Sangyosho (MITI), *1972 Tsusho hakusho* (International Trade White Paper) (Tokyo: Tsusho Sangyo Chosakai, 1972), vol. 1, p. 247.

14. "The Competitive Impact of Japanese Growth," in Jerome B. Cohen, ed., *Pacific Partnership: United States-Japan Trade* (Lexington, Mass.: D.C. Heath, 1972), p. 22.

15. The benefits to participating food producers and processors at a coastal food industries complex such as Konan include (1) considerable reduction in transportation costs made possible by the use of large grain transports, (2) reduction in loading and unloading costs through the use of common silos, (3) economies of scale from volume production at one central location, (4) elimination of conventional transportation costs made possible by the use of conveyors and pipes connecting silos and factories, (5) integration of production from imports to first-stage production to second-stage and third-stage processing, (6) cost reduction made possible by joint transportation of finished products from one central distribution center to wholesalers and retailers, and (7) investment efficiency and cost reduction through joint use of electricity, steam, fire prevention, other facilities, and plant management services.

According to a calculation made in 1973, a 10 percent savings in transportation cost for every ton of wheat can be realized by producers and processors, not including the costs of transportation from processors to the central food distribution center on the complex and to wholesalers and retailers: a 960-yen saving when a 50,000-ton cargo is used in place of a 10,000-ton cargo to transport wheat from U.S. gulf ports in Louisiana to Kobe; a 570-Yen saving when conveyors are used to move wheat from cargo to silos and from silos to flour makers instead of transporting wheat from a cargo to flour makers by truck; a 3,200-Yen saving when pipes instead of trucks are used to move flour from flour makers to noodle and candy factories after it is packed by packers whose wages, too, must be paid. Altogether, this is a 4,730-Yen reduction in transportation cost or a 10 percent saving for every ton of wheat whose cost averaged 50,000 Yen per ton from the U.S. gulf coast to Kobe and to second-stage processors. This is a considerable saving in a highly competitive business and has an important impact on the consumer food price. See Masao Narita, *Nippon no shosha Mitsui Bussan* (Japanese Trading Company: Mitsui & Co.) (Tokyo: Mainichi Shimbunsha, 1973), pp. 47-48. Total integration of consumer goods production, processing, distribution, and marketing (such as exists in the broiler chicken and hog businesses from the import of chicks, hogs, and feed all the way down to retail sales to the consumer) confers the following benefits: (1) rationalization of the hitherto highly complex and inefficient production, processing, distribution, and marketing systems, (2) better production, processing, and marketing planning because of better information on the changing supply and demand situation and on price fluctuations, (3) reduction in personnel, production, and transportation costs because of economies of scale, (4) greater quality control by producers, processors, and distributors, (5) stable employment and income for farmers, including many whose livelihood hitherto depended on insecure seasonal migrant farming, and (6) lower food prices for the consumer. The *sogo shosha* have tieups with large mass merchandise retail chains such as Seiyu, Jasco, and Seibu. The large trading companies supply financing, leasing of store and equipment, information, development services, and large quantities of merchandise. This solves some of the serious problems that retail chains faced during fast expansion, including shortage of capital, lack of continuing supply of large-volume merchandise, need to develop new merchandise to meet shifting consumer tastes that have become more diverse and sophisticated, shortage of trained managers and sales personnel, and development of total management systems required for controlling the movement of manpower, money, and merchandise.

16. Shosha Kino Kenkyukai, ed., *Gendai sogoshosharon* (On Contemporary General Trading Companies) (Tokyo: Toyo Keizai Shimposha, 1975), p. 105.

6
Overseas Natural Resource Development Projects

Chapter 5 considered the *sogo shosha*'s various roles in the post-World War II Japanese economy. One of these roles, the investment in and organization of multimillion dollar overseas natural resource development projects, has been so central to Japan's economic, foreign policy, and strategic interests that it needs to be discussed in greater detail.

Japan's Critical Shortage of Raw Materials

The rapid growth of the Japanese economy during the late 1950s and the 1960s was spurred by Prime Minister Hatoyama's five-year economic plan and by Prime Minister Ikeda's double national income plan. The plans achieved their primary goal: the rapid growth of heavy and chemical industries. But the growth of these energy-hungry and raw material-hungry industries in turn caused tremendous increases in Japan's need for energy and industrial raw materials and a critical shortage of domestic supplies. Raw material and energy import levels rose dramatically and Japan became much more dependent than previously on external sources of supply.

The weight of imports of major industrial crude and semiprocessed materials, excluding agricultural commodities, in Japan's total imports jumped from 28.1 percent ($1,263 million) in 1960 to 42.2 percent ($5,476.7 million) in 1968, a 430 percent increase in eight years. Table 6.1 displays the process vividly. Between calendar years 1960 and 1968 imports of coking coal increased by 430 percent, of crude oil by 450 percent, or iron ore by

Table 6.1 Japanese Imports of Major Raw Materials, 1960-1968

		Quantity			Scale of growth		Value
	Unit	1960	1967	1968	1968 over 1960 (times)	1968 over 1967 (times)	1968 ($ million)
Wood	1,000 CM	6,388	28,279	33,567	5.3	18.7	1,160.7
Lauan	1,000 CM	4,568	12,306	13,024	2.9	5.8	391.7
Pulp	1,000 MT	146.9	724.1	786.7	5.4	8.6	113.4
Coking coal	1,000 MT	7,164	24,030	30,967	4.3	28.9	491.8
Crude oil	1,000 KL	31,121	120,622	139,819	4.5	15.9	1,685.3
Fuel oil	1,000 KL	5,506	15,971	20,779	3.8	30.1	373.0
Iron ores	1,000 MT	15,036	56,695	68,164	4.5	20.2	833.8
Copper ores	1,000 MT	464.9	1,022.2	1,061.1	2.3	3.8	271.2
Copper and copper alloy	1,000 MT	62	277.9	292.7	4.7	5.3	357.6
Nickel ores	1,000 MT	945.9	1,660.6	2,712.2	2.9	63.3	58.0
Nickel and nickel alloy	1 MT	381	14,332	4,974	13.1	65.3	16.8
Bauxite	1,000 MT	1,094.6	2,085.9	2,449.9	2.2	17.5	25.7
Lead ores	1,000 MT	42	130.1	144.2	3.4	10.8	26.5
Zinc ores	1,000 MT	109.5	614.1	856.7	7.8	39.5	62.9

Source: Tsusho Sangyosho (MITI), *1969 Tsusho hakusho* (1969 International Trade White Paper) (Tokyo: Tsusho Sangyo Chosakai, 1969), vol. 1, p. 322.

Note: MT = metric ton; CM = cubic meter; KL = kiloliter.

Table 6.2   Import Dependence Rates for Japan's Major Natural Resources FY 1960–FY 1972 (percent)

	FY 1960	FY 1965	FY 1970	FY 1972
Copper	50.6	57.6	75.6	78.5
Lead	54.6	51.7	54.6	59.1
Zinc	26.3	38.1	54.5	59.7
Aluminium	100	100	100	100
Nickel	100	100	100	100
Iron ores	68.0	80.7	87.9	89.6
Coking coal	51.6	63.8	82.7	82.1
Crude oil	98.6	99.5	99.7	99.7
Uranium	—	—	100	100

Source: The Japan Foreign Trade Council, Inc., *Sogo shosha wa shigen kaihatsu, keizai kyoryoku ni tsutomete imasu* (General Trading Companies are Working Hard in Natural Resource Development and Economic Cooperation), September 1974, p. 2.

450 percent, of copper ore by 230 percent, of copper and copper alloy by 470 percent, of nickel ores by 290 percent, of lead by 340 percent, and of zinc ores by 780 percent. Increases between 1967 and 1968 were equally dramatic. Imports of coking coal, iron ore, nickel ores, and zinc ores all rose by more than 20 percent.

Huge industrial demand and short domestic supplies resulted in a spiral rise of import dependence rates for industrial materials, far beyond the already strikingly high 1960 rates. The import dependence rate of copper rose from 50.6 to 78.5 percent between FY 1960 and FY 1972. During the same twelve-year period the import dependence rate of lead rose from 54.6 to 59.1 percent, of zinc from 26.3 to 59.7 percent, of iron ore from 68 to 89.6 percent, of coking coal from 51.6 to 82.1 percent, and of crude oil from 98.6 to 99.7 percent. There was no change for aluminum, nickel, and uranium, because Japan had to import all of these metals long before 1960.

Japanese imports of foreign grains and meats also increased enormously during the 1960s. Imports of agricultural products for 1972 totalled $4,337 million, a 220 percent increase over 1965 and 19 percent of Japan's total imports for 1972. Imports of corn rose by 140 percent to $370 million between 1965 and 1972, of grain-sorghum by 240 percent to $215 million, of wheat by 140 percent to $361 million, of soybeans by 210 percent to $474 million, of meats by 820 percent to $320 million, and of sugar to $440 million. The enormous rises in imports of grains and meats reflected reduced self-sufficiency as of FY 1972. Self-sufficiency rates, the domestic production/domestic demand rates, for grains and meats dropped sharply between FY 1960 and FY 1972. The self-sufficiency rate of wheat dropped from 39 to 5 percent, of barley and rye from 107 to 18 percent, and of soybeans from 28 to 4 percent. While the self-sufficiency rates of meats (excluding whale meat) did not decline as sharply as that of grains, the drops were also substantial: beef from 96 to 80 percent and pork from 96 to 90 percent. Sugar's rate rose by 12 percent from 18 for FY 1960 to 30 percent for FY 1965, but then declined to 23 percent in FY 1970 and to 20 percent in FY 1972.

Metals Resource Development: Import Projects Before the Mid-1960s[1]

Nonferrous metals smelters were the first among Japanese industries to become alarmed about the inadequacy of short-term spot purchases of ores. Prices fluctuated wildly during business upturns and downturns and there was no assured, long-term stable supply. In 1953 Mitsubishi Metal Mining signed a contract with Atlas, a U.S. mining concern, by which it agreed to extend a 4.4-billion-Yen ($12.2 million) loan as part of the 28.8-billion-Yen ($80 million) financing required to develop a copper mine in Cebu, the Philippines. In return, Mitsubishi received the right to nearly all the mine's copper production. Mitsubishi Metal Mining's participation was limited to the extension of the loan and was a small financial commitment, but it was the pioneer project of the so-called "resource development–import projects" (*kaihatsu yunyu*). A few other nonferrous metals development projects based on similar agreements between Japanese smelters and foreign mining concerns were undertaken.

In the mid-1950s Japanese nonferrous metals smelters expanded into equity participation, which gave them both assured long-term supplies and returns on their investment. Of course, they also thereby shared in high prospecting and development risks.

The supply problem, however, did not become critical until the mid-1960s. Spot purchases remained the dominant pattern of supply for Japanese smelters. As a result the number of resource development–import projects with Japanese participation was very small before the mid-1960s: only four from 1955 to 1964. The scale of projects was also small. Furthermore, Japanese metals smelters, rather than general trading companies, were the leading participants. The role of trading companies was largely limited to shipping developed ores to Japan on a commission basis.

Japanese general trading firms had little involvement in overseas iron ore and coal development projects before 1960. When they began to participate, however, they chose extended involvement from the very first project, through equity participation as well as extension of loans. They participated in only two small-scale iron ore and coal development–import projects between 1960 and 1964. Less than $15 million was involved in both cases. In contrast to nonferrous metals development–import projects, however, general trading companies rather than steel makers were the main Japanese participants.

Huge *Sogo Shosha* Resource Development–Import Projects Since the Mid-1960s

In the mid-1960s there was a dramatic increase in Japanese participation in overseas resource development–import projects, both those involving only a loan extension and those involving a loan extension and equity participation. Many more projects were undertaken, and on a much larger scale, than previously. The total capital requirements, the size of Japanese financial participation, and the production involved rose sharply. Furthermore, the role played by the *sogo shosha* expanded. The trading companies increased their participation in nonferrous metals development projects and assumed a central role in iron ore and coal development projects.

A number of factors led to these sudden increases. One was the greatly diminished supply capacity of domestic sources to meet the rising demand of heavy and chemical industries for industrial raw materials. Another was the active policy and financial commitment of the Japanese government, which had long been concerned with the problem of the nation's paucity of raw materials and the negative impact this had on Japan's economic, foreign policy, and strategic interests.

The government had long been aware that assured long-term stable supplies of industrial raw materials and reduced dependence on foreign supply sources were indispensable to the nation's continuing economic growth, export expansion at an internationally competitive basis, freedom, and independence. It actively encouraged private enterprises in 1964 to form the Overseas Mineral Resource Development Corporation (*Kaigai Kobutsushigen Kaihatsu Kabushikikaisha*) to develop mineral resources abroad. In 1967 the government set up a new overseas resource development section in a government corporation called Metal Minerals Development Promotion Corporation (*Kinzoku Kobutsu Tanko Sokushin Jigyo*). More important, the Japanese government expanded the financing facilities of the Japan Export-Import Bank, the Overseas Economic Cooperation Fund, and others for private enterprise overseas resource development projects.

The new investment and development opportunities that opened up abroad also contributed to the growth in number and scale of overseas resource development–import projects. One of the most important new opportunities resulted from the decision of the Australian government in late 1960 to end its policy prohibiting the export of iron ore and to allow the development of its vast natural resources by foreign firms.

There were several reasons for the *sogo shosha*'s greater involvement in overseas mineral resource development–import projects. One was encouragement from the Japanese government. Another was encouragement from Japanese steel makers who desired to concentrate on steel production rather than spreading limited capital, personnel, and other resources in overseas development of iron ores and coal. Also, the rise in import volume and the diversification in the source of supply, requiring simultaneous transactions with numerous firms and countries of

Southeast Asia, Oceania, Latin America, and Africa, became too complex and cumbersome for the steel makers. As a result, the general trading companies became sole participants in approximately two-thirds of overseas steel raw materials development projects since 1968. The *sogo shosha* greatly increased their participation, both loan extension and equity participation, in nonferrous metals development because of the greatly expanded financing required by and risks involved in the new and much larger projects—financing and risks Japanese smelters found it difficult to bear alone. Many copper projects since the mid-1960s, with annual production capacities of about 100,000 tons rather than 1,000 tons, required development financing in the $100-million to $300-million range rather than the tens of millions of earlier projects.

As the projects expanded in number and grew in scale and complexity, the necessity emerged to organize and coordinate the Japanese participants, provide adequate information, and negotiate with the Japanese government, host governments, and foreign firms. Only the general trading companies, with their global information, communications, and commercial networks and personnel, could provide these services. This led them to play an increasingly central role.

Additionally, the *sogo shosha* could borrow hundreds of millions of dollars from Japanese and foreign financial institutions. They could also both tie down vast sums of money and carry large debt service costs for the several years between prospecting and feasibility studies and the actual production and import of raw materials into Japan.

Perhaps the most important reason, however, was the zeal and special efforts of the trading companies themselves. All *sogo shosha* firms established special natural resource development offices in the mid-1960s and began investing vast human and financial resources to actively expand resource development projects. They hired geological, mining, engineering, and international finance specialists from outside and sent young managers to study at leading mining, engineering, and business schools abroad. They created special resource development funds. The *sogo shosha* showed special zeal because resource development projects provided them with opportunities to create significant forms of supply and demand: demand for and the right to sell mining, infrastructure construction, transportation equipment, and other machines necessary to a project; new sources of supply that would assure long-term stable supply of raw materials to Japanese industries; the ability to import iron ore, coal, copper, bauxite, and other materials into Japan; valuable contacts with large Japanese and foreign project partners (mining concerns, manufacturers, financial institutions, etc.); and returns (dividends and interest) on investment.

Kiyoshi Kojima is correct in stating that Japan's pattern of resource development imports, in contrast to the U.S. and European pattern (independent development aiming at earnings from upstream and downstream integration), meets Japan's national interest well. It satisfies the resource nationalism of the host country that desires to preserve sovereign rights and control over its own natural resources. It benefits from the technologies and capital of U.S. and European mining and engineering concerns. It guarantees a large Japanese market on a long-term basis that makes possible huge resource development projects and large scale transactions. Finally, the relatively small equity participation (big in absolute value but relatively small in share of total financing required) provides Japanese industry with a long-term supply of industrial raw materials from diversified sources.[2]

Mt. Newman Iron Ore Project: The First Big Resource Development Project (Mitsui & Co.-C. Itoh & Co.)

The *sogo shosha*'s first opportunity to participate in a huge overseas resource development–import project came in 1966 when Australian mining and commercial interests extended an invitation to Japanese steel manufacturers to have a 10 percent financial participation in a $252-million iron ore development project at Mt. Newman in northwestern Australia, one of the world's largest iron ore deposits. The Japanese steel makers recommended two general trading companies, Mitsui & Co. and C. Itoh & Co., rather than themselves, as the participants in the Mt. Newman project. The two trading firms reviewed the various Australian proposals and studies (construction of railroad, harbor, ore development, etc.). Following extended negotiations, they reached an agreement with the Broken Hill Proprietary Company and the Colonial Sugar Refinery Company, the two Australian concerns involved. With the permission of the Japanese government, the trading companies established a joint subsidiary called Mitsui–C. Itoh Pty., Ltd. The agreement led to a 10 percent loan ($3.2 million) and equity ($22 million) participation by Mitsui–C. Itoh Pty., Ltd. The well-known U.S. mining concern, AMAX, became the fourth joint venture partner, with a 25 percent participation. Selection Trust of Britain became the fifth.

Actual production started in 1969, but more than 200 million tons of high grade ore had been contracted on a long-term basis by Japanese and Australian steelmakers even before mining started. During FY 1973 ended March 31, 1974, production totaled 35 million tons, of which 22 million tons were shipped to Japanese steel makers. The Japanese steel mills have been the largest customers of Mt. Newman ore, which in turn has been the largest source of iron ore for the Japanese steel industry. Production under a second project agreement started in 1977. Mitsui–C. Itoh Pty., Ltd., again has a 10 percent participation in the new project, which required $216 million in capital. Three-fifths of its annual production is now shipped to Japan.

Efforts Toward Becoming Project Organizers

Despite the dramatic increase in the *sogo shosha*'s involvement in overseas resource development, their participation has been primarily one of investment (extension of loans and equity participation) and only secondarily one of organizing Japanese participants. Since the late 1960s, however, the *sogo shosha* have aimed at becoming global natural resource development project organizers. They want to take the initiative and play a central role throughout the complex organizing process. Among the steps are the following: collecting information on potential projects; conducting preliminary feasibility studies and evaluations; selecting and organizing potential Japanese and foreign project partners (investors, builders of infrastructure, suppliers of equipment, project developers, users of products, etc.); making expert feasibility studies by staff experts or by outside consulting engineering firms; preparing negotiation terms related to capital participation ratio, sharing of risks, supply of equipment and transfer of technologies, selection of infrastructure builders and project developers, ratio of shipment of development products to Japan and other countries, pricing of products, etc.; negotiating foreign direct investments, permits, development project licenses, taxes, etc., with the home and host governments; managing the project; and settling disputes among participants after the start of production.

The trading companies, especially the top six, invested substantial efforts and resources to achieve this goal. One domestic result of these efforts was the establishment in Japan of group natural resource development companies in which each general trading company acts as organizer, coordinator, headquarters, and secretariat. Top *sogo shosha* officials serve as chairmen, presidents, or managing directors. For example, in petroleum, the Mitsubishi Corporation mobilized Mitsubishi group firms to establish the Mitsubishi Petroleum Development Company; Mitsui & Co. set up the Mitsui Petroleum Development Company; the Marubeni Corporation organized the Fuyo Petroleum Development Company; C. Itoh & Co. established the World Energy Development Company; Sumitomo Shoji Kaisha founded the Sumitomo Petroleum Development Company; and Nissho-Iwai Co. organized the Toyo Petroleum Development Company.

Balance of Direct Foreign Investments: March 1975

The *sogo shosha*'s efforts to develop some independent sources of raw material and to diversify foreign sources of supply provided a measure of freedom and independence to a country almost entirely lacking in major domestic food (except rice) and industrial resources. A measure of their efforts is the size of their direct foreign investment in resource development and its weight in Japan's total direct foreign investment. During FY 1975, Mitsui & Co. invested 33.6 percent of its direct investment abroad (both stock investment and loans) or 55.8 percent of its foreign stock investment (excluding loans) in natural resource development.[3] The other top ten trading companies have not invested as heavily as Mitsui in absolute value and percentage share, but their investments also have been sizable.

One result of their substantial investments in overseas resource development, in global commercial networks, and in foreign manufacturing is that the five largest trading companies topped all other Japanese firms in direct foreign investment as of March 1975. They surpassed Japan's manufacturing giants such as Matsushita Electric, Honda Motor, Toray Industries, and Kawasaki Steel. Nissho-Iwai Co., the sixth-largest *sogo shosha*, was the seventh-largest Japanese foreign investor, topped by only one non–*sogo shosha* firm. Ataka & Co. was twelfth. The other three trading firms (Toyomenka Kaisha, Kanematsu Gosho, and Nichimen Company) all ranked among the top thirty.[4] The top ten had a balance of 6,475 billion Yen ($3,160 million) in combined direct foreign investment (stock investment and loans, according to the definition of the Ministry of International Trade and Industry) or 17.1 percent of Japan's total, 37,911 billion Yen. The top six *sogo shosha* together had a 15.3 percent share of Japan's total direct investment abroad. Mitsui & Co., Japan's largest foreign investor, alone had a 5 percent share.

Other Major Overseas Natural Resource Development–Import Projects

The *sogo shosha* have not limited their participation in overseas natural resource development–import projects as investors and as organizers of Japanese participants to nonferrous and ferrous metals. They have participated in developing a wide range of strategic products including iron ore, copper, oil, natural gas, soybeans, lumber, and deep sea manganese nodules. The following examples illustrate some of the different development patterns.

The Mt. Newman iron ore project has been the predominant pattern. It is a joint venture with firms of several companies as partners. Non-Japanese concerns are the leading project organizers and Japanese firms are less active investor-participants. Furthermore, two Japanese trading companies, otherwise fierce rivals, are partners. The copper development project in the island of Bougainville and the Lornex copper ore development project

Table 6.3 Direct Foreign Investments (DFIs) of the Ten General Trading Companies, FY 1972–FY 1975[a]

	FY 1972	FY 1973	FY 1974	FY 1975
Mitsubishi Corporation	716	934	1,451	1,538
Mitsui & Co.	755	1,848	1,862	2,319
Marubeni Corporation	451	686	856	1,201
C. Itoh & Co.	412	540	796	1,003
Sumitomo Shoji	192	342	438	629
Nissho-Iwai Co.	234	188	400	421
Toyomenka	85	137	180	207
Kanematsu Gosho	70	100	140	188
Ataka & Co.	73	107	205	298
Nichimen Company	361	139	183	231
Total of the ten	3,349	5,021	6,475	8,035
Japan's DFIs	16,500	28,800	37,911	48,600
Share of the ten firms in Japan's DFIs	20.3%	17.4%	17.1%	16.5%

Source: Compiled from Information and Research Department, Mitsui & Co., *Nihon keizai ni okeru shosha no yakuwari: genjo to tenbo* (The Role of Trading Companies in the Japanese Economy: Current State and Future Prospects) (Tokyo: Mitsui & Co., 1976), p. 19, and Information and Research Department, Mitsui & Co., *Atarashi sogo shoshazo o motomete* (Seeking a New Image of General Trading Companies) (Tokyo: Mitsui & Co., 1977), p. 86.

[a] In hundred million Yen.

in British Columbia, Canada, are other projects in which rival Japanese copper smelters and rival trading companies are joint venture partners with foreign firms.

There are also projects in which a Japanese trading company is the chief organizer of the entire project and not just an investor and organizer of Japanese participants. An example is the natural gas project in Brunei, organized by the Mitsubishi Corporation. This pattern is rare, however. There are also iron ore and coal development projects in which only one Japanese *sogo shosha* is a joint venture participant with non-Japanese firms. An example is the Robe River iron ore project in Australia, in which Mitsui & Co. is the sole Japanese participant. Such projects are also relatively few. Most of the huge iron ore and coal development projects have rival trading companies as joint venture partners with non-Japanese concerns. The reasons are simple. Joint venture partners share huge capital requirements and high prospecting and development risks that no individual firm can bear alone. For Japanese general trading companies, overseas resource development–import projects provide opportunities to create the supply and demand discussed above. Competition among rival firms is fierce and failure to participate can be costly to future growth and profits. Joint venture with rival firms helps maintain the balance of power among competing firms and provides an opportunity to observe the operational methods of rivals.

The Iraqi Petroleum Development Project

In April 1972 Sumitomo Shoji Kaisha established a new Energy Resource Development Office to promote petroleum development–import projects. In March 1974 the new office acquired 40 percent development-participation rights and obligations from L'Entreprise de Recherche et d'Activités Pétrolières (ERAP), the state-owned French petroleum development company (it changed its name to SNEA in June 1976), which had signed a production and sales contract in 1968 with the Iraq National Oil Company (INOC) to develop oil in the Buzurgan oil fields in Southeast Iraq. Sumitomo Shoji Kaisha had already organized group firms to establish the Sumitomo Petroleum Development Company two months earlier (January 1973) to push the oil development project in Iran. To raise the massive capital required and to spread development risks, Sumitomo Shoji in July 1973 formed the Japan Iraq Petroleum Development Company (JIPD) with an initial capitalization at 12,000 million Yen ($40 million) and with Sumitomo Petroleum Development Company as the largest shareholder (40.7 percent equity participation). Other JIPD shareholders included the Japan Petroleum Development Company (29.9 percent), the Mitsubishi Petroleum Development Company (16.8 percent), Idemitsu Kosan Company (7 percent), the Japan Petroleum Exploration Company (4.9 percent), and Teikoku Oil Company (0.7 percent). Oil production at the Buzurgan oil fields started in late October 1976. They are expected to produce eighty million tons of crude in ten years, 40 percent of which will be shipped to Japan. The fields also produce natural gas.[5]

Tokisaburo Shiina, then vice chairman of Sumitomo Shoji Kaisha, became chairman of the Japan Iraq Petroleum Development Co. Shiina was also chairman of the Sumitomo Petroleum Development Co., the Sumitomo group oil development company in which Sumitomo Shoji Kaisha has a 16 percent equity participation. The Mitsubishi Corporation has a 24 percent interest in the Mitsubishi Petroleum Development Co., the third-largest shareholder of the JIPD. (The pivotal position the two trading companies hold in the JIPD is clear.) JIPD Chairman Shiina, a former official of the Sumitomo Metal Industries, declared in an interview with the author that he was "the happiest man in the world," because Sumitomo Shoji Kaisha, as the project's organizer, handled sales of two critical products he loved: Sumitomo Metal Industries' oil pipes for the 300-kilometer pipeline from the Buzurgan oil fields to the Arabian Gulf Port of Al-Bakr, and crude oil for Japan once production started.

Agribusiness in Brazil

The Marubeni Corporation is the organizer of a large-scale soybean and wheat development project in southwestern Brazil that started production in early 1975. The 20,000 hectares of farmland acquired by Marubeni are on a plateau in the Uniao region of Mato Grosso State, about 1,000 kilometers east of São Paulo. As of 1975, this was the largest agricultural project abroad organized by a Japanese trading company. Marubeni set up a subsidiary called Mato Grosso Commercial e Agropecueuia in July 1975 with an initial capitalization of $3 million, using a loan provided by the Japanese government's Overseas Economic Cooperation Fund. The project produces 39,000 tons of soybeans and 16,000 tons of wheat annually since full production started in 1977. It is part of Japan's efforts to diversify overseas sources of food supply. At the same time it meets Brazil's plan to expand its agricultural production and increase its share of world grain trade. For this reason, the Brazilian government lifted legal controls on foreign acquisition of farmland and issued a special decree granting various construction licenses to the Uniao project.

LNG Project in Brunei

The Mitsubishi Corporation is the chief organizer of one of the world's largest natural gas development projects just off the shore of Brunei on the island of Borneo. The first shipment of liquefied natural gas (LNG) arrived at Osaka, Japan, in December 1972. Mitsubishi has a 45 percent equity participation in the Brunei LNG Co., a joint venture set up with the government of Brunei (10 percent) and Royal Dutch Shell (45 percent), which has the concession on the reserves. The Mitsubishi Corporation did a feasibility study of the project, made detailed technical studies, and negotiated with the Brunei government, Royal Dutch Shell, and the large users of natural gas in Japan to whom the LNG is shipped. Mitsubishi assumed responsibility for establishing the said joint venture company for production and liquefaction of natural gas, furnished the necessary construction materials, built a local liquefaction factory, and established unloading bases in Japan. Finally, it raised its share of the necessary funds for the project.

Natural gas in Brunei is liquefied at a temperature of −161° Celsius, compressed to 1-600th in volume, and transported 4,500 kilometers to Japan in seven LNG tankers. Each tanker has a capacity of 32,000 tons of LNG and is chartered by the Mitsubishi Corporation at a rate of five million tons a year for use by the Tokyo Electric Co., the Tokyo Gas Company, and the Osaka Gas Company. This clean energy project not only meets Japan's growing energy demand but helps solve its critical pollution problem.

Multinational Deep Sea Mineral Resources Development Projects

As the world's natural resources on land become depleted, the development of manganese nodules, lying in abundance on the sea bed a few miles (4,000 to 6,000 meters) below the surface of the sea and containing such valuable minerals as manganese, nickel, copper, and cobalt, has attracted attention in recent years. Many consider manganese nodules the most promising natural resource of the twenty-first century. Tests show that these purplish-black nodules, porous but hard and about the size of a potato, are about 25 to 26 percent manganese, 1.2 to 1.7 percent nickel, 0.75 to 1.3 percent copper, and 0.2 to 0.3 percent cobalt. Estimates of their worldwide deposits range from several hundred billion to a trillion tons. Such almost unlimited reserves would be enough to supply resource-hungry industries of the world for many generations.

Unfortunately, the financial and technological problems involved in the commercial mining and processing of these mineral-rich nodules are enormous. Exploitation alone, not to speak of actual mining and processing, requires tens of millions of dollars. Gathering and bringing the nodules to the surface at a commercially feasible cost presents numerous difficulties. Three methods are currently under study: the continuous line bucket method in which one or two ships operate a chain of buckets like a conveyor system; the suction method in which nodules are sucked up to a surface ship through a pipe; and the airlift method in which nodules are lifted through a pipe by compressed air. None has been perfected as of this writing (fall 1977).

In light of the great potential, which outweighs the financial and technological difficulties, vigorous international efforts have been under way for several years to develop these deep sea mineral resources commercially. In mid-1974 there were four multinational joint venture groups actively engaged in various development projects: the Kennecott group, the Tenneco group, the Ocean Management, Inc. (OMI) group, and the Lockheed group. Each group consists of some of the world's largest mining concerns, metals producers, engineering firms, and Japanese trading companies and, in the case of the OMI group, financial institutions. The four groups differ in the methods of mining they are trying to perfect, but they share similar feasibility studies, timetables, and commercial development target dates. Technical development, the first stage, is from 1975 to 1979; final feasibility studies, the second stage, are planned for 1979 and 1980; and commercialization (mining, refining, processing, and sales) is projected for the third stage in the early 1980s.

Japanese general trading companies, ever eager to find new

natural resource supplies for resource-hungry Japanese industries, have been active participants in these multinational joint venture projects as investors, organizers of Japanese participants, and liaisons between the respective multinational joint venture group and Japanese participants.[6] The Mitsubishi Corporation has a 10 percent equity participation in the Kennecott group project capitalized at $50 million. The chief partner of the joint venture is Kennecott Copper, the well-known U.S. mining concern, with 50 percent participation. Other partners include two British firms, Rio-Tinto Zing Corporation (20 percent) and Consolidated Gold Fields (10 percent), and Noranda Mines, Ltd., of Canada (10 percent).

Three trading companies (Kanematsu Gosho, Ltd., Nichimen Company, and C. Itoh & Co.) and two Japanese manufacturing firms (Hitachi Shipbuilding & Engineering and Nippon Heavy and Chemical Industries) have a 25 percent participation through a Japanese joint venture, the Japan Manganese Nodules Development Company, in the Tenneco group venture, Ocean Mining Associates (OMA). Deepsea Ventures, a Tenneco subsidiary (with 25 percent participation), U.S. Steel (25 percent participation), and Union Minière (25 percent participation), the Belgian mining concern, are other OMA partners.

Five *sogo shosha* (Sumitomo Shoji Kaisha, Ataka & Co., Nissho-Iwai Co., Toyomenka Kaisha, and the Marubeni Corporation) and eighteen other Japanese financial institutions and producers have a 25 percent participation through a Japanese consortium, the Japan Deep Ocean Mining Company, in Ocean Management, Inc. (OMI). OMI was established in 1975 with a $33-million capitalization. Its headquarters are in Seattle, Washington. Membership includes one Canadian firm, one American resource development giant, one West German consortium, and one Japanese consortium, each with a 25 percent equity participation. INCO (International Nickel Company of Canada) Ltd. is the world's largest nickel refiner and possesses the technology indispensable for refining the minerals in manganese nodules. SEDCO, Inc., the American participant, is the world's leader in oil rig and drilling technology and has been developing exploitation methods for manganese nodules since the early 1970s. The West German consortium (AMR) has five members:

four private firms and the West German government, which provided 50 percent of AMR's capital. It is the only West German organization recognized by the federal government to engage in manganese nodule research and development. Two of the private firms, Metallgesellschaft A.G. and Preussag A.G., have been involved in the research of the world's oceans since the mid-nineteenth century. They possess advanced technology and a wealth of data indispensable to deep sea resource mining.

The Japan Deep Ocean Mining Company, the Japanese consortium known as DOMCO, is largely a Sumitomo Shoji Kaisha-led joint venture centering around Sumitomo group firms, although its members include four other non-Sumitomo trading companies and ten other non-Sumitomo financial institutions and producers. Nine out of twenty-three DOMCO partners are Sumitomo group firms: Sumitomo Shoji Kaisha, Sumitomo Ocean Development and Engineering, Sumitomo Heavy Industries, Sumitomo Metal Mining, Sumitomo Metal Industry, the Sumitomo Bank, Sumitomo Marine & Fire Insurance, Sumitomo Trust & Banking, and Sumitomo Life Insurance.

Sumitomo Shoji Kaisha has long spearheaded the ocean resource development efforts of the entire Sumitomo group. It established the Ocean Development Department within the company in 1968 in the expectation that deep sea mineral resources would have a great potential for securing assured long-term supplies to the Japanese industry, and that the Sumitomo group ought to be in the forefront of the new resource development industry. The same year it organized a joint project team with Sumitomo Heavy Industries and Sumitomo Metal Mining to study deep sea mining of manganese nodules. The joint venture sent a mission abroad to study technologies related to the mining of mineral seabed resources and to investigate possibilities of collaboration with leading companies in the field. In 1973 Sumitomo Shoji Kaisha took a giant step forward and organized a group venture called Sumitomo Ocean Development and Engineering Company with Hisashi Tsuda, its chairman, and J. Tamura, manager of its ocean development department, serving respectively as chairman and executive director of the new firm. The new firm took the lead in establishing the Japan Deep

Ocean Mining Company in 1975 and in DOMCO's participation in the INCO group's multinational venture that followed shortly afterward.

In a sense, all of Chapter 6 is a case study of how the *sogo shosha* harnessed their core business and their services and resources to meet Japan's and the world's needs. The patterns by which overseas natural resource development projects have been organized are various, but the central role of the *sogo shosha* remains clear in most patterns and at most levels.

So far this book has examined what the *sogo shosha* are and what they do. It has delved into their evolution and their roles in the post-World War II Japanese economy. Part 3 examines the challenges they face and their prospects in the contemporary world by looking first, in Chapter 7, at strategic changes in their operations since 1973 and then, in Chapter 8, at how they currently function and are likely to function in the future in world commerce.

Notes

1. This section draws heavily on *Kaigai kobutsu shigen kaihatsu* (Overseas Mineral Resources Development) issued by Nihon Boekikai (Tokyo: Sasaki Taipu, 1975), pp. 85-127.

2. Kiyoshi Kojima, "Nihon no shigen hosho to kaigai toshi" (Natural Resource Guarantees for Japan and Japan's Overseas Investment), *Sekai Keizai Hyoron*, April 1977, pp. 4-19.

3. Mitsui & Co. Information and Research Department, *Nihon keizai ni okeru shosha no yakuwari: genjo to tenbo* (The Role of Trading Companies in the Japanese Economy: Current State and Future Prospects) (Tokyo: Mitsui & Co., 1976), p. 18.

4. Toyo Keizai Shinposha, *Kaigai shinshutsu kigyo soran*, 1976 (A Directory of Japanese Multinational Enterprises) (Tokyo: Toyo Keizai Shinposha, 1976), p. 3.

5. Sumitomo Shoji, "Taibo no Iraku genyu iyoiyo seisan kaishi" (The Long-Awaited Iraqi Crude Oil Development Project Begins Production), *Sumisho News*, January 1977, pp. 21-22.

6. This section is based largely on "Nijuitseiki no shigen kaitei mangan-ryu kaihatsu ni idomu" (A Challenge—Developing Deepsea Manganese Nodules—Natural Resources of the 21st Century), *Sumisho News*, March 1976, pp. 2-6.

Part 3
Challenges and Prospects

7
Strategic Changes Since 1973: Management Efficiency and Global Reach

The six-month periods before and after the oil crisis of October 1973 marked a major turning point in the post–World War II history of the *sogo shosha*. As a result of the events of those twelve months, the general trading companies made two major strategic decisions. First they decided to shift emphasis from rapid growth and sales volume to social responsibility, efficient management, and the marketing of high-technology plants, products, and know-how. Second, they decided to accelerate at all levels their efforts to become global enterprises. What these decisions entailed, their immediate consequences, and their likely portents for the future of the *sogo shosha* in world commerce will engage our attention in this chapter and the next.

These decisions represented fundamental changes in the *sogo shosha*'s objectives and strategies. They originated in the radically altered domestic and international environments, including a slower growth economy, the changing structure of Japanese industry, government efforts to limit the *sogo shosha*'s stock holdings and bank loans, growing protectionism abroad, and rising nationalism in the developing countries. The trading companies had coped successfully with numerous environmental challenges after World War II. Among these challenges were the military defeat of Japan and the subsequent Occupation, rapid growth of the Japanese economy in the late 1950s and 1960s, the radical transformation of Japan's industrial structure, manufacturers' thrusts into direct marketing, the emergence of a mass consumer society, and liberalization of the restrictions on foreign investment in Japan. The trading companies became *sogo shosha* and adopted strategies of growth, diversification, demand and supply creation, organization of new industries, thrust into the consumer goods market, and consolidation. The environmental changes the *sogo shosha* encountered in 1973 were more far-reaching in impact. The decisions they made were of even greater strategic importance than those of the 1950s and 1960s. First, the radically altered domestic environment will be described; then the *sogo shosha*'s strategic responses will be analyzed.

A Radically Altered Domestic Environment

The dramatic changes in the domestic Japanese environment in the 1970s had three significant aspects: a slowdown in economic growth; a shift in economic and industrial structure; and a less hospitable political and social climate leading to efforts to restrict the *sogo shosha*'s stock holdings and borrowings. Each aspect will be discussed in some detail.

Slower Economic Growth

The Japanese economy grew rapidly from the mid-1950s to the early 1970s, despite periodic downturns. The annual growth in real terms of Japan's GNP averaged 9.8 percent between FY 1960 and FY 1965 and an astounding 12.4 percent between FY 1966 and FY 1970. Such rapid growth was made possible by technological innovations, by vigorous private investment in plants and equipment in heavy and chemical industries, by an ample supply of cheap raw materials from abroad, and by a tremendous growth in exports.

By the early 1970s, however, there were clear signs that Japan could not maintain this high rate of economic growth indefinitely. Its core industries (steel, shipbuilding, automobile, consumer electronics, chemical, and petrochemical industries) either had already become or were becoming mature industries with slower rates of growth. Consumer electronics faced saturated markets in selected product areas at home and abroad.

It also became clear that the Japanese economy would have to shift its top priority from catching up with the West through rapid growth to raising the social welfare of the people. Their needs and demands could no longer be ignored. Increased investments in the public sector to ease the shortages of housing, highways, schools, and health facilities became imperative. Equally imperative was investment in ameliorating such serious by-products of the high growth economy as industrial, air, and water pollution and transportation bottlenecks. Tough government pollution regulations were passed. By 1975 Japanese industry was spending between 15 and 20 percent of its capital outlays on pollution control.[1] The maturing of the economy, the change in economic priorities, and pollution control measures all led to the slowing down of the Japanese economy.

At the same time that public debates on these issues intensified and pressures for action grew, Japan was hit by critical international developments: the international currency crises of fall 1971 and early 1973 that led to the float system, and the oil crisis of fall 1973 and the subsequent quadrupling of oil prices and simultaneous global inflation and recession that followed. Japan's GNP suffered a -1.2 percent growth in 1974. By mid-1976, Japan had adjusted to the dislocations caused by the oil crisis, but the era of a high-flying economy was clearly over. In September 1974 the prestigious Industrial Structure Council, in its report to the Minister of International Trade and Industry, forecast 6 percent real growth between 1973 and 1980, 6.5 percent between 1980 and 1985, and 6 percent between 1985 and 1990.[2] Six and one-half percent real growth between fiscal 1977 and fiscal 1980 was forecast by the council in August 1976.

Changing Economic and Industrial Structure

The shift in the goals and growth pattern of the Japanese economy led in turn to a basic change in the economic and industrial structure. The Industrial Structure Council in September 1974 predicted that the weight of personal expenditure in the total national expenditure, which saw a gradual decline between fiscal 1955 and fiscal 1970, would rise as housing and miscellaneous expenditures increased. It also predicted an increase in the weight of government investment in the total national expenditure from 8.6 percent in fiscal 1970 (in real terms) to 12.2 percent in fiscal 1985 as investments in pollution control, housing, and other public works rose. The weight of private plant and equipment investment in the total national expenditure would, however, decline from 20.1 percent in fiscal 1970 (real terms) to 18.7 percent in fiscal 1985. The Japanese economy, in a word, would shift to an economy spurred primarily by government investments and private consumption from one propelled primarily by huge private capital investments. The council predicted a shift from a manufacturer-oriented to a consumer-oriented economy.

The shift in the Japanese economic structure, specifically in the structure of demand, led to changes in the structure of Japanese industry. The same Industrial Structure Council report predicted that primary industry would grow by only 1.9 percent between calendar years 1970 and 1985, while secondary industry (mining, manufacturing, and construction) would grow by 6.8 percent and tertiary industry by 6.6 percent during the same period. The weight of primary industry in total production would drop further, while that of secondary and tertiary industries would increase slightly. The industrial structure of Japan is likely to move in two additional significant directions: a declining share of intermediate products (crude steel, primary nonferrous metals products, pulp, and basic chemical products) in total production; and the growth of knowledge-intensive industries (i.e., high-technology industries) and even greater technological innovations in heavy and chemical industries.[3]

Moves To Restrict the Sogo Shosha's *Stock Holdings and Borrowings*

Another major change in the domestic environment that directly affected the *sogo shosha* was a vastly deteriorated business climate, reflected in a series of proposals made by the Japan Fair Trade Commission and the Ministry of Finance. These proposals aimed at limiting the size of the trading firms' stock holdings and bank loans. They were made against a backdrop of rising public criticism of the trading firms in 1973 and 1974. The firms were accused of being speculators in stocks, foreign exchanges, and land; they were attacked as hoarders of the necessities of life from rice to toilet paper, and condemned as tax evaders. The trading firms acknowledged a few violations and some laxity in control over the actions of low-level officials, but they protested vigorously against what they considered extraordinary public ignorance and misunderstanding about the nature and functions

Table 7.1 Domestic Stock Holdings of the Ten General Trading Companies and Holdings Exceeding Limits Proposed by the Japan Fair Trade Commission in 1974[a]

	(A) Capital stock	(B) Net worth × ½	(C) Domestic securities (nonaffiliates)	(D) Domestic securities (affiliates)	(E) Total of C + D	(F) Excess holdings	F/E (percent)
Mitsubishi Corporation	33,477	41,035	121,888	11,950	133,838	92,803	69.3
Mitsui & Co.	33,042	50,109	130,434	33,968	164,402	114,293	69.5
Marubeni Corporation	30,464	26,060	137,931	15,714	153,645	123,181	80.2
C. Itoh & Co.	26,856	40,967	121,323	31,348	152,671	111,704	73.2
Sumitomo Shoji	15,686	21,628	52,904	4,046	56,950	35,322	62.0
Nissho-Iwai Co.	16,448	17,897	61,208	4,202	65,410	47,513	72.6
Toyomenka	10,000	12,589	27,515	3,848	31,363	18,774	59.9
Kanematsu Gosho	7,260	9,634	25,209	6,294	31,503	21,869	69.4
Ataka & Co.	10,000	9,561	54,611	6,145	60,756	50,756	83.5
Nichimen Company	10,010	11,964	31,065	9,649	40,714	28,750	70.6
Total			764,088	127,164	891,252	644,965	72.4

Source: Jutaro Nakamura, Sogo shosha no katsudo kisoku ni tsuite (On Regulations Controlling the Activities of General Trading Companies), unpublished Nikko Research Center paper, October 21, 1974, p. 12.

[a]In million Yen.

of their business. The heads of the top six firms were summoned before a Diet committee and harshly questioned.

What really shook the top officials of the trading firms in 1974, however, were moves of the Japan Fair Trade Commission and the Ministry of Finance to restrict their activities. The FTC, having completed a study of the *sogo shosha* in January 1974, declared that it intended to revise the antitrust law to restrict the stock holdings of two groups: firms whose capital stock exceeded 10 billion Yen, and firms whose total assets were in excess of 200 billion Yen. The proposed revision in the antitrust law would limit the size of stock investment by a Japanese firm in another domestic firm to the investor firm's capital stock (*shihonkin*), or one-half of its total assets, whichever is larger. There was little doubt that the FTC's main target was the *sogo shosha*, since eleven huge trading firms were among the forty-nine target firms (forty-three firms with capital stock exceeding 10 billion Yen and six firms with total assets in excess of 200 billion Yen). More important, the excess stock investments, which were held by the eleven trading firms and would have to be disposed of if the proposed revision became law, were two and one-half times larger than the excess stock investments of the thirty-eight non–*sogo shosha* firms. It was expected that as of September 1974 the *sogo shosha* would have to divest roughly two-thirds of their holdings in domestic securities, or approximately $2.9 billion.

In 1974 the Bureau of Banks of the Ministry of Finance drafted a plan to severely limit the amount of loans a financial institution could lend to a Japanese corporation. Loans of commercial banks were restricted to 20 percent of their equity (*jiko shihon*); those of long-term credit banks and trust banks to 30 percent of equity; and those of foreign exchange banks to 40 percent of equity. Sound banking and protection of depositors were the official reasons given by the Ministry of Finance, but again the main target seemed to be the *sogo shosha*. The new administrative policy, which was adopted and took effect on December 25, 1974, forced eight general trading companies (all of the top ten except Kanematsu Gosho, Ltd., and Nichimen Company) to redeem approximately 600 billion Yen ($2,000 million) worth of bank loans. There was little doubt that the moves announced by the two

Table 7.2 Loans of Japanese Banks to the Ten General Trading Companies and Amount in Excess of the Limits Imposed by the Ministry of Finance as of March 31, 1974

Bank	Mitsubishi Corporation	Mitsui & Co.	Marubeni Corporation	C. Itoh & Co.	Trading Company Sumitomo Shoji	Nissho-Iwai Co.	Toyo-menka	Kanematsu Gosho	Ataka & Co.	Nichimen Company
1. Ratio of loans to bank's net worth + reserves (percent):										
Nippon Kogyo Bank	9.6	15.8	10.4	10.6	8.7	1.7	1.2	2.1	2.5	1.0
Japan Long-Term Credit Bank	14.6	17.1	7.6	21.1	11.9	2.4	3.0	1.0	4.4	—
Japan Real Estate Bank	—	16.9	—	—	20.3	—	1.4	0.9	—	1.4
Daiichi Kangyo Bank	20.8	8.6	—	16.0	—	11.5	—	4.6	0.6	1.2
Fuji Bank	2.5	36.0	24.6	3.3	—	0.5	1.5	—	—	—
Sumitomo Bank	1.4	14.2	—	21.5	17.5	—	—	—	13.8	—
Mitsubishi Bank	42.9	11.2	5.4	1.1	—	1.2	—	—	2.4	1.2
Sanwa Bank	19.3	8.6	3.0	43.5	—	19.2	—	—	—	16.3
Bank of Tokyo	54.1	63.0	44.9	2.1	18.3	17.4	3.4	25.9	9.0	12.3
Tokai Bank	25.4	8.2	8.5	5.1	—	1.3	22.1	3.5	—	—
Mitsui Bank	—	69.9	—	5.6	—	1.6	12.9	—	2.9	2.6
Taiyo Kobe Bank	12.3	—	18.4	18.6	6.1	4.3	—	8.0	—	—
Kyowa Bank	—	—	7.3	—	—	4.0	—	—	27.7	3.4
Daiwa Bank	—	16.8	9.3	—	—	16.7	5.2	2.4	—	6.8
Saitama Bank	—	—	9.3	9.5	7.7	3.9	3.4	4.1	5.5	—
Hokkaido Takushoku Bank	7.5	—	—	—	—	—	2.3	7.6	—	—

(Table 7.2 continues)

174

Table 7.2 (cont.)

Bank	Mitsubishi Corporation	Mitsui & Co.	Marubeni Corporation	C. Itoh & Co.	Trading Company Sumitomo Shoji	Nissho-Iwai Co.	Toyo-menka	Kanematsu Gosho	Ataka & Co.	Nichimen Company
Mitsubishi Trust & Banking	67.9	–	13.2	7.5	6.5	–	–	2.2	–	9.0
Sumitomo Trust & Banking	–	–	17.2	43.3	34.4	–	3.8	–	34.0	–
Mitsui Trust & Banking	–	62.6	–	–	–	–	7.2	6.2	–	–
Yasuda Trust & Banking	–	–	67.8	–	–	–	7.7	–	–	–
Toyo Trust & Banking	41.8	21.6	–	–	–	38.1	–	–	–	23.2
Chuo Trust & Banking	–	–	–	–	–	–	85.1	–	–	–
2. Amount exceeding the 20 percent loan ratio (i.e., 20 percent of bank's net worth + reserves) for city banks (other than the Bank of Tokyo) imposed by the Ministry of Finance in 1974 (million Yen):	92,769	164,266	16,700	5,418	–	–	4,490	–	11,278	–
3. Amount exceeding the 30 percent loan ratio for long-term and trust banks (million Yen):	92,390	101,247	52,610	38,902	4,796	4,322	9,855	–	4,354	–
4. Total amount exceeding the limit imposed by the Ministry of Finance (million Yen):	185,159	265,513	69,310	44,320	4,796	4,322	14,345	–	15,632	–

Source: Jutaro Nakamura, *Sogo shosha no katsudo kisoku ni tsuite* (On Regulations Controlling the Activities of General Trading Companies), unpubliisued Nikko Research Center paper, October 21, 1974, p. 12.

government agencies had a strong negative impact on the *sogo shosha*'s business activities, functions, and profits.

A Less Hospitable International Environment
Growing Protectionism Abroad

The success of Japan's export drive led to a favorable international balance of payments for Japan by fall 1969 and to a rapid expansion in 1971 of Japan's foreign exchange reserves from $7.9 billion in July to $12.5 billion in August. Japan's industrial and export drive successes, however, also led to strong reactions abroad that took the form of realignments of major international currencies and growing protectionism. Japan's success was largely responsible for President Nixon's emergency economic measures of August 1971 that suspended the convertibility of the dollar into gold and imposed surcharges on foreign imports. The system of fixed exchange rates under the Bretton Woods system since 1944 collapsed. To make U.S. goods more competitive in world markets, the dollar was devalued. The Yen was revalued in December by 16.88 percent to 308 Yen to the dollar in a multilateral realignment, but the realigned system did not work long. In early 1973 the major industrial nations shifted to the uncertain and unstable float-rate system in which exchange rates are fixed by demand and supply. The float system itself in part was a protectionist measure designed to guard against a sudden huge shipment of goods and unemployment from another nation. By February 1973, when the float system was adopted, Japan's foreign exchange reserves swelled to a record $19 billion.

The quadrupling of oil prices and the global recession and inflation that followed the war in the Middle East hit Japan even harder than the so-called "Nixon shocks" of August 1971. To get out of the recession of 1974 and 1975 the Japanese mounted another aggressive export drive and cut imports, as they had done in past recessions. Exports in 1974 rose by a hefty 50 percent over the previous year to $55.5 billion, roughly 19 percent of Japan's GNP of $297 billion. However, the increase in imports was even bigger because of the steep increase in oil prices, 62 percent more than in 1973.

The practice of relying on export expansion as an engine of

economic growth and on import reduction as a way of cutting payments deficits had few international repercussions when the Japanese economy was relatively small, but not when it had become the third-largest economy in a closely intertwined world. The impact on a world undergoing the deepest and largest recession since the Great Depression of the 1930s was obvious and reactions were swift. Australia cut imports of Japanese automobiles by 50 percent. Western European countries forced Japanese manufacturers of electronic equipment (TV, tape recorders, radios, etc.) to adopt voluntary quotas.

Nationalism among Developing Nations

The oil crisis was a manifestation par excellence of the growing economic and political nationalism among the resource-rich developing nations of Asia, the Middle East, Africa, and Latin America. It was a manifesto that countries rich in oil and other resources intended to control their own destinies and that they would use resources as instruments of foreign policy when necessary. It was also a declaration that the post–World War II era of ample supplies of cheap energy and other primary commodities, which greatly benefited the economic growth of the industrialized nations, was over.

A fair price for energy and other resources was not the sole demand. The developing countries demanded investments not only in prospecting and development but in local processing of raw materials. They asked for the cooperation of the industrialized countries in economic development, including the construction of infrastructure, the building of huge petrochemical complexes, and selling manufactured products in the world market, in return for supplies of raw materials.

Nationalism was not the only concern of Japanese businessmen in 1974, however. Labor-intensive industries (such as textile and shoe industries), whose exports to the United States caused serious trade disputes in the late 1960s and early 1970s, now found themselves losing ground in the home market to low-priced imports from Korea and Taiwan. Things were bound to get even worse as developing countries further expanded their economies and as Japanese goods lost international competitiveness because of spiraling production costs from rising labor and materials costs and the rising value of the Yen.

The Domestic Response

The radically altered and much less hospitable domestic social, political, and economic environment of 1973 and 1974 led the general trading companies to make three decisions: to emphasize social responsibilities and counterattack against critics; to stress management and functional efficiency; and to expand involvement with future growth industries. Their response to the equally radically transformed international environment was an accelerated push toward becoming global enterprises. These strategic decisions had long-term impacts on the *sogo shosha*'s broad objectives, basic courses of action, and resource allocation. Each decision and its consequences will be discussed in turn.

Emphasis on Social Responsibilities and Counterattacks against Critics

The *sogo shosha*'s first domestic response was to emphasize social responsibilities. Stung by severe criticism by the mass media, which only a short time ago (from the late 1960s to late 1971) had hailed them as investors and organizers of overseas natural resource development projects, and by consumer groups, the trading companies took some joint and some independent actions. The Japan Foreign Trade Council, headed by Tatsuzo Mizukami, former chairman of Mitsui & Co. and an influential figure in Japanese business and political circles, was strengthened to serve as a united front organization. In May 1973 the council issued *The General Trading Company's Code of Behavior* and pledged that the *sogo shosha* firms "shall ensure, through the strengthening of internal auditing system, company personnel training and other systems, the constant self-recognition, throughout the entire organization, of their mission to society; and shall control and regulate themselves by the basic principle of social responsibility." In addition, they pledged that "special care to ensure conformity to management philosophy and functions shall be taken in business dealings involving land, stocks, and goods related to the people's livelihood."[4]

Many *sogo shosha* also issued their own separate and more specific codes of behavior in the next few months. They solemnly pledged to avoid speculation in rice, food, lumber, stocks, and land and to consider the interests of the consumer, the environmental impact of development projects and views of local residents, and the interests of affiliates and medium- and small-size firms when integration and rationalization programs were undertaken.[5]

On July 4, 1973, the board of directors of Mitsui & Co. approved a plan calling for contributions of between 2 and 4 percent of its annual profits before taxes to pollution control and other social service projects. On July 19, then President Fujino of the Mitsubishi Corporation declared that the firm would make contributions in the same areas as part of its annual plan. He urged business and industry to become actively involved in projects with long-term benefits for the people and to sacrifice short-term profits if necessary. The *sogo shosha* also complained that much public criticism was based on ignorance of the fact that worldwide inflation, rather than hoarding or speculation, was the major cause of the spiral rise in the prices of soybeans, food, lumber, and other commodities, and that excess liquidity in the aftermath of the first international monetary crisis of August 1971 was at the root of the firms' large purchases of stocks and land.

In July 1974, the *sogo shosha* shifted to a counterattack against the Fair Trade Commission, using the Japan Foreign Trade Council as the vehicle. It issued two pamphlets, one in July 1974 titled "The Functions and Special Nature of the *Sogo Shosha;*" the second in February 1975 titled "On the Fair Trade Commission's Second Investigation of General Trading Companies." The first was a point-by-point mild rebuttal to the arguments raised by the commission about the firms' considerable financial and marketing power and their potential for restraining the free, orderly, and democratic development of the Japanese economy. The second was a strong frontal assault on the FTC's second investigative report issued in January 1975. After criticizing what it termed the FTC's "lack of understanding," it "refuted" the major issues raised by the FTC. These issues were the vertical integration of affiliated firms through stock holding;

the core position enjoyed by the top six firms in their respective industrial and commercial groups; and potential abuses that could result from the trading firms' power. The second pamphlet concluded with a strong affirmation of the principles of free enterprise, declaring that the *sogo shosha* will be "utterly opposed to any structural control that will affect the trading firms' basic business and weaken their functions at this critical juncture in the Japanese and international economy."[6]

In addition, the *sogo shosha* labored hard jointly and individually to secure the support of their allies and friends in the government (officials in the Ministry of International Trade and Industry, etc.), in the Liberal Democratic Party, and in influential business circles (e.g., leaders of the Federation of Economic Organizations). Business interests and domestic politics are intertwined in the whole complex issue. As of the summer of 1977, the bill to revise the antitrust law had not passed the Japanese Diet. However, as previously noted, the Finance Ministry's policy to restrict the size of bank loans to the trading companies and other firms took effect on December 25, 1974.

Stress on Managerial and Functional Efficiency

The *sogo shosha*'s second domestic response, which involved many facets, can be summarized as an urgent stress on efficiency of management and of functions. The *sogo shosha* had expanded and diversified rapidly without much concern for efficiency of management, functions, and organizational structure during the two decades of economic growth. To achieve their primary objectives of rapid growth of sales volume and diversification, they expanded external debts and the volume of credits and loans to suppliers, customers, and affiliates without undue concern with profitability of transactions or the credit worthiness of suppliers and customers. The system worked as long as enough profits were generated to sustain operations. Similar to pedaling a bicycle, the trading companies (and the Japanese economy for that matter) could keep moving forward without faltering as long as the Japanese economy kept growing.

A slower growth economy thus was perceived as a crisis of major proportions. It would result in a further fall in the trading firms' small profit margins. It would also mean that debt servicing (especially during periods of high interest rates) would become a heavy financial burden, and that defaults on credits and loans extended by the *sogo shosha* would have a larger negative impact. The question of efficiency thus loomed large. It was not the first time the huge trading companies emphasized efficiency, but the stress on efficiency (or rationalization as it is called in Japan) was never more urgent or given greater emphasis by top management than in 1974 and 1975.

The actions taken by the Mitsubishi Corporation and Mitsui & Co. serve as good illustrations. On October 16, 1975, President Bunichiro Tanabe of the Mitsubishi Corporation issued a statement, "On Coping with a Low Growth Era," in which he proposed a seven-point rationalization plan to cope with the continuing drop in the firm's basic business activities and the alarming rise in the number of uncollectable receivables. The rationalization plan called for personnel efficiency, capital efficiency, business transactions efficiency, active business development, the strengthening of corporate internal control functions, the strengthening of corporate staff functions, and the reduction of operating costs. The Management Planning Office worked out detailed plans for flexible companywide implementation of these seven points. The Credit Department was expanded substantially. An audit team was created and placed under the direct jurisdiction of each product division manager. The "Seven Point Rationalization Plan" and follow-up led to the issuing by Mitsubishi Corporation of an "Eight Point Comprehensive Basic Plan" on April 1, 1976, that included detailed plans for profits, capital, personnel, product, investment, prospects of core products, basic policy toward crucial geographic areas, and new business investment.

At Mitsui & Co., President Yoshizo Ikeda issued an urgent message on April 8, 1974, "On Our Firm's Basic Posture," explaining Mitsui's long-term policy. It had been debated and approved earlier at a conference of presidents of three overseas regional headquarters—Mitsui & Co. (U.S.A.), Inc.; Mitsui & Co. (Europe); and Mitsui & Co. (Australia). The message, addressed to the general managers of all divisions, departments, and offices in Japan and around the world, dealt with what President Ikeda called "change in Mitsui's basic policy and posture." It called for a radical transformation of the employees' work posture and orientation in face of the critically changed environment. The message enunciated the following new long-term policies: (1) acceleration of an earlier policy to become a global enterprise; (2) qualitative change in domestic business—shifting from emphasis on quantity to quality, specifically, from emphasis on sales volume to management efficiency and profits; (3) observation of Mitsui's Code of Behavior and cooperation with the government's price policy; and (4) revision of the employee evaluation system.[7]

Expanding the Marketing of High-Technology Industrial Products, Plants, and Know-how

The expected decline in the share of intermediate products in Japan's total production and the predicted growth of the knowledge-intensive industries was another domestic development with a direct negative impact on the general trading companies. Their strength had been in business related to high-volume transactions of raw materials and intermediate products. The *sogo shosha*'s response was to expand the handling of package deals, such as exports of large industrial plants on a turnkey basis as well as to expand involvement in such future growth industries as (1) the knowledge industry, (2) the resource and energy development industry, (3) the environmental industry, (4) the health and leisure industry, and (5) the high-technology industry.

The *sogo shosha* are also sparing no efforts in expanding their sales of plants in foreign markets. They are using even more fully than in the past their global information networks, their contacts with officials of importing countries, their ability to coordinate and organize Japanese and foreign plant manufacturers and engineering firms, their skill at setting up multinational financial consortia, their risk assumption capabilities, and their marketing capacities once the exported plants are in production.

Closely related is the *sogo shosha*'s conscious determination to move beyond the trading of goods into the exchange of capital, softwares, and management know-how. Symbolic of this was Mitsui & Co.'s formal revision of its Articles of Incorporation in May 1975 to add "the acquisition, planning, safekeeping, use, disposal, and agency of industrial rights, know-how, systems technologies and other softwares" as Mitsui's new line of business.

Acceleration of Global Reach

The *sogo shosha*'s international response to the radically altered environment was to accelerate implementation of the decision made in the early 1970s to become global enterprises. In 1970 C. Itoh & Co. adopted a ten-year long-term plan to become "a diversified and integrated world enterprise" (*Sekaiteki takaku sogo kigyo*) by 1980. In 1971 the Mitsubishi Corporation adopted "becoming a multinational enterprise" as its goal for the 1970s.[8] Mitsui & Co. made a similar decision. In September 1972 Hiroshi Ohara, general manager of the Corporate Planning Office (an office in the Corporate Planning Division which was upgraded to a group later) declared in a draft policy sent to the heads of all overseas offices and later adopted that "the 1970s is a decade in which Mitsui ought to actively pursue a global strategy with aim toward becoming a mature capital company." In announcing Mitsui & Co.'s long-term plan on April 8, 1974, President Ikeda declared that "the goal of growing out of a Japanese firm into a world enterprise . . . should be speeded up in response to the changed domestic, international, and corporate environment." Ikeda set as the objective raising the share of exports, imports, and third-country trade in Mitsui & Co.'s total sales from 43.6 to 60 percent by spring 1977.

A year and a half earlier a draft policy (entitled "Greater Efforts Toward Setting Up an Autonomous and Independent Management System Requested") sent out by General Manager Ohara recommended the following steps: (1) local (i.e., host-country) incorporation of overseas branches as a way of participating in the local economy; (2) increasing the capital stock of the locally incorporated subsidiaries as a step toward autonomy; (3) acquisition of stocks of large, influential host-country corporations, establishment of joint ventures with them, and greater retaining of earnings; (4) promotion of business relations with many enterprises, selecting those first-class firms in growth industries as targets, but not excluding transportation, insurance, finance, and other service industries; (5) looking out for investment, loans, and joint venture opportunities in any trading of goods; (6) promotion of business dealings with the socialist states; and (7) active use of U.S. capital. Ohara also recommended autonomy and independence for Mitsui & Co.'s overseas offices. More important, he proposed a shift from Japan-oriented and Japan-led offices to global orientation through greater participation in the host country's economy by exchange of products as well as of capital, technology, and labor.

Mitsui President Ikeda advocated the speedup of the globalization plan by focusing on four specific steps. First, control over foreign investments and extension of loans was to be transferred to overseas offices. Overseas offices would assume control in these two areas with the following exceptions: (1) natural resource development projects; (2) investments and loans exceeding $5 million; (3) projects that require more than five years to become profitable; (4) cases involving countries where government overseas investment insurance is not applicable; (5) cases where institutional financing is required from the total company point of view; (6) cases involving the Middle East, Africa, and Southeast Asia; and (7) investments and extension of loans cases that overseas incorporated subsidiaries cannot extend at their own risk and account but judge worthy of approval on the home office's risk and account. Second, Ikeda recommended a step-by-step transfer of existing joint ventures to the accounts of overseas incorporated subsidiaries, with the transfer of joint ventures of good record to be achieved in three years. Third, he proposed the establishment and strengthening of the primary control system of joint ventures by incorporated subsidiaries overseas and speeding up, through the establishment of fund-raising bases, of the plan to grant autonomy to overseas offices. Finally, he recommended backup (personnel, financial, etc.) by domestic divisions and offices of the plan for global reach.

Other firms made similar decisions to speed up their plans to go global. C. Itoh & Co., for example, convened the Management Conference (its supreme policymaking body consisting of managing directors and up) in early December 1974 to discuss "Implementation of the Internationalization Strategy" for two days. This was immediately followed by a three-day conference on "Comprehensive Overseas Policy" for general managers of regional headquarters in Asia, Oceania, the Middle East, Western

Europe, Africa, North America, and Latin America. The Management Conference decided that internationalization would be the long-term goal of the firm. This goal should be implemented by four "pillars:" overseas natural resource development, joint ventures abroad, third-country trade, and expanded business with foreign-based multinational enterprises.

Global Management, Supply, Marketing, Finance, and Investment

It is difficult for an outsider to get a total picture of how the firms are trying to achieve their long-term goals of internationalization. One gets bits and pieces from their press releases and replies to questionnaires, but not an integrated view of how their long-term goals, mid-term goals, strategies (functional, product, and geographic), and tactical actions interrelate and mesh. President Ikeda's message of April 1974 seemed to have set raising international business in the firm's total sales from about 44 to 60 percent by spring 1977 as Mitsui & Co.'s intermediate goal and the gradual grant of autonomy to overseas offices and other steps as a strategy to attain the mid-term goal, but nowhere was it clearly stated. C. Itoh & Co.'s "four pillars" could be interpreted as mid-term goals or as strategies. The distinction between goals and strategies and between the "four pillars" seemed unclear. Most Japanese firms remain as secretive as their European counterparts and are quite unlike the relatively open American firms. Internal documents are rarely available to outsiders. Thus, the following picture is incomplete and imperfect at best.

Becoming global enterprises required more than the possession of global supply and marketing networks and of global information and communications networks, which they already possessed by the late 1960s. A radical shift from past Japanese orientation to global orientation was necessary at all levels from top management to lower-level managers. This has occurred in at least four functional areas: management, supply and marketing, financing, and investment. Each will be discussed briefly.

The *sogo shosha* have chosen a global management system, although some variations exist among the firms. The Mitsubishi Corporation, which has long emphasized vertical organizational control, has greatly strengthened corporate staff functions, head office coordination, and control of domestic and overseas affiliates with regard to goals and strategies affecting the firm as a whole. But it has also sought to strengthen its offices abroad, especially regional headquarters such as Mitsubishi International in New York, and to grant them gradual autonomy in operational matters that affect them.

Mitsui & Co., where domestic and overseas offices rather than product divisions have long formed its profit centers, took a different path, although arriving at a global management system quite similar to that of Mitsubishi Corporation. First, it granted gradual but considerable autonomy to overseas offices. Then, in August 1974, it established three regional "home offices" (*honsha*) abroad: the North American home office with jurisdiction over North, Central, and South America; the European home office with jurisdiction over Western Europe and Africa; and the Oceania home office with jurisdiction over Australia and New Zealand. The three overseas home offices have been given considerable autonomy and authority to manage business of the region and countries under their respective jurisdictions. In 1975 and 1976 corporate staff functions were greatly strengthened to ensure tighter global coordination and control of functions, products, projects, and geographic areas.

The general trading companies also chose global supply, marketing, and project participation. The goal was to secure supplies of raw materials, manufactures, equipment, and technology anywhere in the world (worldwide sourcing) and to supply goods and services first to their affiliates anywhere in the world, then to Japanese manufacturers anywhere in the world, and finally to firms or governments of any nation. Similar goals and policies applied to marketing, financing, and project organization. Global supply and marketing was a radical shift; the expansion of third-country trade, to which all general trading companies aspired, was its concrete manifestation.

The general trading companies were entirely justified in 1973 in viewing the expansion of third-country trade as the road to becoming global enterprises. They had already built up global commercial networks staffed by thousands of managers sent from the head office and supported by extensive information-gathering

Table 7.3 Trading Activities of Japanese Firms in the United States, FY 1970 and FY 1973[a]

	FY 1970				FY 1973			
	Import from Japan	Export to Japan	Domestic trade in U.S.	Third-country trade	Total	Import from Japan	Export to Japan	Domestic trade in U.S.	Third-country trade	Total
Total business	5,340 (100.0%)	5,150 (100.0%)	1,610 (100.0%)	646 (100.0%)	12,746 (100.0%)	7,531 (100.0%)	5,295 (100.0%)	1,855 (100.0%)	2,531 (100.0%)	17,212 (100.0%)
Wholesalers'/retailers' share	4,665 (87.4%)	4,433 (86.1%)	450 (27.9%)	643 (99.5%)	10,190 (79.9%)	5,574 (74.0%)	5,168 (97.6%)	1,745 (94.1%)	2,521 (99.8%)	15,012 (87.2%)
Manufacturers' share	665 (12.5%)	714 (13.9%)	957 (59.5%)	3 (0.5%)	2,340 (18.4%)	1,940 (25.8%)	113 (2.1%)	108 (5.8%)	5 (0.2%)	2,166 (12.6%)
Activity as percentage of company business:										
Wholesalers/retailers	45.8	43.5	4.4	6.3	100.0	37.1	34.4	11.6	16.8	100.0
Manufacturers	28.8	30.5	40.9	0.1	100.0	89.5	5.2	5.0	0.3	100.0

Source: Compiled from Tsusho Sangyosho (MITI), *1971 Boeki gyotai tokeihyo* (1971 Foreign Trade Statistics by Industries) (Tokyo: Tsusho Sangyo Chosakai, 1971), pp. 156-171, and *1974 Boeki gyotai tokeihyo*, pp. 158-173.

Note: Figures do not add to 100% because of exclusion of figures for department stores and "others" and because of rounding. See footnote 3 on p. 21 on the double accounting system of Japan's foreign trade transactions used in MITI's *Boeki gyotai tokeihyo*.

[a] In thousands of dollars.

Table 7.4 Trading Activities of Japanese Firms in Taiwan, FY 1970 and FY 1973[a]

	FY 1970				FY 1973			
	Import from Japan	Export to Japan	Domestic trade in Taiwan	Third-country trade	Total	Import from Japan	Export to Japan	Domestic trade in Taiwan	Third-country trade	Total
Total business	272,859 (100.0%)	240,444 (100.0%)	40,308 (100.0%)	247,016 (100.0%)	800,627 (100.0%)	557,024 (100.0%)	220,796 (100.0%)	44,474 (100.0%)	517,050 (100.0%)	1,339,344 (100.0%)
Wholesalers'/retailers' share	239,466 (87.8%)	238,609 (99.2%)	5,905 (14.6%)	243,688 (98.7%)	727,668 (90.9%)	510,309 (91.6%)	204,122 (92.4%)	27,618 (62.1%)	485,670 (93.9%)	1,227,719 (100.0%)
Manufacturers' share	33,386 (12.2%)	1,835 (0.8%)	34,403 (85.4%)	3,328 (1.3%)	72,952 (9.1%)	46,222 (8.3%)	16,669 (7.6%)	16,856 (37.9%)	31,380 (6.1%)	111,127 (100.0%)
Activity as percentage of company business:										
Wholesalers/retailers	32.9	32.8	0.8	33.5	100.0	41.6	16.6	2.2	39.6	100.0
Manufacturers	45.8	2.5	47.2	4.6	100.0	41.6	15.0	15.2	28.2	100.0

Source: Compiled from Tsusho Sangyosho (MITI), *1971 Boeki gyotai tokeihyo* (1971 Foreign Trade Statistics by Industries) (Tokyo: Tsusho Sangyo Chosakai, 1971), pp. 156-171, and *1974 Boeki gyotai tokeihyo*, pp. 158-173.

Note: Figures do not add to 100% because of exclusion of figures for department stores and "others" and because of rounding. See footnote 3 on p. 21 on the double accounting system of Japan's foreign trade transactions used in MITI's *Boeki gyotai tokeihyo*.

[a] In thousands of dollars.

systems and highly advanced communications systems. No Japanese manufacturing or financial multinational could match these. They had also long been engaged in third-country trade. More important, their overseas offices enjoyed a near monopoly of multinational trade. Table 7.3 shows that the U.S. offices of all trading companies (not just the big ten, although dominated by them) had a 99.8 percent share of third-country trade conducted by the U.S. offices of Japanese firms during fiscal 1973 ended March 31, 1974, and that those of Japanese manufacturers were responsible for only 0.2 percent. As Table 7.4 shows, the same was true for third-country trade handled by Japanese firms in Taiwan, although the share of manufacturers was larger.

The *sogo shosha* chose global financing, global investment, and global extension of financial services. Global reach requires substantial financial resources to finance operations, to provide financial services to suppliers and customers, and to finance joint ventures and investments in various huge natural resource development projects. They decided to secure financial resources anywhere and from any sources in the world (although not from the communist bloc in the foreseeable future) when they were available at competitive terms, whether the resources be in the U.S., Western Europe, or the petrodollar-rich countries of the Middle East. Similarly, they decided to invest and to extend financial services to suppliers and customers anywhere in the world. In sum, a global orientation meant viewing the whole world as a single production, supply and marketing, financing, and investment unit.

Support Actions for Global Reach

The general trading companies took a series of significant, closely interrelated actions to support the goal of becoming global enterprises. The first was to strengthen the headquarters' global coordination and control functions, as described above. The second was to upgrade and strengthen the overseas offices, especially the regional headquarters established in the early 1970s. Top managers were appointed to head the major overseas regional headquarters. During 1974 the Mitsubishi Corporation appointed Executive Vice President Shunkichi Nishida to head

Mitsubishi International. Mitsui Executive Vice President T. Goto was appointed to head Mitsui & Co. (U.S.A.) Inc. These were epochmaking actions, since home office managing directors had previously headed North American operations and, unlike U.S. firms, the trading companies had only a few executive vice presidents. Nissho-Iwai Co. and the Marubeni Corporation followed with the appointment of Executive Vice Presidents Mitsuo Ueda and Tachita Kawasaki to head their respective North American headquarters.

Another action was to expand the number of host country incorporated subsidiaries (*genchi hojin*)—branch offices converted into host country corporations. The big six alone converted forty-two branch offices into host country corporations between March 1971 and March 1976.[9] During fiscal 1975 Kanematsu Gosho, Ltd., Nissho-Iwai Co., Mitsui & Co., Nichimen Company, and the Mitsubishi Corporation upgraded their branch offices in Hong Kong to local corporations. Nichimen Company also converted its London branch into a British corporation.

Equally important, action was taken to expand the financial resources of major overseas affiliates, especially in the United States and Western Europe. Capital stock of Mitsubishi International Corporation was increased from $75 million in March 1974 to $125 million by March 1976; that of Mitsui & Co. (U.S.A.) Inc. from $65 million in March 1974 to $92.3 million by March 1975 and to $133 million by March 1976; that of C. Itoh & Co. (America) Inc. from $26 million in March 1973 to $50 million by March 1974 and to $78 million by March 1976; that of Sumitomo Shoji America, Inc., from $20 million in March 1974 to $52.5 million by March 1976; and that of Nichimen Co., Inc. (the U.S. affiliate of Nichimen Company, Limited) from $29 million in March 1973 to $33 million by March 1975 and to $36 million by March 1976. By March 1976 capital stock of the U.S. affiliates of the ten firms, the largest and most important among the firms' overseas affiliates, either equaled or surpassed by a slight margin that of the Japan head offices.

The *sogo shosha* also established specialized supply, distribution, and project bases aimed at global sourcing and marketing and at the expansion of third-country trade and host country domestic trade. Mitsui & Co. established two wholly owned

Table 7.5 Capital Stock of the Six General Trading Companies' North American Headquarters, March 1971–March 1976[a]

	1971	1972	1973	1974	1975	1976
Mitsubishi Corporation	33	33	75	75	75	125
Mitsui & Co.	33	50	60	65	92	133
Marubeni Corporation	16	25	50	50	75	77
C. Itoh & Co.	16	25	26	50	53	78
Sumitomo Shoji	10	20	20	20	31	53
Nissho-Iwai Co.	—	—	30	30	33	35

Source: Financial reports of the general trading companies, various years.
Note: Data are as of March 31.
[a] In millions of dollars.

international procurement and service corporations (International Procurement and Service Corporation in Luxemburg and International Procurement and Service America, Inc.) to collect information, secure orders, and procure materials and equipment from all over the world for clients. The Mitsubishi Corporation established the wholly owned Europe Project Coordinator Center in London for similar purposes. C. Itoh & Co. and the Marubeni Corporation did likewise. Toyomenka Kaisha and Kanematsu Gosho, Ltd., however, established procurement corporations on a joint venture basis for promoting trade and investments in the Arab world. The former set up in 1976 Arab-Japanese International Promotion Co., a joint venture with the Arab International Bank, an investment bank established by five Arab governments (Egypt, Libya, Abu Dubai, Oman, and Qatar).

Other specialized channels established for the expansion of global trade included two petroleum companies by C. Itoh & Co. in 1975 (C. Itoh International Petroleum in the United States and the Dragon Petroleum Trading Co. in Britain). Mitsui & Co. established Pacific Resources, Inc., in the U.S. in 1975 to control its tuna fishing bases in the Indian Ocean and South Pacific and its two canning factories and one sales company in America that process and market tuna imported from the two bases and other areas. All the firms established numerous sales companies, warehousing and transportation companies, distribution centers, textile and food processing companies, steel fabrication centers, and grain centers in many parts of the world, either on a wholly owned or joint venture basis.

The *sogo shosha* adopted management systems better suited to global business. Specific measures, not all of which have been implemented, include: (1) a step-by-step grant of autonomy to overseas headquarters; (2) the gradual transfer of authority, both staff and line, to—and the requirement of greater accountability and risk from—presidents of overseas regional headquarters; (3) gradual delegation of authority from regional headquarters to overseas branch offices and subsidiaries; (4) employment of foreign personnel, with gradual increase in their involvement in middle-level management; (5) reduction in the number and stay of Japanese employees and managers abroad, and their replacement by foreign employees as much as possible; (6) a shift from past emphasis on volume transactions to management efficiency and earnings and from high leverage to increase of equity capital; and (7) adoption of a more analytic and strategic approach to business ventures.

Finally, the *sogo shosha* expanded the raising and utilization of funds abroad in line with the new policy of procuring financial resources on a global basis. An objective in doubling and tripling capital stock of the firms' major regional headquarters abroad since 1974, among others, has been to strengthen the credit standing of these major commercial bases to enable them to raise large capital independently at their own risk without the backup of the Japan head office.

To achieve this, the *sogo shosha* stepped up their long-term borrowing in the overseas capital markets since 1974, mostly in Western Europe and the United States but also in the Middle East. They have used both ordinary and convertible debentures. For operations and trading purposes they have expanded the utilization of other vehicles, such as borrowings from foreign commercial banks and the issuing of commercial papers. Noteworthy is the expanded use of special U.S. and European financing facilities such as the U.S. Export-Import Bank and the British Export Credit Guarantee Department.

Notes

1. *Business Week*, July 7, 1975, p. 45.
2. Sangyo Kozo Shingikai, *Sangyo kozo no choki bijon* (The Industrial Structure: A Long-Term Vision) (Tokyo: Tsusho Sangyo Chosa kai, 1974), p. 12; also the 1976 edition, p. 4.
3. Ibid. (1974), pp. 36, 51-54.
4. Alexander K. Young, "Internationalization of the Japanese General Trading Companies," *Columbia Journal of World Business*, IX, 9 (Spring 1974), p. 82.
5. One example of a more specific code of behavior is Mitsui & Co.'s "Mitsui Bussan kodo kijun yoko," issued in August 1973.
6. Nihon Boekikai, "Kosei Torihiki Iinkai no 'sogo shosha ni kansuru dainikai chosa hokoku' ni tsuite" (On the Fair Trade Commission's Second Investigation of General Trading Companies) (Tokyo: February 6, 1975), p. 28.
7. Qualitative change in domestic business meant a reexamination and gradual abandoning of the various forms of low-profit transactions (such as credit sales and purchases that yield low profit, small-profit transactions conducted for the sake of expanding sales volume, numerous small transactions, etc.) and emphasis on profits and profit ratio. It also involved the strengthening of the management system and financial position of affiliated firms, including their integration and write-offs if necessary, so as to reduce Mitsui's financial burden. The message asked for strict observation by employees of the Mitsui & Co.'s Code of Behavior adopted in August 1973 and for freezing the prices of general consumer goods by all divisions and offices in cooperation with the Japanese government control of spiraling inflation.

The existing employee evaluation system was changed to support the new policy emphasizing management efficiency and profits. The new policy removed the size of sales contracts and volume of realized transactions as employee evaluation criteria during the period of transition to when the goal of emphasizing quality is realized (i.e., from September 1974 to at least September 1977). It also removed the following as the basis of evaluation: lower profits due to streamlining of business and profit loss due to cooperation with government inflation control policy and other measures. The following were added to the employee evaluation criteria: (1) the strengthening of affiliates; (2) improvement of capital efficiency and profit ratios; and (3) contributions to society. (Yoshizo Ikeda, "Tosha kihon shisei ni tsuite," April 8, 1974.)

Preceding the issuing of the president's message, Mitsui & Co. had earlier (March 1, 1974) set up an Investment and Loans Committee (*Toyushi iinkai*) consisting of general managers of four important departments: corporate planning, finance, accounting, and credit. The committee was given two tasks: (1) prior evaluation of all investment and loan extension proposals by all line divisions before official submission for consideration and approval, and (2) establishment of companywide investment and loan extension standards. The committee issued a list of investment and loan extension standards in January 1975 that emphasized the following: (1) adequate investment returns in cases where Mitsui & Co. takes initiative and participates in management; (2) avoidance of overcommitment in manufacturers-led investments; (3) adequate returns in "simple investments;" and (4) strict screening and approval of loans according to the criteria of Mitsui & Co.'s functions and responsibilities, the safety of funds, the acquisition of commercial rights, profitability, and long-term plans of the line and office involved.

Mitsui & Co. also upgraded the Office of Affiliates Management to strengthen the management of domestic affiliates. More specific criteria and guidelines were also worked out by the greatly strengthened Corporate Planning Division to raise the efficiency of distribution, marketing, and other functions.

8. The new goal was recommended by a task force headed by Hiro Minagawa and approved by then President Chujiro Fujino.

9. Information and Research Department, Mitsui & Co., *Atarashii sogo shoshazo o motomete* (Seeking a New Image of General Trading Companies) (Tokyo: 1977), p. 85.

8
The *Sogo Shosha* in World Commerce

The efforts of the *sogo shosha* to become global businesses have already yielded impressive results. These achievements, substantial though they are, would have been even greater had there not been a worldwide recession in 1974-75 that lingered on into 1977 in the form of a sluggish Japanese economy. Chapter 8 examines in detail several aspects of the decision by the general trading companies to become global. It is in the context of this decision that the major challenges of the late 1970s are described and their implications for the present status and future prospects of the *sogo shosha* are drawn. The book concludes with a discussion of the meaning of power and of responsibility for the *sogo shosha*.

The Results of the Global Reach

This survey of the results of the *sogo shosha*'s effort to become global businesses will look at their position in world trade, third-country trade, the trading of industrial plants and equipment, the growth of United States affiliates, and their changing pattern of direct foreign investment.

Position in World Trade

The importance of the ten *sogo shosha* in world trade is striking. Their export and third-country transactions (customs clearance basis) during FY 1975 totaled $47 billion and amounted to 5.3 percent of world export trade (calendar year). Their international transactions (including imports) were larger than

Table 8.1 Consumption and Import Shares of Japan, the United States, and West Germany in the World's Major Primary Products, 1974 (percent)

	Japan		United States		West Germany	
	Consumption share	Import share	Consumption share	Import share	Consumption share	Import share
Meats	2.1	6.1	20.6	10.9	3.9	15.7
Wheat	1.6	9.1	6.6	0.1	2.5	2.9
Corn	2.7	16.3	30.1	0.1	1.2	6.9
Wool	4.1	17.2	2.6	1.3	1.1	5.0
Cotton	5.8	19.2	10.1	0.2	1.3	4.8
Iron ore	16.8	39.9	15.8	12.9	8.0	17.6
Copper	10.0	23.2	23.5	9.2	8.8	16.7
Lead	5.2	13.7	23.7	12.6	6.1	16.0
Zinc	11.4	15.6	19.7	24.2	6.5	12.5
Aluminium	9.3	11.1	37.0	14.6	6.3	15.9
Tin	14.0	21.0	22.2	27.6	6.5	10.2
Nickel	16.1	14.3	27.7	28.3	8.7	8.7
Coal	3.4	28.7	19.8	2.1	4.5	4.0
Crude oil	8.6	15.4	21.8	11.3	4.0	6.8
Natural gas	0.6	4.4	48.6	24.6	3.4	20.3

Source: Tsusho Sangyosho (MITI), *1976 Tsusho hakusho*, (1976 International Trade White Paper) (Tokyo: Okurasho, 1976), vol. 1, p. 278.

the foreign trade aggregates of most countries and were surpassed only by such major trading countries as the U.S., West Germany, Britain, France, Canada, and Italy.

The *sogo shosha* have significant weight in world raw materials trade because of their dominant position in Japan's huge imports of raw materials. Share of Japanese imports of major raw materials during 1974 ranged between 16 and 40 percent of the world's import trade: 29 percent of world coal trade, 23 percent of world copper trade, 40 percent of world iron ore trade, 17 percent of world wool trade, 19 percent of world cotton trade, and 16 percent of world corn trade. Because of the widely varied commodity classification standards employed by different trading firms and because of the other limitations on data discussed in Chapter 1, no exact estimates are possible. It should be recalled, however, that during FY 1975 ten *sogo shosha* dominated Japan's foodstuffs, chemical, and textile imports (81.3, 78.2, and 73.5 percent respectively) and had a majority share in Japan's imports of metal ores and fuel.

The share of Japan's steel exports in world steel trade during 1972 was 22 percent, while that of Japan's textile product exports in world textile trade in 1971 was 11.8 percent.[1] Again, we will recall that during FY 1975 the ten general trading companies were responsible for 81.8 percent of Japan's metals exports (much of which was steel).

Third-Country Trade

Third-country trade marks the difference between a global or multinational and a Japan-oriented trading company. A trading firm whose third-country transactions amount to 20 percent of its total trade can be considered a genuinely global trading company. Growth of this type of business has been the most important single specific target of all the *sogo shosha* since the early 1970s.

The growth of the *sogo shosha*'s third-country trade has been impressive. Total third-country trade of the big ten amounted to only $35 million in FY 1956. It grew steadily each year, broke the $1-billion mark in FY 1967, and rose to $2.7 billion by the end of FY 1970. The most striking growth, however, came after the oil crisis of 1973: from $6.4 billion during FY 1972 to $10.9 billion by

Figure 8.1 Third-country trade of the ten general trading companies, FY 1956–FY 1976

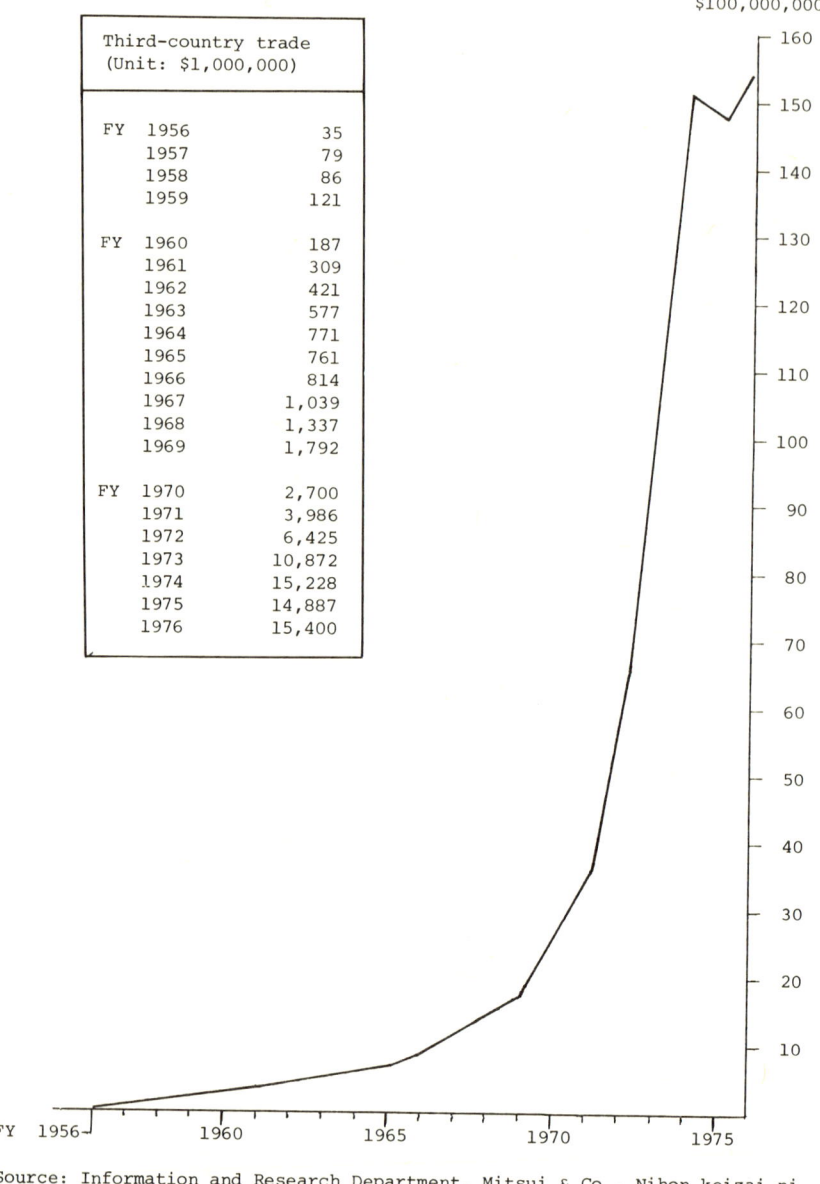

Source: Information and Research Department, Mitsui & Co., Nihon keizai ni okeru shosha no yakuwari: genjo to tenbo (Tokyo: Mitsui & Co., 1976), p. 15.

Table 8.2 Third-Country Trade of the Ten General Trading Companies, March 1971–March 1977 (volume and share in total transactions, six months ended March 31)

	1971		1972		1973		1974		1975		1976[a]		1977[a]	
	Million Yen	Percent	Million Yen	Percent	Million Yen	Percent	Million Yen	Percent	Million Yen	Percent	Million Yen	Percent	Million Yen	Percent
Mitsubishi Corporation	985	4.6	1,132	5.1	2,080	7.5	2,490	6.0	3,278	7.1	6,685	7.3	6,277	6.5
Mitsui & Co.	721	3.8	831	4.0	1,726	6.5	2,737	7.0	4,408	10.3	5,917	7.5	6,483	7.2
Marubeni Corporation	383	2.7	508	3.5	966	5.3	1,314	5.3	2,112	7.6	6,265	10.9	8,338	12.9
C. Itoh & Co.	892	6.8	1,103	8.0	1,182	6.9	1,312	5.5	1,910	7.2	4,051	7.2	6,904	10.8
Sumitomo Shoji	302	3.5	571	5.7	1,835	14.1	2,329	10.7	2,340	9.0	5,586	10.2	3,302	5.7
Nissho-Iwai Co.	727	8.0	706	7.0	1,374	11.0	1,838	10.0	1,857	9.0	3,860	9.7	4,806	10.6
Toyomenka	534	7.7	610	8.9	614	7.4	1,041	9.9	2,007	17.0	4,796	20.0	4,644	18.4
Kanematsu Gosho	332	7.7	368	7.4	350	5.4	999	9.6	1,369	11.8	2,290	9.9	1,848	8.0
Ataka & Co.	250	5.6	301	6.3	636	9.8	1,092	11.9	1,631	15.7	3,024	15.5	818	5.5
Nichimen Company	311	7.0	487	10.5	1,287	19.6	1,861	21.0	2,172	21.0	2,008	11.9	1,343	7.4
Share average of the ten firms	5,437	5.7	6,617	6.6	12,050	9.3	17,013	10.7	23,084	11.6	44,483	9.6	44,762	9.0

Source: Compiled from financial statements of the firms.
[a] Volume and share in total transactions, twelve months ended March 31.

Table 8.3   Overseas Trade (Third-Country and Overseas Domestic Trade) of the Ten General Trading Companies by Commodities (fiscal six months ended March 31, 1971, vs. fiscal six months ended March 31, 1974)

	Fuel		Metals		Machinery	
	100 million Yen	Percent	100 million Yen	Percent	100 million Yen	Percent
Mitsubishi Corp.						
1971	39	4.0	44	4.5	30	3.0
1974	261	10.5	365	14.6	52	2.1
Mitsui & Co.						
1971	—	—	70	9.7	37	5.2
1974	—	—	282	10.3	284	10.4
Marubeni Corp.						
1971	—	—	12	—	19	—
1974	—	—	205	15.6	35	2.7
C. Itoh & Co.						
1971	—	—	59	—	36	—
1974	—	—	92	7.0	90	6.9
Sumitomo Shoji						
1971	—	—	147	48.7	20	6.6
1974	—	—	321	13.8	210	9.0
Nissho-Iwai Co.						
1971	—	—	218	—	167	—
1974	—	—	382	20.8	366	19.9
Toyomenka						
1971	—	—	—	—	—	—
1974	—	—	180	17.3	181	17.4
Kanematsu Gosho						
1971	—	—	—	—	—	—
1974	29	2.9	230	23.0	95	9.6
Ataka & Co.						
1971	—	—	—	—	—	—
1974	—	—	330	30.2	39	3.6
Nichimen Company						
1971	—	—	27	—	12	—
1974	—	—	354	19.0	239	12.8

Source: Compiled from financial statements of the ten general trading companies for March 31, 1971, and March 31, 1974.

Note: See footnote 3 on p. 20 on the various commodities systems used by the general trading companies.

Food		Textile		Chemicals		Wood & other materials		Total
100 million Yen	Percent	100 million Yen	Percent	100 million Yen	Percent	100 million Yen	Percent	100 million Yen
612	62.1	68	6.9	44	4.5	148	15.0	985
1,330	53.4	118	4.8	167	6.7	197	7.9	2,490
332	46.0	128	17.8	29	4.1	124	17.2	721
1,367	49.9	172	6.3	192	7.0	441	16.1	2,737
195	–	94	–	53	–	10	–	–
334	25.4	193	14.7	457	34.8	90	6.9	1,314
353	–	267	–	68	–	109	–	892
292	22.3	543	41.4	189	14.4	106	8.1	1,312
41	13.5	3	1.0	63	20.8	28	9.4	302
956	41.0	124	5.3	500	21.5	218	9.4	2,329
119	–	63	–	–	–	160	–	727
601	32.7	110	6.0	–	–	378	20.6	1,838
–	–	–	–	–	–	–	–	–
172	16.5	295	28.3	94	9.1	112	10.7	1,041
	–	98	29.6	–	–	–	–	332
370	37.0	199	19.9	9	0.9	67	6.7	999
–	–	–	–	–	–	–	–	–
–	–	189	17.3	453	41.5	81	7.4	1,092
202	–	35	–	13	–	22	–	311
816	43.9	161	8.7	114	6.1	177	9.5	1,861

the end of FY 1973, and to a staggering $15.2 billion by the end of FY 1974, the year the trading companies launched a concerted drive for expansion. There was a slight decline during FY 1975 and a small increase during FY 1976 because of the global recession and the continuing sluggishness of the world economy. Third-country trade of the ten firms stood at $15.4 billion during FY 1976.

The share of third-country trade in the trading companies' total transactions has grown at an equally impressive rate since the early 1970s. The ten firms' average was 5.7 percent as of March 1971. It began to rise sharply: 6.6 percent by March 1972, 9.3 percent by March 1973, 10.7 percent by March 1974 (the first settlement term after the oil crisis), and 11.6 percent by March 1975. It dropped to 9.6 percent by March 1976 and to 9 percent by March 1977 because of the slow recovery of the world economy.

Even more striking has been the rapid growth achieved by a few individual firms. The Marubeni Corporation's third-country trade and its share in total transactions rose from less than 3 percent during FY 1971 to about 13 percent during FY 1976. Toyomenka Kaisha's rose from about 9 to 18 percent, the best among the ten firms in terms of percentage share, during the same period. Nichimen Company's rose to 22 percent during fiscal six months ended March 1974 but then dropped to 7.4 percent in March 1977.

The ten firms' third-country trade amounting to over $15 billion, while constituting only 9 percent of total transactions, is a very sizable trade indeed. It is larger than the foreign trade of many nations, including that of the People's Republic of China.

During the six months ended March 1974 the ten firms had third-country foodstuffs trade of more than $2 billion, a substantial part of it U.S. grains to other parts of the world; third-country-metals trade amounting to close to $1 billion; third-country chemicals and fuel trade amounting to over $800 million; and third-country textile trade amounting to over $700 million. Foodstuffs and metals remain the largest items in the *sogo shosha*'s third-country trade. The firms have, however, stepped up their efforts to increase third-country trading of machinery required in exports of industrial plants and equipment, and of energy.

Table 8.4 Share of the Ten General Trading Companies in Japan's Plant Exports, 1966-1974 (contract basis)[a]

	(A) Japan's total	(B) Contracts by ten general trading companies	Share of B in A (percent)
Fiscal year 1966	260	229	88.1
Fiscal year 1967	519	497	95.8
Fiscal year 1968	367	332	90.5
Fiscal year 1969	567	491	86.6
Fiscal year 1970	827	620	75.0
Fiscal year 1971	1,047	738	70.5
Fiscal year 1972	829	507	61.2
Calendar year 1973	1,935	1,331	68.8
Calendar year 1974	2,463	2,454	99.6

Source: Information and Research Department, Mitsui & Co., *Nihon keizai ni okeru shosha no yakuwari: genjo to tenbo* (The Role of Trading Companies in the Japanese Economy: Current State and Future Prospects) (Tokyo: Mitsui & Co., 1976), p. 13.

Trading of Industrial Plants and Equipment

The *sogo shosha*'s trade in industrial plants and equipment also has grown substantially in the past few years. During 1974, the year after the oil crisis, the *sogo shosha* increased their share of Japan's plant exports, acting mostly as agents and organizers-coordinators, from 68.8 percent to an unbelievable 99.6 percent.

The trading companies have long acted (and still act) as agents-organizers-coordinators of Japan's plant exports in close cooperation with Japanese plant manufacturers and three of the country's largest engineering firms (Toyo Engineering Corp., Nikki, and Chiyoda Chemical Engineering and Construction). In the last few years, however, they have also consciously aimed at expanding joint plant trade with large non-Japanese plant manufacturers and engineering firms. For example, in 1977 the Nissho-Iwai Co. acted as the procurement agent for the purchase of about $200 million worth of equipment, about half of the equipment required, for the well-known U.S. engineering firm Pullman Kellogg in one of the latter's LNG plant exports to

Algeria. In 1975, C. Itoh & Co. organized an international consortium of C. Itoh & Co., Sasakura Engineering of Japan, and Brown Boveri of West Germany, and won a bid to construct a 50-billion-Yen desalinization plant in Saudi Arabia. Nichimen Company has obtained an order to export, with the Flour Corporation of California and Japan Steel Works of Japan, a 73-billion-Yen LPG plant to the Soviet Union.

Perhaps the most unusual example was the contract Toyomenka Kaisha signed with Rumanian officials in 1977 as prime contractor to export a pyrolysis furnace for an ethylene plant, using the engineering know-how of Head Research Corporation, a subsidiary of Pullman Kellogg. As prime contractor, Toyomenka Kaisha assumed responsibility to procure the necessary equipment, construct the plant, and provide operating instructions to its Rumanian manager. This represents a new strategy designed to strengthen the position of the trading company vis-à-vis plant manufacturers and engineering firms. The other trading companies will surely follow Toyomenka Kaisha's example.

Growth of U.S. Affiliates

Overseas affiliates (majority-owned subsidiaries and minority-owned related firms according to the Japan Fair Trade Commission's definition) of the trading companies have grown tremendously in the past few years, although their development has been somewhat slowed by the global recession following the oil crisis and the continuing sluggishness of the world economy. Their American affiliates, the largest of the firms' foreign affiliates, may be cited as examples.

The U.S. affiliates, whose headquarters are all located at the choicest and most prestigious sites in midtown New York or at the World Trade Center in lower Manhattan, have become global enterprises in their own right. As of early 1977, their assets ranged from several hundred million dollars to more than one billion dollars each, while shareholders' equity ranged from more than $38 million to about $160 million. The largest were Mitsubishi International Corporation and Mitsui & Co. (U.S.A.), Inc. Thanks to substantially strengthened financial positions during the past several years, Mitsubishi International, Mitsui & Co. (U.S.A.), and a few other firms can now issue commercial papers in their own right without guarantees of the parent company. Furthermore, the commercial papers of a number of firms have been given top ratings by Standard & Poor's and by Moody's. Mitsubishi International became the first affiliate of a Japanese firm to be given the top A-1 rating on its commercial papers by Standard & Poor's.

The *sogo shosha*'s American affiliates enjoy extensive business relations (trading, financing, joint venture, etc.) with many American firms large and small. For example, Sumitomo Shoji America, Inc., has more than 10,000 American customers, including about half of the top 200 on the *Fortune* list of 500 leading industries.

They have all become multibillion dollar traders. No precise comparison of the American affiliates of the six largest firms is possible because of differences in settlement periods and in methods of classifying types of business. Their annual transactions during 1976 ranged from more than $2 billion (Sumitomo Shoji America) to about $7 billion (Mitsubishi International). The U.S. affiliates of the big six had total sales amounting to about $24 billion during 1976, a growth of about $9 billion over 1973. Despite the substantial decline in total transactions from the previous year, Mitsui & Co. (U.S.A.) had the largest net income during 1976, $12 million.

Trade with Japan (much of it with parent firms) remains the largest component of total transactions: 47 percent (contract sales basis) for Mitsui & Co. (U.S.A.) and about 74 percent for C. Itoh & Co. (America), Inc. The weight of domestic transactions (i.e., transactions in the domestic American market) in total transactions has grown steadily, however, from an average of about 1 percent in 1971 to about 2 percent in 1976. This remains small in percentage share but not in absolute values, $111 million for Mitsui & Co. (U.S.A.), contract sales basis, and $113 million for C. Itoh & Co. (America). Approximately two-thirds of C. Itoh & Co. (America)'s domestic trade in the U.S. was in energy.

The weight of C. Itoh & Co. (America)'s third-country trade rose from about one-seventh to close to one-quarter of total transactions (15 to 23 percent). Mitsui & Co. (U.S.A.)'s saw an even larger growth, attaining about two-fifths of total transactions (contract sales basis) or $1.7 billion during 1976. Nissho-Iwai

Table 8.5 Sales, Assets, Income, and Equity of American Affiliates of Six General Trading Companies, 1973-1976 ($ millions)

	Mitsubishi International[a]	Mitsui & Co. (U.S.A.)[a]	Marubeni American[b]	C. Itoh & Co. (America)[c]	Sumitomo Shoji America[b]	Nissho-Iwai American[c]	Total
Gross sales							
1973	4,306	3,298	3,257[d]	474	1,530[d]	1,714	14,579
1976	6,821	3,929	4,634[e]	3,239	2,659[e]	2,526	23,808
Gross profits							
1973	48	n.a.	99	46	51	47	
1976	77	85	95	102	55	48	462
Net income							
1973	5.5	8.1	4.0	2.8	3.1	3.1	
1976	6.5	12.0	4.2	2.0	6.7	0.7	
Assets							
1973	778	826	1,098	2,245	366	447	3,760
1976	1,127	1,304	1,121	541	448	746	5,287
Shareholders' equity							
1973 capital stock	75.0	63.0	50.0[d]	50.0	20.9[d]	30.0	
1973 retained earnings	11.7	5.0	4.4	4.9	5.2	4.9	
1973 total	86.7	68.0	54.4	54.9	26.1	34.9	325
1976 capital stock	125.0	132.5	77.0[e]	78.1	53.4[e]	34.7	
1976 retained earnings	30.9	27.7	8.3	3.9	13.2	3.2	
1976 total	155.9	160.2	85.3	82.0	66.6	37.9	587.9

Source: Compiled from financial statements of the firms.
[a] Data for fiscal year ended September 30.
[b] Data for fiscal year ended December 31.
[c] March 1974 data.

Table 8.6 Transactions of C. Itoh & Co. (America) by Types of Business, 1974-1976 (year ended December 31)

	1974		1975		1976	
	Million dollars	*Percent*	*Million dollars*	*Percent*	*Million dollars*	*Percent*
Imports from Japan	590	18.1	619	20.5	833	25.7
Exports from U.S. to Japan	2,133	65.6	1,712	56.6	1,560	48.1
Third-country trade	496	15.3	576	19.1	735	22.7
Domestic U.S.A.	33	1.0	116	3.8	113	3.5
Total	3,251	100.0	3,022	100.0	3,241	100.0

Source: Corporate Planning Division, C. Itoh & Co. (America) Inc.

Table 8.7 Trade with Japan, C. Itoh & Co. (America) and Mitsui & Co. (U.S.A.), 1975-1976[a]

	C. Itoh & Co. (America) (year ended Dec. 31)			Mitsui & Co. (U.S.A.) (year ended Sept. 30; contract sales basis)		
	1974	*1975*	*1976*	*1974*	*1975*	*1976*
Exports from U.S. to Japan	2,133	1,711	1,560	—	1,380	1,302
Imports from Japan to U.S.	590	619	833	—	954	732
Contribution to U.S. trade surplus	1,543	1,092	757	—	429	570

Source: C. Itoh & Co. (America) and Mitsui & Co. (U.S.A.).
[a] In million dollars.

Table 8.8 Export and Import Transactions of Nissho-Iwai American Corporation and Mitsui & Co. (U.S.A.), 1975-1976[a]

	Nissho-Iwai American (year ended Dec. 31)		Mitsui & Co. (U.S.A.) (year ended Sept. 30; contract sales basis)	
	1975	1976	1975	1976
Exports	1,376	1,353	1,720	1,561
Imports	977	1,044	1,082	923
Contribution to U.S. trade surplus	399	306	638	638

Source: Nissho-Iwai American and Mitsui & Co. (U.S.A.)
[a] In million dollars.

American Corporation's grew from about one-eighth in 1975 to one-sixth in 1976.

The American affiliates of the *sogo shosha* dominated U.S. trade with Japan. According to the 1976 report of the U.S. Secretary of Commerce to the Congress, U.S. affiliates of Japanese trading companies accounted for 85 percent of U.S. exports to and 50 percent of imports from Japan during 1974.[2] Their much smaller share in Japanese imports resulted from direct import of

Table 8.9 Transactions of C. Itoh & Co. (America) by Types of Business and Commodities, Year Ended December 31, 1976

	Import from Japan			Export to Japan		
	Amount ($ thousands)	Share of division (percent)	Share of total (percent)	Amount ($ thousands)	Share of division (percent)	Share of total (percent)
Textile	135220	16.2	33.6	43017	2.8	10.7
Machinery	436732	52.4	81.2	52531	3.4	9.8
Metal and ore	216919	26.0	46.5	210463	13.5	45.1
Grain	4758	0.6	0.6	534311	34.2	67.7
General merchandise	19314	2.3	7.8	183204	11.7	73.8
Energy	1197	0.1	0.2	509022	32.6	69.1
Chemical	19977	2.4	28.6	33901	2.2	48.5
Construction				1	–	0.2
Special asset	-885	–	9.5	-6824	-0.4	73.3
Total	833233	100		1559625	100	

Source: C. Itoh & Co. (America)

Japanese automobiles and electronic equipment by U.S. subsidiaries of Japanese manufacturers.

No detailed breakdowns are available, but it can be safely assumed that U.S. affiliates of the ten *sogo shosha* dominate U.S. trade with Japan conducted by U.S. affiliates of all Japanese trading companies. A major part of their activity has been exporting U.S. grains and industrial raw materials and importing and marketing manufactured products from Japan.

Each U.S. affiliate of the six largest *sogo shosha* has accounted for between 1 and 2 percent of U.S. exports ($115.2 billion).[3] More important, each has consistently shipped more goods from the U.S. to Japan than they imported from Japan. They have thus contributed significantly to the U.S. trade surplus vis-à-vis Japan. The same is true for trade with other countries.

The ten trading companies together operate 100 headquarters and branch offices in the United States. Their U.S. affiliates employ more than 4,000 people of whom slightly over one-third are Japanese managers dispatched from parent companies; the remainder are hired locally. They own numerous affiliates (subsidiaries and related firms) in the United States. More important, they have changed the pattern and objectives of investments in the U.S. since the early 1970s from minority ownership aimed at gaining commercial rights (sales rights) without active management participation to total ownership aimed at management control and investment returns in addition to gaining commercial rights.

Third Country			Domestic			Total		
Amount ($ thousands)	Share of division (percent)	Share of total (percent)	Amount ($ thousands)	Share of division (percent)	Share of total (percent)	Amount ($ thousands)	Share of division (percent)	Share of total (percent)
211236	28.7	52.6	12405	10.9	3.1	401879	12.4	100
40993	5.6	7.6	7815	6.9	1.4	538071	16.6	100
29525	4.0	6.4	9536	8.4	2.0	466443	14.4	100
244873	33.3	31.0	5825	5.1	0.7	789767	24.3	100
41708	5.7	16.7	4123	3.6	1.7	248349	7.7	100
152115	20.7	20.7	73516	64.8	10.0	735849	22.7	100
15800	2.1	22.6	250	0.2	0.3	69928	2.2	
196	–	46.5	225	0.2	53.3	422	–	100
-1225	-0.1	13.2	-375	-0.3	4.0	-9309	-0.3	100
735222	100		113320	100		3241400	100	

Table 8.10 Number of Employees of U.S. Affiliates of the Ten General Trading Companies, March 31, 1976

	From Parent Company	Hired locally	Total
Mitsubishi International	216	484	700
Mitsui & Co. (U.S.A.)	238	401	639
Marubeni American	185	326	511
C. Itoh & Co. (America)	150	235	385
Sumitomo Shoji America	176	254	430
Nissho-Iwai American	194	292	486
Toyomenka (America)	92	129	221
Kanematsu Gosho (U.S.A.)	95	211	306
Ataka America	81	110	191
Nichimen Co., Inc.	100	110	210
Total	1,527	2,552	4,079

Source: Compiled from Isamu Kato, ed., *1976 Sogo shosha nenkan* (1976 General Trade Company Yearbook) (Tokyo: Seikei Tsushinsha, 1976), pp. 564-598.

The Changing Pattern of Direct Foreign Investment

Pursuing their goal of becoming global enterprises, specifically of expanding business in the overseas host country domestic markets and third-country trade, the *sogo shosha* have altered their pattern of overseas investments since the early 1970s. According to Yoshi Tsurumi, between 1950 and 1971 the ten *sogo shosha* accounted for about three-quarters of the 1,154 overseas affiliates (Tsurumi seems to include both subsidiaries and related firms as subsidiaries) set up by all Japanese trading companies. Most of those set up in the first half of the 1950s were sales rather than manufacturing affiliates. Sales affiliates were established abroad to develop export markets for Japanese manufactured goods. The number of manufacturing affiliates, however, rose suddenly to about one-third of all foreign affiliates or about three-fifths of sales affiliates set up during 1956-1961. During the next decade foreign manufacturing affiliates established by the ten largest trading companies outnumbered their new sales affiliates by about three to one. Manufacturing affiliates were established abroad by Japanese manufacturers and large trading companies,

Table 8.11   Number of Offices Operated by Affiliates of the Ten General Trading Companies, March 1976

	Number of offices
Mitsubishi International	14
Mitsui & Co. (U.S.A.)	12
Marubeni American	13
C. Itoh & Co. (America)	10
Sumitomo Shoji America	9
Nissho-Iwai American	11
Kanematsu Gosho (U.S.A.)	10
Ataka America	7
Nichimen Co., Inc.	7
Toyomenka (America)	7
Total	100

Source: Compiled from Isamu Kato, ed., *1976 Sogo shosha nenkan* (1976 General Trading Company Yearbook) (Tokyo: Seikei Tsushinsha, 1976), pp. 564-598.

which functioned as the international marketing channels of Japanese manufacturing firms, to defend export markets in response to attempts by host countries, especially the developing countries, to expand domestic production in place of imports. By far the largest number of manufacturing affiliates of the big trading companies (slightly over two-thirds) were established in Asia and Latin America.[4]

The *sogo shosha*'s investment patterns in the developing countries did not change drastically after 1972. No single wholly owned subsidiary was set up in Asia before or after 1971 except in Hong Kong, a free trade zone, and in Singapore. Most investments of all types (sales, manufacturing, and others) in Asia continue to be joint ventures with Japanese manufacturers and host country firms because of host government restrictions on foreign ownership. Sales and manufacturing affiliates in Asia and other developing countries will no doubt grow in importance as bases for trade with Japan, the United States, and Western Europe and as third-country trade bases.

Investment patterns by the *sogo shosha* in Western Europe have undergone a moderate change, however. After 1972 the number of wholly owned and majority owned affiliates increased slightly, although a majority of the affiliates remained minority owned.

The pattern and objectives of the ten *sogo shosha*'s investments in the U.S. changed dramatically, however. While the ten general trading companies had a few wholly owned subsidiaries in the U.S. before 1971, their number was extremely small compared with the number of minority and majority owned affiliates. The number of newly established majority and wholly owned subsidiaries suddenly rose, however, after 1972, outnumbering partially owned firms. The increase in the number of wholly owned subsidaries was especially marked. Mitsui & Co. established one-half of all new subsidiaries as wholly owned subsidiaries.

During the 1950s and the 1960s the general trading companies were content to establish joint ventures in the United States with Japanese manufacturers. The trading companies served as the manufacturers' marketing arms and left management in the hands of their joint venture partners. The exceptions were the trading companies' wholly owned American-incorporated subsidiaries, such as Mitsui & Co. (U.S.A.), Inc. and Mitsubishi International Corporation. Beginning in the early 1970s, especially since 1973, the *sogo shosha* switched their policy and began setting up wholly owned subsidiaries in the United States. These subsidiaries were mostly sales companies, but included a few manufacturing enterprises. The short-term goals of the trading companies were to ensure full management control by themselves, maximize returns on their investments, and strengthen their management, sales, procurement, and manufacturing capabilities. The intermediate goals were to expand business in the domestic American market and to increase third-country trade. The trading companies viewed success in achieving these intermediate goals as significant steps toward realizing their long-term goal—becoming genuine global enterprises.

The *sogo shosha* are taking full advantage of the favorable American business environment—the huge domestic market, the large capital market, the liberal American policy on foreign investment, and political and economic stability (despite recent deterioration in United States–Japan trade relations)—to grow in

Table 8.12 Wholly-owned Affiliates in Selected Countries of Three General Trading Companies

	1971 and before	1972-1976	Total
C. Itoh & Co.			
United States	0	9	9
Canada		1	1
Panama		3	3
Curacao		1	1
Britain		1	1
Hong Kong	1	2	3
Singapore		1	1
Australia		1	1
Total	1	19	20
Marubeni Corporation			
United States	1	8	9
Canada		1	1
Brazil		3	3
Britain		2	2
West Germany		1	1
Belgium	1		1
Liberia		1	1
Australia	1	1	2
Total	3	17	20
Mitsui & Co.			
United States	2	14	16
Canada	1		1
Colombia	1		1
Brazil	1		1
Britain	1		1
West Germany		1	1
Hong Kong	1		1
Australia	1	2	3
Total	8	17	25

Source: Compiled from *Sogo shosha Yearbook 1977* (Tokyo: Tokyo Information Service, 1977), pp. 90-126.

America and in world business. The dramatic change in their investment pattern and objectives in the United States is likely to result in even greater growth.

Challenges in the Late 1970s

The *sogo shosha* have served Japan's national interests well since World War II. They will continue to grow as Japanese firms even as they exert even greater efforts to become global enterprises. The challenges they face today have never been greater, however, and these challenges will continue into the foreseeable future. Six of the most significant challenges will be discussed briefly: the crisis of identity, the changing Japanese economy, the thrust by manufacturers into direct marketing, nationalism in the developing nations, global management and control, and the management of overseas affiliates.

The Crisis of Identity

As the trading companies strove to become global enterprises in the 1970s, the nature of their business and their role in the Japanese economy became blurred in the eyes of the general public. From their inception in the 1870s to the late 1960s, the trading companies had a clear notion of their chief objectives and main business. Service to Japan's national interests was a chief objective. Operating as Japan's major supply and distribution channels, primarily as importers of industrial raw materials and as exporters of manufactured goods, was their main business.

Now, however, the *sogo shosha* have taken on new roles. Striving to become organizers and coordinators of natural resource development projects, exporters of plants and other huge industrial projects, and managers of greatly expanded financing, information, and other services seems to have blurred for some *sogo shosha* officials the nature of their business. But in fact, whatever the future may hold, trading remains the *sogo shosha*'s main business. The hundreds of subsidiaries and related firms in manufacturing, processing, financing, leasing, subcontracting, and sales all have one primary purpose: to support the main business of selling and buying and to generate new business. The *sogo shosha*'s role as organizers-coordinators of natural resource development projects, urban and regional development, plant exports and numerous other projects also serves the same purpose: to secure and expand supply and marketing opportunities. Top management should clarify this relationship between the firms' main business and secondary businesses for the benefit of both those within and those outside the firms.

The ambiguity surrounding the objectives and the nature of the *sogo shosha*'s business has resulted in wide shifts of opinion about them in Japan. In the early 1960s, observers predicted their gradual decline—even eventual demise—because of the rising trend among manufacturers toward direct marketing. In the late 1960s and early 1970s, they were hailed by the Japanese mass media as organizers of overseas natural resource development projects to meet the demand of Japanese industry. Then in 1974, the trading firms suddenly found themselves under severe public attack as speculators, hoarders, and tax evaders. In the mid-1970s, top officials were summoned before the Diet for insulting interrogations. The Japan Fair Trade Commission conducted two investigations during 1974 and 1975 that questioned not only the *sogo shosha*'s business behavior but the validity of their very existence. What battered the trading companies most, however, was the so-called "Lockheed incident," the biggest political and business scandal to hit post–World War II Japan. The revelation in early 1976 that Lockheed had allegedly made huge illegal payments to Japanese politicians through the Marubeni Corporation, among others, caused widespread shock and indignation.

The ambiguous public image of the trading firms' business has been one of the root causes of the wide swing of opinion. The public has a relatively clear notion of what banks, shipbuilders, steel makers, and electric power companies do. The general public and even some government officials, however, often have only a dim notion of what the *sogo shosha* do. Top officials of the firms have an important task of explaining to the public and to close observers the objectives, nature, and methods of their business.

The Changing Japanese Economy

As noted earlier, the Japan Industrial Structure Council

Table 8.13 Trends in Japanese Industrial Production, 1970-1985, 1970 Price Basis (percent)

	CALENDAR YEAR							
	Share (percent)				Average Annual Growth Rate (percent)			
Industry	1970	1974	1980	1985	1975/1970	1980/1970	1985/1980	1985/1970
Agriculture, forest, marine	4.4	3.7	2.9	2.4	1.3	1.5	2.3	1.8
Mining	0.6	0.6	0.5	0.4	10.6	4.0	3.8	3.9
Food	6.0	5.8	5.5	5.4	6.2	4.9	6.0	5.2
Textile	3.3	2.0	2.5	2.2	7.1	2.6	3.5	2.9
Paper and pulp	1.6	1.5	1.6	1.6	12.7	5.6	5.9	5.7
Chemicals	3.2	3.5	3.4	3.5	16.8	6.4	6.5	6.5
Oil and coal products	1.9	2.0	2.0	2.0	17.0	6.5	5.9	6.3
Pottery	1.7	1.6	1.7	1.7	17.1	6.0	6.7	6.2
Steel	7.0	7.0	6.9	6.0	18.2	5.6	3.4	4.8
Nonferrous metals	1.1	1.2	1.4	1.3	16.6	7.4	4.5	6.5
Metal products	2.3	2.5	2.8	2.9	17.6	7.5	7.1	7.3
General machinery	5.1	5.8	5.6	5.9	22.9	6.6	7.3	6.8
Electric machinery	4.7	4.7	6.2	6.9	24.1	8.7	8.4	8.6
Transportation machinery	4.7	5.8	4.8	4.4	17.0	5.9	4.0	5.3

Precision machinery	0.7	0.7	0.7	0.8	13.7	6.3	7.7	6.9
Other manufacturing industries	6.3	6.3	6.6	7.4	13.3	6.2	7.5	7.0
Construction	10.1	7.7	10.3	11.1	13.4	5.9	7.8	6.6
Electricity, gas, and water	1.6	1.8	1.6	1.6	12.1	5.8	6.3	6.0
Commerce	8.8	9.4	9.3	9.3	15.6	6.2	6.2	6.2
Finance, insurance, and real estate	6.7	8.3	6.0	5.7	9.7	4.5	5.3	4.2
Transportation and communications	4.6	4.4	4.7	4.7	11.2	5.9	6.1	6.0
Service	10.6	10.6	10.3	10.3	7.5	5.4	6.2	5.7
Others	3.0	3.1	2.5	2.5	—	—	—	—
Primary industries	4.4	3.7	2.9	2.4	1.3	1.5	2.3	1.8
Secondary industries	60.3	58.8	62.6	63.4	14.7	6.1	6.5	6.2
(manufacturing industries)	(49.6)	(50.4)	(51.8)	(51.9)	(15.1)	(6.1)	(6.3)	(6.2)
Tertiary industries	32.3	34.5	31.9	31.6	10.6	5.6	6.0	5.7
Total	100.0	100.0	100.0	100.0	12.7	5.7	6.2	5.7

Source: Sangyo Kozo Shingikai, *Sangyo kozo no choki bijon* (The Industrial Structure: A Long-Term Vision) (Tokyo: Tsusho Sangyo Chosakai, 1976), pp. 82-83.

predicted in 1974 that the Japanese economy would grow by 6 percent during the rest of the 1970s, by 6.5 percent between 1980 and 1985, and by 6 percent between 1985 and 1990. The council later raised its forecast for the period between 1977 and 1980 to 6.5 percent—a slight increase, but still a much slower growth rate than experienced during the decade before 1972.

The end of Japan's rapid economic growth signaled the end of the *sogo shosha*'s rapid growth and a corresponding decline in their revenues. Of even greater potential negative impact on the trading firms were the council's forecasts of even slower growth and reduced weight for raw materials industries and intermediate industries (steel, primary nonferrous metals, pulp, and basic chemicals) and the rising weight of consumer goods and high-technology industries.

The council predicted similar trends for Japanese exports and imports. The shares of steel and textiles in Japan's total exports will decline respectively from 17 to 7 percent and from 8 to 5 percent between 1974 and 1985, while that of machinery (especially high-technology machinery and industrial plants) and chemicals will rise. The weight of metals raw materials (iron ore and nonferrous metals ore), coal, foodstuffs, and textile materials in Japanese imports will drop between 1974 and 1985 (from 13.2 to 9.8 percent, 4.9 to 4.4 percent, 13 to 10.7 percent, and 3 to 2 percent, respectively), while that of machinery will rise. The *sogo shosha*'s traditional stength has been in the supply and marketing of large-volume raw materials, intermediate products, and capital goods that are highly sensitive to Japan's economic cycles and growth rates rather than in the trading of consumer goods or high-technology products.

As was discussed in Chapter 7, the *sogo shosha* have responded to the changing Japanese economic environment by a concerted drive to raise managerial and functional efficiency; by entering the consumer goods industry; by expanding trade in high-technology products, industrial plants, and know-how; by stepping up transfer of labor-intensive manufacturing subsidiaries to the developing countries, by increasing exports of light industrial products from developing countries to Japan, U.S., and Western Europe; by increasing third-country trade; and by expanding their business in overseas host-country markets. These are impressive initial steps, but the question remains of how

Table 8.14 Trends in Commodities Exports of Japan, 1970-1985[a]

	Exports ($ millions)				Share structure (percent)				Average annual growth rate (percent)		
	1970	1974	1980	1985	1970	1974	1980	1985	1974/1970	1980/1974	1985/1980
Food	648	478	490	490	3.3	1.6	1.1	0.8	△7.3	0.3	0.2
Textiles	2,408	2,480	2,770	3,000	12.4	8.1	6.4	5.0	0.7	1.8	1.6
Chemical	1,234	1,607	3,070	5,350	6.3	5.3	7.1	9.0	6.8	11.4	11.7
Nonferrous metal products	373	342	450	520	1.9	1.1	1.0	0.9	△2.2	4.7	3.0
Metals and metal products	3,805	6,537	6,800	6,200	19.6	21.4	15.8	10.4	14.5	0.7	△1.8
Steel	2,844	5,252	5,130	4,150	14.7	17.2	11.9	6.9	16.5	△0.5	△4.2
Metal products	714	865	1,260	1,730	3.7	2.8	2.9	2.9	4.9	6.4	6.5
Machinery	8,941	17,042	26,810	40,510	46.2	55.8	62.2	67.8	17.5	7.8	8.4
General	2,006	4,463	8,210	12,150	10.3	14.6	19.0	20.4	22.1	10.7	8.2
Electric	2,866	4,052	7,640	12,500	14.8	13.3	17.7	20.9	9.0	11.1	10.3
Transportation	3,443	7,485	8,900	12,700	17.8	24.5	20.6	21.3	21.4	2.9	7.4
Precision	626	1,042	2,060	3,160	3.2	3.4	4.8	5.3	13.6	12.0	9.0
Others	1,909	2,036	2,710	3,630	9.9	6.7	6.3	6.1	1.6	4.9	6.0
Total	19,318	30,552	43,100	59,700	100.0	100.0	100.0	100.0	12.1	5.9	6.7

Source: Sangyo Kozo Shingikai, *Sangyo kozo no choki bijon* (The Industrial Structure: A Long-Term Vision) (Tokyo: Tsusho Sangyo Chosakai, 1976), p. 163.
Note: △ = minus.
[a]In real terms; 1970 prices; customs clearance basis.

Table 8.15 Trends in Commodities Imports of Japan, 1970-1985[a]

	Imports ($ millions)				Share structure (percent)				Average annual growth rate (percent)		
	1970	1974	1980	1985	1970	1974	1980	1985	1974/ 1970	1980/ 1974	1985/ 1980
Food	2,574	3,457	4,690	5,950	13.6	13.0	12.0	10.7	7.7	5.2	4.9
Textile raw materials	963	806	1,050	1,090	5.1	3.0	2.7	2.0	△4.3	4.5	0.8
Metal raw materials	2,696	3,521	4,520	5,410	14.3	13.2	11.5	9.8	6.9	4.3	3.7
Iron ores	1,208	1,682	2,140	2,450	6.4	6.3	5.5	4.4	8.6	4.1	2.7
Nonferrous metal ores	1,064	1,368	1,790	2,270	5.6	5.1	4.6	4.1	6.5	4.6	4.8
Other raw materials	3,018	3,371	5,100	6,890	16.0	12.6	13.1	12.4	2.8	7.2	6.2
Pulp	161	265	460	560	0.9	1.0	1.2	1.0	13.3	9.6	4.0
Lumber	1,572	1,715	2,250	2,770	8.3	6.4	5.7	5.0	2.2	4.6	4.2
Mineral fuel	3,905	5,159	7,630	9,540	20.7	19.3	19.5	17.2	7.1	6.8	4.6
Coal	1,010	1,292	1,940	2,460	5.3	4.9	4.9	4.4	6.3	7.0	4.9
Crude oil	2,236	3,157	4,280	5,180	11.8	11.8	10.9	9.4	9.0	5.2	3.9
Petroleum products	550	449	450	450	2.9	1.7	1.1	0.8	△5.0	0.0	0.0
Natural and manu-factured gas	105	261	960	1,450	0.6	1.0	2.4	2.6	25.6	24.2	8.5
Chemical products	1,080	2,407	2,890	4,470	5.7	9.0	7.4	8.1	22.2	3.1	9.1
Machinery	2,296	3,881	6,730	10,860	12.2	14.6	17.2	19.6	14.0	9.6	10.0
General	1,262	1,845	3,170	5,310	6.7	6.9	8.1	9.6	10.0	9.4	10.9
Electric	477	1,143	2,140	3,500	2.5	4.3	5.5	6.3	24.4	11.0	10.3
Transportation	406	578	940	1,340	2.2	2.2	2.4	2.4	9.2	8.5	7.3
Precision	151	315	480	710	0.8	1.2	1.2	1.3	20.2	7.2	8.1
Others	2,349	4,058	6,490	11,190	12.4	15.3	16.6	20.2	14.6	8.1	11.5
Steel	276	206	910	2,360	1.5	0.8	2.3	4.3	△7.1	28.2	20.9
Nonferrous metals	945	1,314	2,140	3,420	5.0	4.9	5.5	6.2	8.6	8.5	9.8
Textile products	315	1,333	2,180	3,690	1.7	5.0	5.6	6.7	43.4	8.5	11.1
Total	18,881	26,660	39,100	55,400	100.0	100.0	100.0	100.0	9.0	6.6	7.2

Source: Sangyo Kozo Shingikai, *Sangyo kozo no choki bijon* (The Industrial Structure: A Long-Term Vision) (Tokyo: Tsusho Sangyo Chosakai, 1976), p. 166.
Note: △ = minus.
[a]In real terms; 1970 prices; customs clearance basis.

Thrust by Manufacturers into Direct Marketing

Another serious problem facing the *sogo shosha* is the trend among Japanese manufacturers to discontinue indirect marketing through trading companies and to engage in direct marketing, especially in exporting to the U.S. market. The trend has been especially pronounced in the past decade among consumer goods industries such as automobile and electronics industries that require considerable technical know-how, close consumer service, and unified production and marketing strategy covering a wide range of products. The trend is expected to spread to other industries, including such growth industries as computers and ocean development.

The desire of industrial plant manufacturers to engage in direct exports of industrial plants in the future presents another problem. The *sogo shosha* currently participate in practically all Japanese plant exports as organizers-coordinators and procurement agents working in close cooperation with Japanese plant manufacturers and engineering firms. The past weakness of Japanese heavy machinery makers in softwares and the late start of Japanese engineering firms necessitated the participation of the *sogo shosha*. To further strengthen their position, the trading companies have in the past few years expanded joint plant exports with U.S. and European plant manufacturers and with engineering firms and have raised the level of equipment procurement abroad. Most significant was the recent attempt to become prime contractors (not merely organizers and equipment procurement agents) in plant exports, with the trading companies assuming responsibilities not only for supplying equipment but also providing installation and operational services (i.e., instructions on plant operation, management, and maintenance).

The plant export capabilities of Japanese plant manufacturers and engineering firms have grown substantially in the last few years, however. Japan's three largest engineering firms (Toyo Engineering Corp., Nikki, and Chiyoda Chemical Engineering and Construction) entered the ranks of the world's top forty engineering firms in 1976. Japanese steel manufacturers (such as Nippon Steel and Nippon Kokan) have substantially strengthened their engineering divisions in the past few years, changing from plant users to steel plant exporters in cooperation with shipbuilding and heavy machinery manufacturers (such as Ishikawajima Harima Heavy Industries and Hitachi, Ltd). The steel makers provide engineering, operational, and maintenance services, and the other manufacturers supply machinery and equipment. Chemical firms (Mitsui Toatsu Chemicals, Mitsubishi Rayon, Mitsubishi Petrochemical, Shinetsu Chemical Industry, Kuraray, etc.) have also established chemical engineering firms for the export of chemical plants.

In the immediate future, Japan's plant manufacturers and engineering firms will require the global information and financing resources and the organization and coordination skills of the trading companies. Conversely, the trading firms cannot acquire overnight the engineering, operational, and maintenance know-how that a prime contractor requires. The pattern of close cooperation among the *sogo shosha*, engineering firms, and equipment makers will thus continue. The trading companies, however, will have to continue to develop their financing, organizing, and engineering capabilities and resources to ensure the future dependence of importers, engineering firms, and plant manufacturers on their services.

Nationalism in the Developing Countries

During the 1960s, the general trading companies set up the majority of their foreign manufacturing and sales affiliates (about two-thirds) in the developing countries of Asia, Latin America, the Middle East, and Africa to defend the markets they had already developed for exports of Japanese manufactured goods. The developing countries, especially those of Southeast Asia, continued to be the major target of their direct foreign investments in the 1970s, but the objective of the investments changed. In the 1970s developing countries were seen as export bases for sales of textiles and other light industrial products (and eventually of higher-technology industrial products) to Japan, the United States, and Western Europe. They were also seen as third-country trade bases to support the firms' global strategy.

These new goals replaced the defense of already established markets as primary objectives of direct investments in the developing countries. This trend is likely to grow. The developing countries are projected to receive about 40 percent of the world's total direct foreign investments by 1985, a 9 percent increase over 1967.[5]

A number of barriers may hinder the *sogo shosha*'s objectives in the developing countries, however. One is growing competition in the third-country market (for instance, the U.S. and Western European markets) between Japanese products (e.g., electronics equipment and, eventually, automobiles, ships, and steel) and products from developing countries as their industrialization efforts bear fruit. Another is growing competition from U.S. and Western European multinational corporations as they expand investments in the developing countries to take advantage of lower manufacturing costs.

Yet another is the various restrictions imposed on the trading companies' operations by the host governments, partly out of a desire to maintain national control over operations of foreign firms and partly in reaction to some past abuses.[6] The growing trend by governments and private enterprises to establish their own channels of international supply and marketing and their own engineering firms will also hinder the efforts of the Japanese trading firms to expand sales of manufactures from developing countries.

Global Management and Control

The general trading companies also face many problems of global management and control. These include how to plan on a global basis, how to manage overseas affiliates, how to develop global methods of financing and investment, how to establish suitable organizational structures, and how to secure the resources they need. As noted previously, the trading companies have shown a remarkable ability to adapt to changing domestic and international environments. In the late 1950s and 1960s they acted to become general trading companies through growth, diversification, and demand and supply creation, and the thrust into consumer industries. In the early 1970s, their goals shifted to social responsibilities, management and functional efficiency, the marketing of high-technology products, exports of industrial plants, and becoming global enterprises. Since the early 1960s they have adopted mid-term and long-term plans. Top officials meet regularly to analyze the situation facing the firms, to make plans with the assistance of *gyomu-honbu* (usually translated as "corporate planning and coordination division"), and to formulate business strategies. This disproves the occasional assertions of some foreign observers that simple reaction to environmental stimuli rather than strategic planning characterizes the behavior of Japanese businessmen.

The impression (and it is only an impression because of lack of full access to the firms' internal documents and the resulting inability to make a more accurate overall judgment) is that past formulation of corporate plans and strategy has not been fully systematic and comprehensive, and that the primary focus has been on expanded volume of sales. If this impression is correct, the *sogo shosha* need a more systematic and conceptual approach to the formulation of global strategies. As William A. Dymsza suggests, specific mid-term and long-term plans and strategies for overall company, divisions, and affiliates should be based on and derives systematically from company philosophy, the nature of the business, broad objectives, a managerial audit of strengths and weaknesses, analysis of national and regional environments, a competitive audit, and identification of key future opportunities and problems in major countries.[7] Formulation of functional, product, and geographic strategies and programs should be based on and derived from specific intermediate and long-term goals and should in turn lead to tactical planning, to allocation of budgets, personnel and other resources, and to operating in a dynamic process. The *sogo shosha* should monitor and evaluate performance of plans and modify strategies and tactics and perhaps even their goals if radical environmental changes so require. The coordination and integration of the whole company, including its divisions, affiliates, functions, products, and geographic areas, should be more systematic.

Another management problem is that of orientation. Chapter 4 showed that the trading companies have long had sizable international transactions. Until the early 1970s, however, these transactions centered almost exclusively on Japan and the *sogo*

225

Figure 8.2 Model for international strategic planning and control

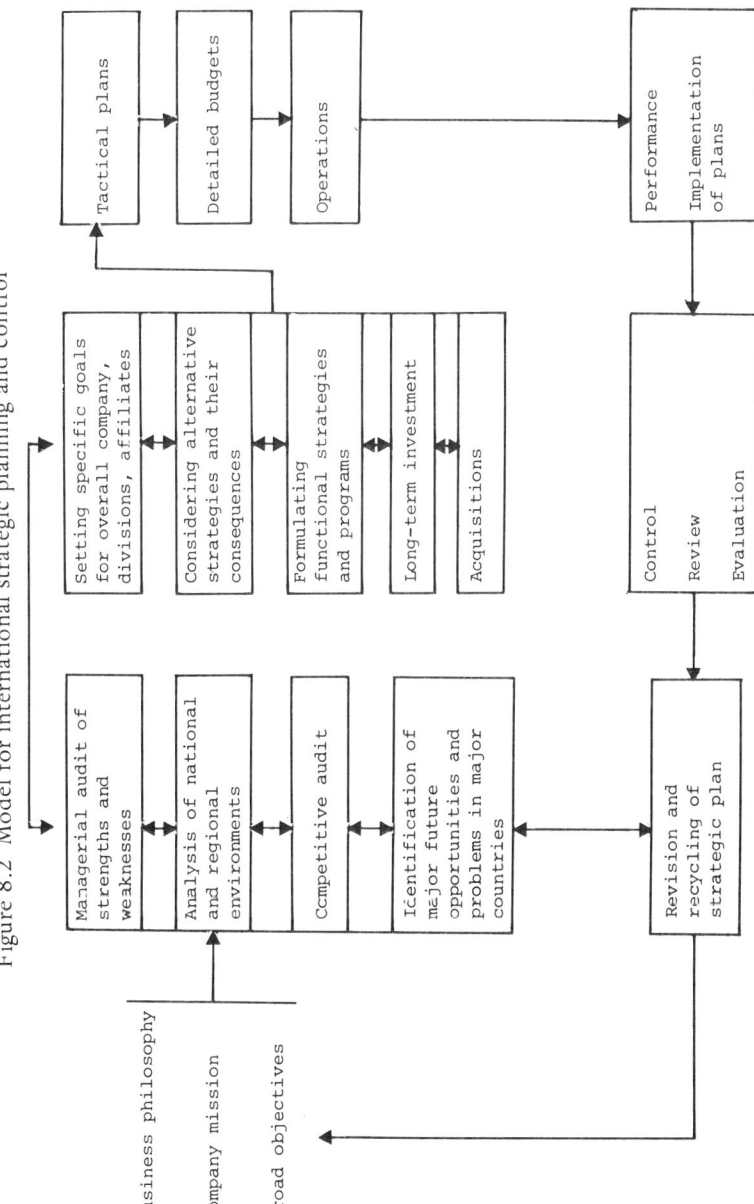

Source: William A. Dymsza, Multinational Business Strategy (New York: McGraw-Hill, 1972), p. 65.

shosha's home offices. Imports and exports were almost always imports into Japan and exports from Japan and served Japan's national interests. Overseas offices were set up to promote many sets of two-country trade with Japan (Japan-U.S. trade, Japan-Indonesian trade, Japan-Brazilian trade, etc.) and not third-country or global trade. The primary concern of company officials stationed abroad had been to follow home office instructions rather than assume local initiative, and to strengthen personal ties with home office top management in hope of eventual promotion to the home office board of directors.

Becoming global enterprises requires a shift from Japan orientation to global orientation to increase transactions in host country domestic markets and third-country trade. Japan's direct foreign investment is expected to increase to $80 billion by 1985, according to a revised estimate of the Japan Industrial Structural Council.[8] The need for a global orientation will rise as direct foreign investments by the trading companies increase. The long legacy of Japan-centered and home office–oriented overseas management systems and operations, latent nationalism, and the high proportion of company officials abroad who are Japanese nationals, however, makes one wonder whether the *sogo shosha* can become truly globally oriented in the near future.

The question of the *sogo shosha*'s past style of financing and investment is still another problem. The demise of Ataka & Co. and its absorption by C. Itoh & Co. in October 1977 (triggered by Ataka America Inc.'s huge bad loan to John M. Shaheen's Newfoundland Refining Company[9]) called into serious question the *sogo shosha*'s postwar high leverage capital structure. Equity often was only 3 percent of the total capital employed, and the financing and investment criteria were loose, to put it mildly. Ataka & Co.'s uncollectable funds eventually totaled almost 224 billion Yen (slightly over $800 million). High leverage, despite heavy debt servicing cost (tax deductible), has been a less costly way of raising capital than equity capital that pays an average of 12 percent in dividends. It is not as risky as in the West because of the strong backup by large commercial banks, which in turn can expect the firm support of the Bank of Japan.

High leverage has been a source of the *sogo shosha*'s strength during two decades of rapid economic growth. It enabled them to expand their market share through ever-increasing financing and other services to customers and suppliers, to serve as risk buffers for banks and manufacturers and to play other roles in the Japanese economy, to increase investments in subsidiaries and other affiliated firms, and to expand natural resource and other project financing. Japan's rapid economic growth enabled the firms to expand business rapidly at small profit margins.

A critical question, however, is whether the *sogo shosha* can maintain the same pattern of high leveraged business operation in periods of sluggish Japanese and world economics accompanied by skyrocketing operational and debt servicing costs and an increasing number of bad loans to customers and affiliates that go bankrupt. Previously, the extension of loans to and investments in group firms, group joint ventures and affiliates, and customers was often made more on the basis of promoting friendly and closer business relations than on strict criteria of sound growth, diversification, and earnings. This may have worked in Japan during two decades of rapid economic growth when the *sogo shosha* had nearly unlimited sources of borrowing and good cash flow and when they were backed up by their main banks. However, loose financing and investment will not work in other parts of the world, as Ataka America's costly loan to Newfoundland Refining Co. proved. The risks are too great. Strict international financing and investment criteria will have to be adopted and continuing internal control maintained.

Yet another problem is designing a more viable organizational structure to carry out their strategies and achieve their objectives. Each firm must manage and control global operations involving between 1,000 and 20,000 products, hundreds of huge projects that cut across product lines, numerous functions including marketing, financing, and insurance, thousands of suppliers and customers around the globe, and hundreds of offices and affiliates at home and abroad. Despite global communications systems, problems of communications across numerous national and cultural boundaries and of global planning, management, and control are enormous.

The general trading companies, because of the wide range of product lines they handle, have long used worldwide organizational structures along major product lines. Product divisions served as profit centers. As overseas natural resource development, plant exports, and other complex projects cutting across product lines increased and as the number of overseas affiliates and the scale of overseas operations expanded since the late 1960s, the *sogo shosha* have taken three important actions to plan, coordinate, and control their global operations. First, they strengthened the planning and coordination functions of the head office staff. Second, they increased the use of project teams of specialists from various product divisions. And third, they established country and regional offices at the Japan head office and set up overseas regional headquarters, such as Toyomenka (America) Inc. and Kanematsu Gosho (U.S.A.) Inc.

Some observers have advocated changing to a global organizational structure along functional lines, with assistance from product and geographic staffs. This might facilitate exports of complex industrial plants and the organization of huge natural resource development and other projects, but it does not seem to be a viable overall solution for firms with thousands of products and hundreds of offices around the world.

Others advocate less head office centralization of authority, responsibility, and control, and more decentralization, giving greater autonomy to overseas regional headquarters and affiliates. Excessive decentralization, however, may lead to competition between the Japan head office and overseas regional headquarters on the one hand and between overseas regional headquarters and among affiliates on the other hand. It may also lead to the weakening of one of the *sogo shosha*'s basic assets: the ability to integrate global operations by product lines. A more viable organizational structure suitable to global planning, coordination, and control with respect to the head office, overseas regional headquarters and affiliates, functions, products, and projects will have to be designed in the future.

Management of Overseas Affiliates

Perhaps the most critical problem facing the *sogo shosha* as they go global is managing overseas affiliates, especially in the area of management-labor relations. Trading companies have largely transplanted the Japanese management system abroad. Furthermore, for years officials dispatched from the Japan head office virtually monopolized all the top management positions abroad, except where they were prevented by law or where political pressure forced the appointment of a certain number of host country employees to top-level positions. The situation has changed somewhat in the past few years as the number of appointments of host country employees to middle-level management positions has increased. In the United States, however, American employees tend to be functional specialists in law, marketing, or accounting rather then general managers with broad responsibilities in planning or divisional management.[10]

There are understandable reasons for the past practice. Transfer of technologies and manufacturing operations, requiring little personal communication, is easier than transfer of management skills requiring extensive communications (both personal and impersonal). Matsushita Electric can build a highly automated color television plant in New Jersey and have it run almost exclusively by American employees and still turn out high-quality products. For the trading companies, however, people rather than industrial plants are the greatest asset. Communications between the parent company and global affiliates, and among managers abroad, is their lifeblood. Smooth business operations require a smooth flow of communications. Japanese employees, who are hired for life fresh out of college, have been trained in the philosophy, objectives, organization, management system, and business methods of the company. They share the Japanese cultural heritage and common company goals, values, and experience. Thus, these trained Japanese employees will operate almost automatically in the Mitsubishi manner or in the Mitsui manner. They are the *sogo shosha*'s greatest assets and are indispensable in the smooth operation and coordination of their worldwide business. Computers can be replaced. Loyal and highly trained Japanese employees cannot be.

The transfer of the Japanese management system and the occupation of middle- and top-level management positions by Japanese ensures the flow of communications (including whom to send a telex to or talk to in the consensus oriented decision-making process), avoids misunderstandings (so easy in a culture where unspoken words and gestures can be more important than spoken and written words), and saves much time. Despite the remarkable improvement in the foreign language ability of Japanese managers and the rise in the number of managers with many years of experience abroad, language and cultural differences persist as major barriers to communications and to the integration of host country employees into overseas affiliates.

One can view with sympathy and understanding the past transfer of the Japanese management system and the near monopoly of Japanese employees in top management positions at overseas affilates. The current situation requires modification of past practice, however. Economic realities demand reduced stationing of head office–dispatched Japanese officials abroad who cost considerably more than those locally employed. With the increase of global transactions (such as third-country trade and host country domestic business), trading companies need more host country personnel as managers and not simply as functional specialists. Furthermore, host country employees want advancement to positions of greater management responsibility and higher monetary reward commensurate with their capabilities and years of service. Job dissatisfaction leads to low morale and poor job performance. It may lead to serious nationalist agitation in the developing countries and to costly and highly damaging antidiscrimination lawsuits in the U.S. and other industrialized countries.

The development of a more viable management system for overseas affiliates is clearly a critical problem requiring the close attention and action of the *sogo shosha*'s top management. Their future success may well be in proportion to their ability to confront and solve this problem.

Power and Responsibility

There is no question that the *sogo shosha* possess enormous power in world commerce. While their position in the world's total exports is not dominant, their power in the world's agricultural and indusrial raw material trade is considerable because of their dominant position in Japanese imports. Although the size of their transactions in Japan's raw material imports is dictated by the shifting demands of Japanese industry, they possess significant power to affect the price movements of the world iron ore, coal, grains, lumber, and textile raw materials and products trade. They also possess considerable power in trade with nations that are highly interdependent with Japan, namely, those nations from which Japan imports an extraordinarily large amount of raw materials and which export an extraordinarily large share of Japan's imports.

During FY 1973, for example, the U.S. supplied 88 percent of Japan's soybean imports, 29 percent of cotton imports, and 25 percent of lumber imports; Australia supplied 48 percent of Japan's iron ore imports, 43 percent of coal imports, 64 percent of bauxite imports, 89 percent of wool imports, and 40 percent of meats imports; Canada was responsible for 54 percent of Japan's uranium imports and 27 percent of copper imports; Iran supplied 31 percent of Japan's oil imports; and Brunei supplied 58 percent of Japan's natural gas imports.[11] The result is a high degree of mutual dependence. Just as a sudden export embargo of critical raw materials could have a severe negative impact on Japan, so shifts in Japan's import pattern could have equally adverse consequences for its major suppliers of raw materials.

Conclusion

Sogo shosha whose top management is unable to cope with the new requirements and responsibilities of global business can expect to fall behind and be absorbed by others. One thing is certain: the ranking of the firms by total transactions and earnings in 1985 will be different from that of March 1977, even if they all survive. Greater weight will be given to ranking by earnings than by transactions.

Sogo shosha that survive will become true global enterprises, serving as the supply and marketing channels of the world. They should become the world's most important multiproduct, multimarket, multiservice, and multinational traders, making significant contributions to the now evolving global system of supply, production, and marketing. By 1990 (if not by 1985), they should attain their goal of establishing a structure of business in which transactions in the Japanese domestic market, imports into and exports from Japan, multinational trade, and business in overseas domestic markets will have equal 25 percent shares of their total transactions.

The *sogo shosha* will become global traders of commodities, capital, technologies, managerial skills, and labor. Their head offices in Japan will become global operating, investment, and management companies. Their major overseas regional headquarters, such as those in North America and Europe, if not hindered by local laws, will develop into holding companies chiefly concerned with investment, management, and control of subsidiaries. Operations will be left largely to subsidiaries. Many more service departments, such as financing, processing, packaging, warehousing, transportation, insurance, real estate, and even today's commodity groups will spin off from the parent company to become independent businesses. The weight of manufacturing business, too, will rise as more manufacturing subsidiaries are established. A few general trading companies might eventually evolve into integrated global conglomerates possessing global production, marketing, financing, information, and other capabilities.

The *sogo shosha* are a unique knowledge-intensive service industry. They developed in a country isolated from the world for more than two centuries until pried open by Commodore Perry in the mid-nineteenth century, ignorant of foreign languages, cultures, and world trade customs, poorly endowed with natural resources, but blessed with a rich supply of intelligent and hard-working people and in perpetual need of foreign good will and markets. They have served Japan and the Japanese people well in the last hundred years. They should have a bright future if they serve the needs and welfare of the world community and mankind equally well in the years to come.

Notes

1. Shosho Kino Kenkyukai, *Gendai sogoshosharon* (On Contemporary General Trading Companies) (Tokyo: Toyo Keisai Shinposha, 1975), pp. 110 and 160.

2. U.S. Department of Commerce, *Foreign Direct Investment in the United States*, vol. 1 (Washington, D.C.: U.S. Government Printing Office, 1976), p. 37.

3. *International Economic Report of the President* (Washington, D.C.: U.S. Government Printing Office, January 1977), p. 148.

4. Yoshi Tsurumi, *The Japanese Are Coming* (Cambridge: Ballinger Publishing Co., 1976), pp. 138-141.

5. Sangyo Kozo Shingikai, ed. *Sangyo kozo no choki bijon* (The Industrial Structure—A Long-Term Vision) (Tokyo: Tsusho Sangyo Chosakai, 1974), p. 192.

6. See a long list of criticisms of Japanese business operations in Southeast Asia in Raul S. Manglapus, *Japan in Southeast Asia: Collision Course* (New York: Carnegie Endowment for Interntional Peace, 1976).

7. William A. Dymsza, *Multinational Business Strategy* (New York: McGraw Hill Book Co., 1972), p. 65.

8. The council's original estimate of $93.5 billion made in 1974 was reduced to $80 billion in 1976. See Sangyo Kozo Shingikai, *Sangyo kozo no choki bijon* (The Industrial Structure: A Long-Term Vision) (Tokyo: Sangyo Chosaki, 1976), p. 177.

9. *Business Week*, February 2, 1976, p. 27.

10. "The Japanese Multinational Experience," unpublished research paper by Jun Imanishi, John Miller, Cynthia Morrill, and Peter Ryus, Columbia Graduate School of Business, 1977, p. 9.

11. Shosha Kino Kenkyuakai, *Gendai sogoshosharon* (On Contemporary General Trading Companies), p. 72.

Selected References

Following is a list of selected references on Japanese business in English. Those interested in Japanese sources on the sogo shosha *may consult the footnotes and tables.*

Abbegglen, James C., ed. *Business Strategies for Japan.* Tokyo: Sophia University Press, 1971.

Adams, T. F. M., and Iwao Hoshii. *A Financial History of the New Japan.* Tokyo: Kodansha International, 1972.

Adams, T. F. M., and N. Kobayashi. *The World of Japanese Business.* Tokyo: Kodansha International, 1969.

Ballon, R. J., and C. H. Lee, eds. *Foreign Investment and Japan.* Tokyo: Sophia University Press/Kodansha International, 1972.

Ballon, R. J., I. Tomita, and H. Usami. *Financial Reporting in Japan.* Tokyo: Kodansha International, 1976.

Bank of Japan. *Money and Banking in Japan.* London: Macmillan, 1973.

Caves, Richard E., and Masu Uekusa. *Industrial Organization in Japan.* Washington, D.C.: The Brookings Institution, 1976.

Cohen, Jerome B., ed. *Pacific Partnership: United States-Japan Trade.* Lexington, Mass.: D. C. Heath Company, 1972.

Hadley, Eleanor M. *Antitrust in Japan.* Princeton, N.J.: Princeton University Press, 1970.

Henderson, Dan F. *Foreign Enterprise in Japan—Laws and Policies.* Chapel Hill: University of North Carolina Press, 1973.

Japan External Trade Organization, ed. *The Role of Trading Companies in International Commerce,* JETRO Marketing Ser. 2. Tokyo: JETRO, 1976.

Japan Fair Trade Commission. "FTC Unveils Revealing Data on Nation's Leading Trading Firms," *The Antitrust Bulletin* 20, p. 1 (Spring 1975).

Kaplan, Eugene J. *Japan: The Government-Business Relationship.* Washington, D.C.: U.S. Department of Commerce, 1972.

Manglapus, Raul S. *Japan in Southeast Asia: Collision Course.* New York: Carnegie Endowment for International Peace, 1976.

Monroe, Wilbur F. *Japan: Financial Markets and the World Economy.* New York: Praeger Publishers, 1973.

Ohkawa, Kazushi, and Henry Rosovsky. *Japanese Economic Growth—Trend Acceleration in the Twentieth Century.* Stanford, Calif.: Stanford University Press, 1973.

Okochi, Kazuo, Bernard Karsh, and Solomon B. Levine, eds. *Workers and Employers in Japan.* Tokyo: University of Tokyo Press, 1973.

Patrick, Hugh, ed. *Japanese Industrialization and Its Social Consequences.* Berkeley: University of California Press, 1976.

Patrick, Hugh, and Henry Rosovsky, eds. *Asia's New Giant: How the Japanese Economy Works.* Washington, D.C.: The Brookings Institution, 1976.

Roberts, John G. *Mitsui: Three Centuries of Japanese Business.* New York: John Weatherhill, 1973.

Sethi, S. Prakash. *Japanese Business and Social Conflict.* Cambridge, Mass.: Ballinger Publishing Co., 1975.

Tokyo Economic Information Service Co., ed. *Sogo-shosha Year Book, 1977.* Tokyo: Tokyo Economic Information Service Co., 1977.

Tsurumi, Yoshi. *The Japanese Are Coming.* Cambridge, Mass.: Ballinger Publishing Co., 1976.

Vogel, Ezra, ed. *Modern Japanese Organization and Decision-Making.* Berkeley: University of California Press, 1975.

Yanaga, Chitoshi. *Big Business in Japanese Politics.* New Haven, Conn.: Yale University Press, 1967.

Yamamura, Kozo. "General Trading Companies in Japan—Their Origins and Growth," in Hugh Patrick, ed. *Japanese Industrialization and Its Social Consequences.* Berkeley: University of California Press, 1976.

Yoshino, M. Y. *Japan's Managerial System.* Cambridge, Mass.: MIT Press, 1968.

——— *The Japanese Marketing System.* Cambridge, Mass.: MIT Press, 1971.

——— *Japan's Multinational Enterprises.* Cambridge, Mass.: Harvard University Press, 1976.

Young, Alexander K. "Internationalization of the Japanese General Trading Companies." *Columbia Journal of World Business*, IX, 1, (Spring 1974).

———, trans. "General Trading Company's Code of Behavior" ("Sogo shosha no kodo kijun"), in *C. Itoh Challenging with Ideas*. Tokyo: The Mainichi Newspapers, October 1973.

Index

The references to the various *sogo shosha* are so numerous in the text that an exhaustive index to all references is impractical. It is suggested that the reader wishing to find information on the individual firms consult subentries under *sogo shosha* for items common to all the firms. Subentries under the individual firms (e.g., Toyomenka Kaisha: export of industrial plants as prime contractor) direct the reader either to activities peculiar to one firm or activities common to all for which a single firm was chosen for purposes of illustration (e.g., Mitsui & Co.: Konan food industries complex).

Abegglen, James, 135
Accumulated producton experience, 135
Affiliates (subsidiaries and related firms)
 definition, 44
 sogo shosha's in U.S., 204-209
Alaska oil pipeline, 131
Allis-Chalmers Corporation, 125
AMAX, 9, 153
Ataka & Co. *See also Sogo shosha*
 absorption by C. Itoh & Co., 226
 reorganization, 25
Ataka America, Inc.
 comparison with U.S. trading companies, 19
 loans to Newfoundland Refining Company, 226, 227
Atlas, 148
Australia, 111, 121, 185, 231

Bank-centered conglomerate groups, 36-37
 relations with the *sogo shosha*, 42-44
Barter trade, 11
Benichu, 31
Bisson, T. A., 56
Boeing, 108
Brazil, 120, 158-159
Britain, 100, 197
British Export Credit Guarantee Department, 191
British General Electric, 125
Broken Hill Proprietary Company, Ltd., 153
Brown Boveri, 204
Brunei, 231
Brunei LNG Co., 159

Canada, 197, 231

239

Caves, Richard E., 56
Cebu, 148
China, People's Republic of, 9, 202
China, Republic of. *See* Taiwan
Chiyoda Chemical Engineering and Construction Co., 203, 221
Chori Co., Ltd., 23, 32
Cohen, Jerome B., 143
Colonial Sugar Refinery Company, 153
Conglomerates, 36-37
 relations of groups with the *sogo shosha*, 42-44
 trading conglomerates, 11-13
 U.S. and West European conglomerates, 13
Consolidated Goldfields, Ltd., 161
Cuba, 111
Currencies, float of major world, 63, 175

Daiichi Kangyo Bank group, 36, 37, 44, 115
Dairy Queen, 114
Deepsea Ventures, Inc., 161
Dragon Petroleum Trading Co., 190
du Pont, 105
Dymsza, William A., 224, 233

Echigo, Masakazu, 55
Engineering firms, 203-204

Federation of Economic Organizations, 179
Flour Corporation, 204
Ford Motor Co., 105
Foreign domination of Japan's foreign trade in early Meiji period, 24
France, 197
Fujino, Chujiro, 55, 178, 193
Furukawa Aluminium, 121
Fuyo group, 36-37, 42, 44, 66, 115
Fuyo Petroleum Development Company, 154

General Electric Co., 105, 108

General Motors Corporation, 48, 105
Goto, T., 189
Groups, conglomerate, 36-37, 115. *See also* President Clubs
 relations with the *sogo shosha*, 42-44

Hadley, Eleanor, 56
Hasegawa, Norishige, 55
Hatoyama, Ichiro, 99, 145
Head Research Corporation, 204
Hitachi, Ltd., 66, 72, 222
Hitachi Shipbuilding & Engineering Co., Ltd., 105, 121
Honda Motor Co., Ltd., 155
Hong Kong, 211
Hyuga, Hosai, 55

IBM, 17, 48, 105
Idemitsu Kosan, 157
Ikeda, Hayato, 99, 131, 145
Ikeda, Yoshizo, 55, 180, 182, 183, 192
INCO Ltd., 161, 163
Indonesia, 9, 11, 121
International Nickel Company, 161
International Procurement and Service America, Inc., 190
International Procurement and Service Corporation, Luxemburg, 190
Ishikawajima-Harima Heavy Industries, Co., Ltd., 115, 222
Italy, 197
Itoh & Co., C. *See also Sogo shosha*
 absorption of Ataka & Co., 266
 export of industrial plants, 204
 international strategy, 183-184
 long-term plan, 182
 mergers by, 109
 Mt. Newman iron ore project, 152-153
Itoh & Co. (America), C., 189, 205
Itoh International Petroleum Co., C., 190
Itohman & Co., Ltd., 23
ITT, 12, 105
Iwai Sangyo, 31, 116

Index

Iwai Shoten, 31
Iwasaki, Koyata, 119
Iwasaki, Yataro, 31

Japan
  Export Council, 129
  Export Council for Individual Industry, 129
  export expansion measures, 129
  export trends in late 1970s and 1980s, 218
  foreign investment liberalization, 105
  future growth industries, 181
  government assistance to overseas resource development projects, 150
  industrial and export structures, 99-100, 169-170
  interdependence with other countries, 231
  mass consumer society and mass merchandise stores in, 103-105
  post–World War II economic system, 142
  rapid economic growth of, 98-99
  slower economic growth in the 1970s, 168-169, 218
Japan Deep Ocean Mining Company, 161
Japan Fair Trade Commission
  attack on the *sogo shosha*, 12, 44, 46
  moves to restrict the *sogo shosha*'s stockholdings, 170-172, 178, 204, 215
Japan Foreign Trade Council, Inc., 19, 21, 177-178
Japan Industrial Structure Council, 169-170, 215, 226
Japan Manganese Nodules Development Company, 161
Japan Petroleum Development Company, 157
Japan Steel Works, 204
Japanese trading companies, MITI statistics on, 13

Jardine Matheson & Co., Ltd., 17, 18

Kanematsu Gosho, Ltd. *See also Sogo shosha*
  commodities / classification standards, 20
  deep sea manganese development project, 161
  merger of Kanematsu and Gosho, 116
Kansai Steel, 72, 130
Kawasaki Heavy Industries, Ltd., 115
Kawasaki Steel Corp., 107, 155
Kawasaki, Tachita, 189
Keihin Electric Express Railway, 66
Kellogg, Pullman, 203, 204
Kennecott Copper Corporation, 161
Kentucky Fried Chicken, 114
Kinsho Mataichi Corporation, 23, 32
Kobe Steel, 107, 130
Kojima, Kiyoshi, 152, 163
Konan food industries complex, 111-112, 143, 144
Konan Pier (Konan Futo, Ltd.), 111
Konan Utility, Co., Ltd., 112
Kooperativa Foroundel, 18, 25
Korea, 176
Kuraray, 222

Liberal Democratic Party, 179
Litton Industries, Inc., 12
Lockheed Aircraft, 108
Lockheed incident, 215

Maku, Takashi, 113
Manglapus, Raul S., 233
Manufacturers
  mergers of, 115
  share in Japan's foreign trade, 100
  thrust into direct marketing, 100-103
McDonnel Douglas Corporation, 108
Manganese, deep sea development of, 159-163
Marubeni Corporation. *See also*

Sogo shosha
 agribusiness in Brazil, 158-159
 joint venture with Dairy Queen, 114
 Lockheed incident, 215
 mergers by, 109
Marubeni Reizo, 66
Matsui, Kiyoshi, 56
Matsushita Electric Industrial Co., Ltd., 72, 155, 229
Mexico, 120
Minagawa, Hiro, 193
Ministry of Finance step to limit loans of financial institutions, 172-175
Ministry of International Trade and Industry (MITI), 8, 13, 15, 20, 90, 127, 130, 155, 179
 Foreign Trade Statistics by Industries published by, 20-21
Mitsubishi Corporation. See also *Sogo shosha*
 business principles, 119
 business ventures, scope of, 4-5
 dissolution of Mitsubishi Trading Company, 108
 five-year contract with Seiyu, 114
 information from Zambia, 63
 international seminar, 71
 LNG project in Brunei, 159
 merger of former firms, 109
 Seven Point Rationalization Plan, 180
 share in Japan's foreign trade before World War II, 24
 share in Japan's GNP, 25
Mitsubishi International Corporation, 189, 204, 205, 212
 ratings of commercial papers, 205
Mitsubishi group, 37, 42, 154
Mitsubishi Heavy Industries, 72, 121
Mitsubishi Metal Mining, 148
Mitsubishi Petrochemical Company, 222
Mitsubishi Petroleum Development Company, 154, 157, 158
Mitsubishi Rayon, 222
Mitsui-C. Itoh Pty., Ltd., 153
Mistui & Co. See also *Sogo shosha*
 dissolution of, 108
 foreign investments, 154-155
 global communications systems, 77-80
 global reach, 182-183, 189
 Konan food industrise complex, 111-112, 143-144
 long-term policies for management and functional efficiency, 180-181, 192-193
 merger of former firms, 109
 share in Japan's foreign trade before World War II, 24
Mitsui & Co. (U.S.A.), Inc., 189, 204, 205, 212
Mitsui group, 37, 42, 44
Mitsui, Hachiroeman Takakimi, 51
Mitsui, Takasumi, 51
Mitsui Toatsu Chemicals, Inc., 222
Mizukami, Tatsuzo, 177
Moody's, 205
Morinaga Milk Industry, 111
Morioka Kogyo, 109
Murakami, Yoshishige, 21
Myojo, 111

Nagano, Shigeo, 115
Nagase, 23
Narita, Masao, 144
Nationalism among developing countries, 176-177, 222-223
Newfoundland Refining Company, 226, 227
New Zealand, 185
Nichimen Company, Ltd. See also *Sogo shosha*
 deep sea manganese development project, 161
 export of industrial plants, 204
Nichimen Co., Inc., 189
Nikki, 203, 221
Nippon Electric Co., Ltd., 46
Nippon Feed Co., 111

Index

Nippon Flour Mills, 111
Nippon Kokan K.K., 66, 72, 105, 121, 130, 222
Nippon Steel Corporation, 72, 121, 130, 139, 222
Nishida, Shunkichi, 188
Nissan Motor Co., Ltd., 72
Nisshin Flour Milling Co., Ltd., 66
Nisshin Steel, 130
Nissho-Iwai Co., Ltd. See also Sogo shosha
  global commercial networks, 74-75
  imports of industrial plants and equipment, 124-125
  merger of Nissho Co. and Iwai Sangyo, 116
  procurement agent in industrial plant exports, 202-203
  sales margins, 124
Nissho Co., 31, 107, 109, 116
Nixon, Richard, 83
Noda, Kazuo, 56
Noranda Mines, Ltd., 161
Nozaki & Co., Ltd., 23, 32

Ohara, Hiroshi, 182, 183
Oki, Yasuo, 142
Okura & Co., Ltd., 23, 32
Oligopoly, 49-50
Organization of Economic Cooperation and Development (OECD), 105, 114
Osaka Gas Company, 159
Overseas Economic Cooperation Fund, 158

Pacific Resources, Inc., 190
Perry, Matthew, 105, 232
Peterson, Peter, xiii
President Clubs, 42, 44, 49-50, 55. See also Conglomerate groups
Protectionism, 175-176

Rapp, William, 135
Related firms, definition of, 44

Rio-Tinto Zing Corporation, 161
Roberts, John G., 56
Royal Dutch Shell, 159
Rumania, barter trade with *sogo shosha*, 11, 204

Sack Maschinenfabrik, 125
Safeway Stores, Inc., 113
Sanwa Bank group, 36, 37, 42
Sapporo Breweries Ltd., 66
Saudi Arabia, 204
Schloeman, A. G., 125
SEDCO, Inc., 161
Selection Trust, 153
Senshu Kaisha, 31, 119
Shibayama, Yukio, 107
Shiina, Tokishiro, 158
Shinko Menka, 109
Shinetsu Chemical Industry, 222
Showa Shipping Co., Ltd., 66
Singapore, 9, 211
Sloan, H. S., 56
Sogo shosha
  advance guard of Japan's export drive, 129-131, 131-136
  affiliates (subsidiaries and related firms), 44-45; changing character of in developing countries, 222-223; overseas problem in managing, 228-230; U.S., 204-209; U.S., position of in U.S. trade with Japan, 208
  agribusiness in Brazil, 158-159
  assistance to small and medium-size firms, 140-141
  auxiliary services, 65-66
  bank-centered conglomerate groups, relations with, 36-37, 42-44
  borrowings, from group financial institutions, 42-44
  capital efficiency services, 67-68
  capital structure, high leverage, 74, 93; characteristics of, 3; danger of, 226-227
  Code of Behavior, 177-178

Sogo shosha (cont'd.)
  commodities classification standards, 20
  communications between parent company and global affiliates, 229
  comparisons with other Japanese trading companies, 13-17
  comparisons with U.S. and other non-Japanese trading companies, 17-19
  consolidation strategy, 114-116
  consumer goods industry and market, thrust into, 112-114
  core business, 3-4, 214-215
  criticism of, public, 170, 215
  critics, counterattacks against, 177-179
  demand and supply, creation of, 109-110, 151-154
  diversification, 4-6; strategy, 107-109
  dividend rates, 31
  domestic distribution system, rationalization of, 136-138
  and domestic trade, 28
  economic growth, role in Japan's rapid, 131-136
  economies of scale and cost reduction services, 66-67, 135
  as financial intermediaries, 58-60, 62, 138-142
  financial resources, 71-74; of overseas offices, 189
  financial services, 58-60. *See also Sogo shosha*: financial intermediaries
  food industries complexes, 111-112
  foreign investments, 154-155, 210-211; changing pattern in the 1970s, 211-214
  foreign trade by geographic areas, 8-9, 86
  full-cargo policy, 131
  future prospects, 233-234
  global commercial networks, 74-77. *See also Sogo shosha*: overseas commercial networks
  global communications systems, 77-80
  global financing, 191
  global management and control, problems of, 184-185, 191
  global orientation, necessary, 224-226
  global reach, acceleration of, 182-184
  global reach, support actions for, 188-191
  global spread of business, 6-9
  global supply and marketing, 185-188
  group enterprises and affiliates, 48-49
  groups, relations with (stockholdings, borrowings, business), 42-44
  growth: trends of the firms compared, 84-86; strategy, 106-117
  high technology industrial products, plants, and know-how, marketing of, 181-182, 203-204
  historical origins, 24-25
  histories of various, 31-33
  human resources, 68-71
  identity crisis, 214-215
  information services of, 60-62
  imports: of foodstuffs, 120; foreign technology, 126-127; of plant and equipment, 124-127; of raw materials, 121-124
  industrial plants, exports of, 65, 181-182, 203-204
  integration (upstream and downstream) by, 110, 113
  investments in the U.S., 212-214
  Iraqi petroleum development project, 157-158
  Japanese economic system, integral part of post-World War II, 142
  LNG project in Brunei, 159
  loans. *See Sogo shosha*: borrowings
  managerial and functional effici-

Index

Sogo shosha (cont'd.)
ency, emphasis on, 179-181
and manufacturers' thrust into directing marketing, 100-103, 221-222
mergers of, 108, 116
Mt. Newman iron ore development project, 152-153
natural resource development-import projects, 65; multinational deep sea, 159-163
objectives, 119-120
oligopolies, loose, 49-51
organization of new industries, 110-112
organizational and coordination services, 65, 151
organizational structure, 75
organizational structure needed, viable global, 227-228
overseas commercial networks, expansion of, 124-125. See also Sogo shosha: global commercial networks
owners of stocks, 51-55
problems in the late 1970s, 214-230
product structure, 90-93
profits, 93, 98
and protectionism abroad, 175-176
ranking: by profits, 28-31; by sales, 23
rationalization of domestic distribution system, 136-138
regrouping after World War II, 37
research problems, 19-21
resource development-import, 124; projects before mid-1960s, 148-149; projects since mid-1960s, 149-152
restrictions: on loans to, 172-175; of stockholdings by the Japan Fair Trade Commission, 170-172
risk reduction services, 58, 62-64
size, absolute and relative, 25-31. See also Sogo shosha: stratification
social responsibilities, emphasis on, 177-179
steel fabrication centers of, 110, 136-138
and the steel industry, 150-151
stockholders. See Sogo shosha: owners
stockholdings, 42-44, 170-172
strategic response, 1950s-1973, 106-154; consolidation, 114-116; creation of demand and supply, 109-110, 151-152, 153-154; diversification, 107-109; growth, 106-107; organization of new industries, 110-112; thrust into consumer goods industry and market, 112-114
strategic response, since 1973, 177-191; acceleration of global reach, 182-184; emphasis on social responsibilities and counterattacks against critics, 177-179; expanding the marketing of high technology industrial products, plants, and know-how, 181-182; global management, supply, marketing, finance, investment, and support actions, 184-191; stress on managerial and functional efficiency, 179-181
stratification of, 25-26, 86
strengths of each, 26
strengths and weaknesses of each, 6, 218-221
subsidiaries, purposes of, 12-13, 46
third-country trade of, 86-90, 185-188, 197-202. See also Third-country trade
tieover import system, 141
trade, multi types of, 9-11, 86
trading conglomerates, 11-13
transaction, trends, 83-98; changing structure by types of trade, 86
tribute to, from mass media, 215; from MITI, 130
U.S. offices and employees, number of, 208-209

Sogo shosha (cont'd.)
  world trade, position in, 195-197
  zaibatsu background of, 33-35
Specialized trading companies
  comparisons with the *sogo shosha*, 16
  diversification of, 32-33
  MITI's definition of, 15-16
Standard & Poor's Corporation, 205
Steel distribution in Japan, 137-138
Steel industry, reliance on the *sogo shosha* for resource development, 150-151
Subsidiaries
  benefits of, 48-49
  definition of, 44
Sumitomo Chemical Co., Ltd., 107
Sumitomo Corporation. See Sumitomo Shoji Kaisha
Sumitomo group, 37, 42, 44
Sumitomo Metal Industries, 46, 55, 72, 107, 125, 130, 158
Sumitomo Petroleum Development Co., Ltd., 154, 157
Sumitomo Shoji America, Inc., 189, 205
Sumitomo Shoji Kaisha (name changed to Sumitomo Corporation in summer 1978). See also *Sogo shosha*
  Iraqi petroleum development project, 157-158
  Summit Store, 113
  three-year economic plans, 105
  training of recruits, 70-71
Switch trade, 11

Taiken Industries, 31
Taito Co., Ltd., 111
Taiwan, 120, 176, 188
Taiwan Sugar Refinery, 111
Taiyo Bussan, 109
Takashimaya Iida, 109
Tamura, J., 162
Tanabe, Bunichiro, 55, 180
Teikoku Oil Company, 157

Thailand, 111
Third-country trade, 9-10, 185-188, 197-202
Tobu Railway, 66
Tokai Bank group, 42
Tokyo Bank group, 42
Tokyo Gas Company, 159
Tokyo Electric Company, 159
Tokyo Shibaura Electric Co., Ltd., 72
Tonya, 16-17
Toray Industries, 155
Toyo Engineering Corporation, 203, 221
Toyo Petroleum Development Company, 154
Toyomenka Kaisha, Ltd. See also *Sogo shosha*
  Arab-Japanese International Promotion Co., 190
  export of industrial plant to Rumania as prime contractor, 204
  origin of, 32
  third-country trade, 28
Toyota Motor Co., Ltd., 72
Toshoku Ltd., 23, 32
Tozaki, Seiki, 8, 55
Trading companies (both *sogo shosha* and other Japanese trading companies), 13-17
  declining share in Japan's foreign trade, 100-103
  non-Japanese, 17-19
  specialized, 15-16
Triland Metals, Ltd., 63
Tsuda, Hisashi, 8, 55, 162
Tsuji, Yoshio, 55
Tsurumi, Yoshi, 210-211, 233

Ueda, Mitsuo, 189
Uekusa, Masu, 56
United States, 99, 100, 111, 120, 121, 130, 131, 176, 197, 212-214, 231
  conglomerates, 13
  Export-Import Bank, 191

Foreign Trade Council, 19, 21
multinationals, 223

West European conglomerates, 13
West European multinationals, 223
West Germany, 99, 100, 197
Westinghouse, 108
World Energy Development Company, 154

Yasuda Fire & Marine Insurance Co., 66
Yoshiwara Oil Mill, 111
Yoshino, M. Y., 117
Young, Alexander K., 192

Zaibatsu, 33-36